Also by Richard Price

Poetry

Sense and a Minor Fever
Perfume & Petrol Fumes
Lucky Day
Rays
Small World
Moon for Sale

Artist's Books

Gift Horse (with Ronald King)
The Mechanical Word (with Karen Bleitz)
Folded (with Julie Johnstone)
Wake Up and Sleep (with Caroline Isgar)
Little But Often (with Ronald King)

Fiction

The Island (Two Ravens Press)

Non-fiction

British Poetry Magazines 1914-2000 (with David Miller)
The Star You Steer By: Basil Bunting and British Modernism
(editor, with James McGonigal)

Is This a Poem?

Richard Price

Molecular Press

Copyright © 2016 by Richard Price. The moral right of the author has been asserted.

ISBN 978-2-9700376-1-3

The author wishes to thank all those who originally commissioned or accepted the pieces gathered here, plus Gerry Cambridge www.gerrycambridge.com for the cover design and Ian Neil for copy-editing. 'The Wasp Trap: Edward Thomas, William Carlos Williams, Philip Larkin, and Denise Riley' was a keynote lecture given at the Expanded Lyric Conference 2014 at the Seamus Heaney Centre for Modern Poetry, Queen's University, Belfast. 'War Damage: Edward Thomas, Wilfred Owen, Guillaume Apollinaire, David Bomberg' was a keynote lecture given at the British Comparative Literature Association's International Conference 2010 and later published in *Comparative Criticism*. 'His Care for Living English' first appeared in *Ford Madox Ford, Modernist Magazines and Editing* (International Ford Madox Ford Studies 9), 2010; this version of 'CAT-Scanning the Little Magazine' first appeared in *The Oxford Handbook of Contemporary British and Irish Poetry*, ed. Peter Robinson, 2013; 'Sylvia Pankhurst and Germinal' was presented at Modernism, Cultural Exchange and Transnationality: 2nd conference of the AHRC Modernist Magazines Project, 2009.
'Migrant the Magnificent' and 'Beyond La Grille: France and Four Contemporary Poets: David Kinloch, Peter McCarey, Donny O'Rourke, and Iain Bamforth' were first published in *PN Review*. 'Some Questions about Literary Infrastructure in the 1960s' was published in *The Scottish Sixties: Reading, Rebellion, Revolution?*, eds. Bell and Gunn, 2013. 'Generosity' was first published in *Poetry Review*. 'Edwin Morgan: Is this a Poem?' was first published in *The Scottish Literary Review*, while 'Margaret Tait: Film-maker and Poet' was published in *Painted, spoken*. 'Ear-Jewels Catch a Glint: Roy Fisher's Half-year Letters' was published in *An unofficial Roy Fisher*, ed. Robinson, 2010. 'Robin Fulton: Light Years' first appeared in *Poetry International*; 'Arc Editions: the artists Karen Bleitz, Victoria Bean, and Sam Winston' was published in *Artist's Book Year Book 2008-9*, ed. Bodman, 2007. *Vennel Press: the autobiography of a poetry press* appears on the website hydrohotel.net

Contents

FOREWORD vii

MODERN LYRIC
The Wasp Trap 3
War Damage 16
His Care for Living English: Ford Madox Ford 40

MAKING
CAT-Scanning the Little Magazine 63
Sylvia Pankhurst and Germinal 91
Migrant the Magnificent 104
Literary Infrastructure in the 1960s 115
Poetry Pamphlets as Public Private Spaces 137
Vennel Press: The Autobiography of a Poetry Press 140
Arc Editions 156

POETS, ARTISTS, LYRICISTS
Generosity 165
Edwin Morgan: Is This a Poem? 177
Margaret Tait: Film-Maker and Poet 188
Ear-Jewels Catch a Glint: The Half-Year Letters 200
Beyond La Grille: France and Four Contemporary Poets .. 213
Robin Fulton-MacPherson: Light Years 235

AFTERWORD 239

INDEX 242

Foreword

When you open a book on poetry that ranges from the First World War to the millennium, there are names you expect to see and traditions you don't. 'Edward Thomas' might bring in the Hardy–Frost–Thomas phalanx of approachable verse, and the suspicion of a reactionary move to steal the ball from the high-modernist owners of 20th century English poetry. Ez & Tom, indeed, are out; in this book, Bunting considers Ford more as a craftsman and mentor than as an experimenter, and even high modernists who were never really welcome in the club — Hugh MacDiarmid and David Jones — are not invoked where they might have been expected: Jones among the First World War bards and artists with 'In Parenthesis'; and MacDiarmid as one who dazzled others discussed in this book, rather than as the old stick-in-the-mud we see here. The reason for this might be the importance Richard Price attaches to tradition in the sense of making and giving — something where generosity is valued higher than all-encompassing ambition (which is not to say that ambition is absent).

This book shows how a range of artists has made things for themselves and for their friends, and how those processes create diffuse communities. It is the processes rather than the people that do this: most of the people studied here were not acquainted with the others — the exceptions being Gael Turnbull, who knew William Carlos Williams, Basil Bunting, Roy Fisher and Edwin Morgan; Morgan who knew Hamilton Finlay and the gaggle of Informationists; and Price himself.

I'd highlight two aspects of these traditions. When we turn to how the procedures of art bring artists into community, we might think of Turnbull, Migrant and its ramifications. When art is live, when you see it being made, you can feel there's something unique or perhaps unrepeatable about it. It's part of the changing world, not an item on the shelf. That is what Richard Price works to recover in these pieces on a unique constellation of artists.

On Montale's poems to his late wife, which linger on trivial keepsakes, Price notes, 'What the gift, what generosity is, shifts and almost evades us: presents always end up conventionally useless, they become, ideally, tags to the real gifts, the memories to which they, and we, have become so attached'. We're not talking about products to shift at market, but about the intangibles that link us, so frailly, to the real.

This mirror-ball of a book casts some light also on the poetry of Richard Price himself — how it reaches out, through artists' books, through the production and distribution of small magazines and publications, through lyrics set to music and through some of the improvisational readings he has performed of his own work, to whoever will take to this poetry which, while steadfastly rejecting the high-modernist career path, goes to work on all the major events in our small lives.

PMcC

Modern Lyric

The Wasp Trap

The word 'lyric' faces two ways, one looking back to kinds of poetry written to be sung or at least intoned to the sound of a musical instrument. The instrument in question is that ancient contraption, the lyre. When we talk of lyric poetry there is, I believe, the authority of that appeal to the time-honoured. Some poets and some readers may well like to be associated with that authority, but there is also a kind of old-fashioned flavour to it, a Christmas pudding stolidity to the term: lyric poetry is traditional, yes, and the tradition probably has to be observed in some sort of over-indulgent feast now and again, but, if the tradition can't modernise itself, let us hope this sort of Christmas does not go on for too long.

Lyric poetry is delivered through the first person, the 'I', and, in the same way that no poetry simply transacts information or — unlike journalism for instance — pretends to, it is as much about the lateral and contextual as about the declared subject. The self itself is a key subject for lyric poetry, which often deals with attempts to organise feelings that are so strong or so aberrant that they challenge such organisation; or else, the lyric poem is a stylisation of feelings which in their natural state would never actually appear so distorted. Although the apparent autobiographical can be one source of the lyric poem's concentrated emotional energy, it can also be the source of its aesthetic inertia.

Although every self-respecting reader knows that the 'I' in any poem cannot be the I of the actual poet — selectivity, language itself, never mind its particular rules in poetry, could not possibly allow that — still, lyric poetry asserts emotional realism and personal reaction, with the person doing the reacting being the minimally constructed person of the poet. Even within the 'me, me, me' faction of lyric poetry, confessional poetry, the poet appears as a literary character — when the poem becomes aural, he/she appears as a character in a version of drama. Not to spoil certain kinds of reading and listening pleasure — and psychological succour, since, in vulgar contradiction to 'art for art's sake', I do believe that poetry is a therapeutic force founded in kinds of empathy and kinds of witness, even that of pattern recognition — the writer may not want to make too much of this fictiveness, may not want to suggest that the central perceiving energy at the heart of the form is hardly central, barely perceives, and has derived pretty much all the apparently unitary realistic energy of the poem from a host of different and artificial pre-sets.

Lyric poets may feel it is bad enough being caught in a struggling, stalling art form — poetry itself — one that is regarded with indiscriminate ill favour as distant and academic – without deliberately encouraging those views. Post-modern depersonalisation in poetry is not for everyone, even if everyone must depersonalise themselves to some degree to have a personality. And the lyric poet's lot can be a particularly uncomfortable one because if poetry isn't being criticised for being too knowing, too intellectual, it's being criticised for being too personal, too simple, a little-mediated outpouring of selfish emotions.

When the word lyric stands on its own, though, without the suety clog of the word 'poetry', it becomes a much lighter thing altogether — the words of a song are quite clearly in the air 'now', and, unlike lyric poetry, 'now', the contemporary, seems to be a key construction material. Even though song is so often concerned with the singer as 'I', the singer is not held down by the personal nature of the song and listeners seem better able to hold the contradiction in place — that they are listening to an intense affecting lyric, often with extraordinarily sophisticated musical production, that touches and amplifies emotional reality with a stylisation that is wildly artificial but somehow 'true'. Or at least true for that extraordinary trance state of listening absorption, as powerful as it is fleeting.

When lyrics are written down they seem more fragile, more transient than their vocalisations. The physical manifestation of the lyric sheet — crammed into eight-point or less on a CD-case or, more likely in this download age, supplied by one of those online behemoths that seem to supply every lyric to every song in the instant of a tippety-tap in a search engine: they are there but for the grace, virtually, as the song is virtual in the disturbance of air any melody makes. And with song of course, why should anyone look up a text? Instead we live with misheard lyrics, with fragments of songs, we live with them and we love them — often the chorus, or the bridge — in a way that we can seldom accept with poems, fixed as they are in dullard print solidity, with no hook or refrain which — though they are still pulsing with modernity and expressive power in song in poetry are seen as a throwback, like the prehistoric lungfish in C.L. Dallat's wonderful poem on that theme[1], or a poetic version of the anatomical appendix, once useful, they say, for digesting wood. Maybe poetry would love the craft of Song to be outmoded but it would be an accusation born out of self-interest and insecurity, the secret despair that maybe poems themselves will never thrive in the way that song clearly does.

In fact, because song appears so prolific, almost all-present but somehow insubstantial, self-renewing, date-stamping so many experiences of its listeners — and it has many many followers, while poetry, like literature and even books, has comparatively few — song can almost seem too light, in the sense of trivial, anti-gravity, not only because it lacks pomposity but because it lacks the discrimination of true seriousness. At the extremes, while lyric poetry is caught in its own venerable drag, a form made to plummet, lyric at its worst cannot be caught because it seems so throwaway, like a kite made from a newspaper.

As both a lyric poet and a lyricist, my texts try to make sense of these tensions, these lacks and lifts. I'll concentrate on lyric poetry here and below present some lyric poems that illustrate what I've made of these contradictions, and what others have, too. I should also say that there are forms which are neither lyric poetry nor song but which seem to draw on both but for the moment I want to offer some simple observations about lyric poetry itself through some examples.

First of all, some translations from Sappho. Here is my version of one of Sappho's more well-known poems:

---

[1] 'Throwback', in *Morning Star*, Belfast: Lagan Press, 1998.

As if the equal
after Sappho

As if the equal — more than the equal — of a god is facing you,
sitting with you (she's listening close) —
and you're speaking sweetly

oh and her beautiful laugh –
now the heart in my chest is fluttering, I'm winging this,
and then I look, just for a second,
and that's my voice gone –

as if –

no, the tongue is broken, there are just licks
of fire under my skin,
my eyes are blind, drumming and only drumming
fills my ears.

A chill of sweat is gripping me, shaking me,
I'm as pale as grass.
I am dead. It's as if
I am dead.

Risk... everything.

My approach in lyric poetry, and in contemporary translation, is actually to underplay lyric poetry's historic connection to music. Although some poems are said to have musicality, cadence does exist, and while Bunting, say, certainly deployed musical analogies for the structures of his poems, I don't see the poem as a musical object — though I do see it as a sonic work and so one which can learn from song a little. With certain exceptions, I don't really believe in the viability of an actual connection to music today, whatever it may have been in past. Poetry is much much more about speech than it is about music and so I concentrate on the stylisation of speech patterns when I involve myself in lyric poetry. The stylisation is important — I want to make it very clear that the lyric poem is not a colourless, objective carrier of properly considered emotional information, is not the executive summary of the final report from the 'Royal Commission on Humane Smart-casual'. Repetitions, enjambed hesitations, syncopation, non-verbal transcription — some of which may well have been borrowed from the macrostructure of song but are as likely to have come from speech patterning — re-inscribe the lyric poem at the micro-level and become speech activations. To write in this way risks a mistaken accusation of naivety — but I will try to show the properties of the form itself shaped by the weight of its message, both an integral part of that expression and a clear marker that the reader or listener is now orienting him or herself towards a made object. 'All must be risked' Sappho says and here is the extreme, the superlative again in Fragment 150, 'Sweet apple ripening'.

> **Sweet apple ripening**
> *after Sappho*
>
> Sweet apple ripening, blushing, high high up –
> high up the highest branch, neglected, forgotten.
> No, not forgotten – none could possibly reach....
>
> (Mountain hyacinth the shepherds trample,
> blue hyacinth...)

The isolated, the superlative — the lyric poem is an emphatic form, a categorical form — all must be risked, there is only ONE apple up there and it is right at the TOP. There are more Exceptional Services to Exceptionality in lyric poetry than in the

New Year's Honours List, though with less astonishment of servility. Lyric poetry is abject, desperate — sometimes covered with a serenity of observation or even, as with Philip Larkin sometimes, a broken-hearted cynicism, but it is barely able to contain its extremes. '*So*' is a very important word in lyric poetry. Here is Edward Thomas's poem, 'The Wasp Trap', from 1915, which mutates Sappho's tree-fruit into something much darker, much more cruelly civilised. Look again, for all the superlatives of the classic lyric poem:

The Wasp Trap

This moonlight makes
The lovely lovelier
Than ever before lakes
And meadows were.

And yet they are not,
Though this their hour is, more
Lovely than things that were not
Lovely before.

Nothing on earth,
And in the heavens no star,
For pure brightness is worth
More than that jar,

For wasps meant, now
A star — long may it swing,
From the dead apple-bough,
So glistening.

What is the wasp trap to Thomas? It's an ugly thing by day — alone among the objects he names, Thomas tell us. It is not lovely naturally, so while moonlight enhances those objects which are already beautiful, we are talking wholesale transformation. This is because the wasp trap is in daylight simply a variation on a jar, pasted with jam on its inside walls and containing a quantity of water, then slung with a wire over a tree branch in the orchard. It is a cruel object, designed to take advantage of the sugar addiction wasps have, luring them to their prolonged deaths by drowning them in the liquid into which they inevitably slip. Thomas may or may not have known that it is also a foolish object, as although wasps may damage fruit they also consume large quantities of the aphids that are so destructive in an orchard.

All these qualities are utterly changed in the moonlight, however. Contrast this with Sappho's orchard poem — its jump-cut to the trampled hyacinths does have the melancholic pang that closes 'The Wasp Trap' (the jump-cut is probably because of its fragmentary survival, although as we all know ruins are often more attractive than well-kept buildings) — but Sappho's poem emphasises a growing, living thing in the orchard, and suggests that the orchard is still very much a going concern, a way of life. In this way her poem is about the rare vitality of the beloved, albeit contrasted with his or her fragility among men (those galumphing shepherds!); while Thomas's poem is about something made by humans in a pastoral world that is passing — 'the dead apple-bough' suggests this apple tree has not been cared for for some time. It is perverse to say that it is lovelier than the stars or anything on earth — and I suppose that does mean lovelier than any human being. To me, it's as if Thomas is downgrading a loved one and also himself and yet that is what Thomas insists. This is a temporary vision but a dark and barbed one, ambiguously seeming to be misanthropic and yet a paean to humankind's weird sense of invention. This thrawn, awkward message is delivered in a poem that melds lyric repetitions and rhyme with a kind of philosophical tone, influenced by Hardy and an Elizabethan rhetorical turn, which so much of the lyric poetry to come appears to have found reinvigorating and has continued to adopt.

William Carlos Williams's red wheelbarrow poem would later develop this focus on a trade object in a different direction, pouring Japanese print primary colour into the picture:

> so much depends
> upon
>
> a red wheel
> barrow
>
> glazed with rain
> water
>
> beside the white
> chickens[2]

Williams cartoonises the scene with those blocks of tone (simple red barrow, simple white chickens — no nuance here, but a fantasy Persil purity which has its own attractions, its own charm, and, because of the artist's print effect, perhaps confirms visually an oriental element that is there in the poem's extended-haiku-like form). This is in preference to the Samuel Palmer haloising of moonlight and glisten you see in Edward Thomas, with the bittersweet weakness of trying to rhyme swing with glistening; but if anything Williams likes that sense of gloss more. Thomas

---

[2] 'The Red Wheelbarrow' (poem XXII of *Spring and All* (1923).

finishes his poem with the wasp trap lingering in glisten and Williams breaks cover from a more objectivist style to poeticise with his idea that the wheelbarrow is 'glazed with rain / water' (drawing attention to a kind of artisan effort, and perhaps adding further to the idea in the poem of the far east, this time with its tradition of exquisite pottery). In both cases this is a clarifying and intensifying polish, which occurs in other stripped-down lyric poems. It's there in the 'petals, on a wet, black bough' in Ezra Pound's 'In a Station of the Metro' (1913) and by the time of Philip Larkin's well-known poem, 'Water' (1964) the look of wetness has become a gush — you have to ford a river to get to Larkin's new church —held back only by a cool philosophical eye: water now a hypothetical religion, a witness to lyric poetry's thirst. The lyric poem is itself a glistener. It shines and distorts, it is a work of highlight and glint, of emphasis and so extreme filtering out, of extreme concentration. Larkin's poem ends with a magnifying focus in which Edward Thomas's impure, unsettling jar with its unspoken wasp corpses yet moonlight beauty has become an indoors glass, catching the light of the rising sun, a glass whose radiance is derived from water's ever dynamic, ever restless life:

> I should raise in the east
> A glass of water
> Where any-angled light
> Would congregate endlessly.[3]

Like Larkin, Denise Riley's poem, entitled 'Lyric', maintains a ghost of the traditional four-line quatrain and, like Larkin's poem

---

[3] *Collected Poems,* London: Faber and The Marvell Press, 1988, p.93. Originally published in *The Whitsun Weddings,* 1964.

'Water', avoids rhyme, by using a whispering assonance. Here the dynamic tension isn't in the topic only, it's in the idea of the lyric poem itself, with wild and mixed metaphors and syncopated enjambement reflecting the sense of emotional turmoil of the subject struggling before a form which is half alive, half artificial. After the surprising hope of Larkin's daylight water poem, the speaker and therefore the reader is back in the night with the all too demanding lyric. As the last stanza declares, it is the lyric's ' burden and subject / to listen for sweetness in hope/ to hold it in weeping ears though /each hurt each never so much.'

A much shorter poem by Riley, 'Song', continues this sense of striving 'to listen for sweetness in hope', even within what is identified as a field of struggle within the lyric itself. 'Song' returns the reader to those trampled hyacinths in Sappho — 'Some very dark blue hyacinths on the table / A confession or two before dusk', flowers trod underfoot by men, but this time it is children, and the speaker herself, who have been attacked, are being attacked, as the poem speaks:

> A warm disturbing wind cruises the high road
>
> where in curtained rooms children
> are being beaten then so am I again [...]

The poem begins with a basic four-line structure again but can't maintain it, is both damaged and remaking itself, renewing its political force as it renews its poetic form. To continue that line:

are being beaten then so am I again but no-one's
asking for it, I'm asking for something different now.[4]

I suppose that should be the end of this thinking aloud. But as a coda I would like to mention some of the interesting areas that the lyric poem has visited in recent times, though space does not allow me to detail the hows and whys.

Clearly the prose poem, which conventionally depersonalises, has moved into a very interesting lyrical space with the autobiographical catch-phrasing of Lyn Hejinian's *My Life,* Fiona Templeton's complex tribute to her mother *Airdrie Mum* and David Kinloch's *Dustie-fute* sequence in which a *lettriste* love of individual letters collages with testimony in the first years of the AIDS pandemic and a fascination with old obsolete but beautiful words in Scots. The artist's books of Stevie Ronnie, particularly those in which he isolates resonate words on the keyboard — such as *Home* or *Shift* — are worth contemplation, too. Is the artist's book itself a new kind of lyric poem?

A topic that I have wholly evaded until now is the pang of wit in lyric poetry — from John Donne to Norman MacCaig and the post-MacCaig group, known in England as the Martian school. Robin Fulton's 'wit' — which is to say, a kind of cleverness of analogy, so clever it is naturalised as instinctively 'true' — applies to time and memory, instead of visuality.

Enigmatic and funny Tim Atkins's book *Folklore* allows what I can as yet only call a flavour of lyricism to occupy these strange

---

[4] *Mop Mop Georgette,* London: Reality Street, 1993, p.38.

and comedic poems about the pastoral. The comedy in many of the poems of Frank Kuppner mingles unexpectedly with surprising moments of lyricism, too, sometimes unsettling the sincere seriousness of the lyric register, but by no means always. Tom Leonard's sequence *nora's place* sketches both a lyrical and political identity for the eponymous nora as she goes about her day, as alive and as isolated as Woolf's Mrs Dalloway but in a very different milieu. When they read out their work, poets as various as Mimi Khalvati, Donny O'Rourke, and Paula Claire, reintroduce the collectivity of the poem, perhaps getting closer to the choral function the lyric poem may once have had, by assigning part of their poems to the audience itself — the audience isn't just there to listen or even clap, but to lend its voice to the live event of a poem as it happens.

I mentioned Stevie Ronnie earlier — Work which might be as usefully described as text-based art, for example in J. H. Prynne and Caroline Bergvall, arguably still deploys the lyric pang however depersonalised it becomes. It is striking that in electronic music the synthethised treatment of the human voice, from Herbie Hancock's 'I Thought It Was You' to the songs of Daft Punk, seems to heighten the frailty, the sorrow, of the semi-human voice, and I think that as the lyric poem evolves it may also find technical innovation reflects back on tenderness, on anguish: the life of humanity going further and further out into innovated spaces, while moving further and further within itself, as cyber-humanity, is surely replacing the old doubleness with a new one, and that is the future of the lyric.

War Damage

Four poets of the First World War — Guillaume Apollinaire, Wilfred Owen, Edward Thomas and David Bomberg — mark different points within a range of complex reactions to that conflict. With the exception of David Bomberg, whose reputation as a visual artist far outweighs his little-known poems, each has been widely reprinted and anthologised again and again. I think it's fair to say that the framing of those republications has positioned Owen as almost entirely a war poet, while Apollinaire is viewed as a poet of varied subject matter who also wrote war poetry. Thomas is different again, being judged to have written work that has a bearing on the war but almost always in a very specific sense, specifically oblique. Perhaps only one poem by him, 'This is no petty right or wrong,' addresses the War absolutely directly and the shock of its largely head-on, public tone within Thomas's oeuvre confirms its status as an exception to the rule:

> This is no case of petty right or wrong
> That politicians or philosophers
> Can judge. I hate not Germans, nor grow hot
> With love of Englishmen, to please newspapers.[5]

The relatively recently surfaced poems penned by David Bomberg suggest that almost all of his surviving poems — about a dozen —

---

[5] Edward Eastaway [i.e. Edward Thomas], *Six Poems*, Printed by hand at the Pear Tree Press, [1916], p.[4]. British Library shelfmark: 11642.h.49. Subsequent references to this book appear in the text using the abbreviation *Six Poems*.

are war poetry and that the War itself made Bomberg a poet, even more than it did Owen. Given that his poems came to light only in the early 1990s, when Neville Jason discovered them in the Tate Archives[6], and that Bomberg is almost exclusively understood within a framework of art criticism (a point reinforced by the specialist location of archival material relating to him), it is not surprising that wholesale incorporation of his work into what might be called the canon of English war poetry has failed to take place. The canon-making process probably solidified some decades before.[7] His poems were, however, published by the Gillian Jason Gallery in 1992. His poetry is of interest and in discussing it I'd like to offer a slight fine-tuning of our understanding of stylistic changes in English poetry at that time.

But let's start in France, with Apollinaire's manifesto-like poem, 'La jolie rousse'. This begins as a testimony of the poet's experience of the extremes of existence, extremes which are of mortality, of love, of art, and, specifically, of war:

> Me voici devant tous un homme plein de sens
> Connaissant la vie et de la mort ce qu'un vivant peut connaître
> Ayant éprouvé les douleurs et les joies de l'amour

---

[6] David Bomberg, *Poems and Drawings from the First World War* (London: Gillian Jason Gallery, 1992). p.5. British Library shelfmark: Cup.512.b.66. Subsequent references to this book appear in the text using the abbreviation *Poems and Drawings*.

[7] Examples of war poetry anthologies pre-dating the Bomberg discovery include Maurice Hussey (ed.) *Poetry of the First World War* (London: Longmans, 1967) and Jon Silkin (ed.) *The Penguin book of First World War Poetry* (London: Allen Lane, 1979). There is also the monumental bibliography by Catherine W. Reilly, *English Poetry of the First World War* (London: Prior, 1978).

Ayant su quelquefois imposer ses idées
Connaissant plusieurs langages
Ayant pas mal voyagé
Ayant vu la guerre dans l'Artillerie et l'Infanterie
Blessé à la tête trépané sous le chloroforme
Ayant perdu ses meilleurs amis dans l'effroyable lutte
Je sais d'ancien et de nouveau autant qu'un homme seul
pourrait des deux savoir
Et sans m'inquiéter aujourd'hui de cette guerre
Entre nous et pour nous mes amis
Je juge cette longue querelle de la tradition et de l'invention
De l'Ordre et de l'Aventure[8]

I translate this as:

Here I am before you all a man of some intelligence
Who knows life and of death what any living man can know
Having probed the sorrows and joys of love
Having known now and again how to impose my ideas
Fluent in several tongues
Travelled not a little
Having seen battle as gunner as foot soldier
Wounded in the head trepanned under chloroform
Having lost my dearest friends in that serious struggle.
I know the old and the new as much as one man can know
And without fretting today about that war
Between you and me and for you and me my friends
I stand judge of that long quarrel between tradition and modernity
Between Order and Adventure

---

[8] Guillaume Apollinaire, 'La Jolie Rousse', in *Oeuvres Poétiques*, Paris: Gallimard, 1965. p.313. 'La Jolie Rousse' was originally published in *Calligrammes* (Paris: Mercure de France, 1918).

If world weariness and insouciance can be combined, Apollinaire combines them in that phrase 'Et sans m'inquiéter aujourd'hui de cette guerre' ['And without fretting today about that war']. There are subject and tonal shifts across the poem, too. The voice is moody, up and then down. The poem soon veers, for instance, into an advocacy of the adventuring spirit in art, figured as 'le mystère en fleurs s'offre à qui veut le cueillir,' (*Oeuvres Poétiques*, p.313) ['the flowering mystery that offers itself for those who'd pluck it']. In such 'étranges domaines' [strange territories], 'Il y a là des feux nouveaux des couleurs jamais vues' (*Oeuvres Poétiques*, p.313) [There are new fires colours never seen before].

Far from being led by the War to an experienced repudiation of the avant-garde's interest in spectacle, Apollinaire, if it is he who is the voice of the poem, holds firm to his pre-war artistic ideals. He uses his knowledge of the War — middle-distance knowledge as a gunner, close-hand knowledge as one who also served in the infantry — to place himself above the dispute, 'that long quarrel', between conservative aesthetics, which emphasise order, and liberal ones, which emphasise exploration. Such exploration is a discovery through and of the senses — heat sensation, colour, dramatic vistas — and it's also an aggressive domination, implicitly through art, of time: 'le temps qu'on peut chasser ou faire revenir' (*Oeuvres Poétiques*, p.314) ['time which can be either exiled or brought back'].

Soon, though, the tone has changed again and Apollinaire is mourning his childhood, and perhaps the childhood of humankind: 'Voici que vient l'été la saison violente / Et ma jeunesse est morte ainsi que le printemps / O Soleil c'est le temps de la Raison ardente' (*Oeuvres Poétiques*, p.314) ['Now summer's coming the violent season / And my childhood is dead just like spring / Oh

Sun it's the time of scorching Reason.']. If Reason is 'scorching' it's also 'la forme noble et douce', 'noble' and the 'gentlest form', and now it's a seductive, irresistible element, with the attractive powers a magnet has on iron, but no, it's transmuting once more — into the golden hair of the red-headed woman of the poem's title — a strawberry blonde, perhaps — and this the colour of lightning. Finally, something much slower, much softer: the optics are now without temperature, the heat has been transformed, almost de-natured, into petals, and I think the first intimation of autumn arrives as the poem starts to come to a close, returning to the image of the exotic flower: 'ces flammes qui se pavanent / Dans les roses-thé qui se fanent' (*Oeuvres Poétiques*, p.314) ['those flames that glow / In the shed petals of the tea-rose.'].

Anne Hyde Greet and S. I. Lockerbie point out in their edition of *Calligrammes* that this is where the poem probably finished originally.[9] Although it can be read therefore as the original resolution to the poem, an upbeat one which somehow resolves the fight between Order and Adventure through the perpetual mutability of life itself (a parallel, therefore, to Edmund Spenser's Mutabilitie fragment of the uncompleted *The Faerie Queene*), I find the use of the rose here more melancholy than that. The tea-rose is, after all, an ornamental flower that is not hardy: it needs to be defended not from scorching reason but from the cold. Apollinaire's love of things Chinese, of things exotic, may be at play here because Chinese roses are thought to be ancestors of the

---

[9] Guillaume Apollinaire, *Calligrammes* (Berkeley: University of California Press, 1980), Translated by Anne Hyde Greet, with an introduction by S. I. Lockerbie and Commentary by Greet and Lockerbie, p.507. Future references to this edition's commentary appear in the text with the abbreviation Greet and Lockerbie.

tea-rose. Its palette has cream, yellow and apricot tones, hence the flame-like look. Equally importantly, it's a rose that was created with particularly active hybridisation by experimental gardeners, if not avant-gardeners, in nineteenth century France: with that in mind you can imagine that for Apollinaire it was a symbol that braided internationalism, nationalism, experimentation, heat and visual sensation and even a kind of bohemian dandyism, all concentrated in that glorious flower. That the rose has all these qualities adds further aesthetic subtext to this subdued ending: the adventuring spirit is fragile, after all, a lot more fragile than the 'fighter' it was imagined to be in an earlier part of the poem. So, while the poem as a whole 'believes' in the new territories of sensation and asserts a control over time, the apparently final mood swing is not quite so confident. Despite Apollinaire's early bluster, he now recognises that Nature, the Earth, Time, are in real command.

There is, however, a further curtain call, these apparently extra lines:

> Mais riez riez de moi
> Hommes de partout surtout gens d'ici
> Car il y a tant de choses que je n'ose vous dire
> Tant de choses que vous ne me laisseriez pas dire
> Ayez pitié de moi
> (*Oeuvres Poétiques*, p.314)

Which I'd translate as:

> But laugh at me laugh
> Men from everywhere especially folk from here
> Because there are so many things I can't risk telling you
> So many things you wouldn't let me tell you
> Have pity on me

Greet and Lockerbie note that in Apollinaire's manuscript, held at the Bibliothèque Littéraire Jacques Doucet, this last stanza is written in a different ink (Greet and Lockerbie, p.507). They suppose, rightly I think, that this is because it was written rather later, in moments of further reflection. However, there *could* be other explanations: the poet simply ran out of ink and replenished the well with a different colour; or, more excitingly, it might be that Apollinaire was just beginning to experiment with different tones of ink and that this movement, yet again to a different part of the emotional spectrum, is being emphasised by colour. If Apollinaire had lived longer who knows that his already well established interests in visual aspects of poetic texts — the space of the page, the shaping of poems, the use of printed handwriting — would not have developed further, and further into colour. The concrete poets, inheritors much later of other aspects of his legacy, did exactly that in various examples of their work.

Apollinaire has already heard his readers sniggering: 'laugh at me laugh.' And it isn't just an immediate and parochial audience Apollinaire has to contend with. The man who had worked recently as a government censor certainly knew about the processes of banning. The difference in peace time was that the fear that military secrets might be divulged to an enemy had become another kind of anxiety: the fear that common but private civilian thoughts might be aired publically, that the private life of a people might become public. Those thoughts of course range from the experimentally hedonistic aesthetics Apollinaire has signalled, including the examples of erotic poems that were indeed deemed unsuitable for publication for decades after Apollinaire's death. His poem suggests, correctly as it turned out, that there is more that he can't say because his immediate audience and its mediators have a great degree of control over publication and are *actively against him*. The archive, which did save his poetry, was a sad last resort: his last, desperate, and surely ill-fated resort was to appeal to his audience's sense of pity.

In war poetry, the word 'pity' is not usually first associated with this most delightful of praise poets. Rather 'pity' is attached to a poet from the northwest of England whose angry, sonically sensitive poems describe the 'Pity of war': Wilfred Owen.

Here is the beginning of his famous statement about poetry and the conflict.

> This book is not about heroes. English Poetry is not yet fit to speak of them.
> Nor is it about deeds, or lands, nor anything about glory, honour, might, majesty, dominion, or power, except War.
> Above all I am not concerned with Poetry.
> My subject is War, and the pity of War.
> The Poetry is in the pity.[10]

The original manuscript, held by the British Library, has been digitised and is available as part of the online First World War Poetry Digital Archive.[11] [12] The text is clearly titled 'Preface' and it is placed in an appendix to Owen's manuscript poems and

---

[10] Wilfred Owen, edited and introduced by Jon Stallworthy, *The Poems of Wilfred Owen*, (London: Hogarth, 1985), p.192.
[11] Wilfred Owen, 'Preface', [May 1918]. British Library shelfmark: Add.43720. f.1.
[12] 'The Wilfred Owen Collection', in *The First World War Digital Archive,* www.oucs.ox.ac.uk/ww1lit/collections/owen.

fragments in Jon Stallworthy's scholarly edition of Owen.[13] Actually, 'fragment' would be a nicely indeterminate designation except that literary criticism, biography, and the format designation in the digital archive's catalogue record tend to take it as more confidently prose than perhaps it may be. Implicit, I think, in Dominic Hibberd's excellent biography of Owen is that, although the content of the text would be unconventional, its format is the traditional one of prose: 'Wilfred roughed out some notes for a preface. Prefaces to books of war poetry had usually made grand statements about heroes and national glory, offering traditional consolations, but Wilfred's would be different.'[14]

At least in the confidence of this format attribution I think this may be mistaken, or rather, not the whole story: there is more poetry in this fragment than such a classification would allow.

It was a chance rendering of this text that made me question the usual understanding: in at least two printed versions I noticed that 'Preface' comes to fourteen lines, sonnet-length. There is a lot more to a sonnet that such simple arithmetic of course and I am not suggesting that Owen's statement is anything so specific. Yet that talismanic quantity, and something else I couldn't immediately articulate, made me re-read this fragment as if it were at least a poem and then go back to the manuscript to double-check. It was then that I saw that the manuscript is a *very* different animal from most published versions and, beyond problematising genre, this is the bigger point I would like to make.

---

[13] Wilfred Owen, ed. Jon Stallworthy, *The Complete Poems and Fragments*, (London: Chatto & Windus / Hogarth, 1983), p.535-6.
[14] Dominic Hibberd, *Wilfred Owen: A New Biography* (London: Weidenfeld and Nicolson, 2002), p.317.

What you find is that line endings, punctuation and even several extra words, all of which are clearly there in the original manuscript, are not registered in the readily available printed versions and, except for the digital manuscript facsimile itself, nor are they there in various digital transcriptions. Jon Stallworthy's printed scholarly edition does observe more of the nuances, though awkwardly and ambiguously. I guess typesetting limitations forced a simple printed 'translation' on a spatially more complex master. All the other published versions I have seen, including Jon Stallworthy's version in the edition he made for a wider readership, make this text more conventionally prose-like than it actually is; and certainly more settled. Stallworthy does, however, include a facsimile of the fragment, reduced in size and positioned as a photographic frontispiece. Because reading is not always a linear practice, especially for a collected volume, you could easily miss this.

Owen was fascinated by the sonnet, wrote several, and made an edgily stunted double sonnet in 'Dulce et Decorum Est'. You can't, I think, make an argument for 'Preface' being *certainly* the beginnings of a sonnet but I think there are good grounds to believe in its qualities as a kind of *poem*. I don't think it is certainly the beginnings of the prose piece it has 'become'. There is something creatively unstable about this text — to think of it as either a poem or prose is too categorical an approach — but the manner of its instability makes me think that poetry is nevertheless a good deal of what it *is*, never mind a good deal of what it is *about*.

It seems to be an early draft of something that never went on to exist fully: the manuscript is matted with deletions and corrections but there is nothing to say that what remains is what Owen felt he had completed. That it parallels Owen's own tragically unfinished life is part of its poignancy. One of the phrases Owen scores out is 'I have no hesitation'; but this deletion is an indication that, on the contrary, he had many second-thoughts about the detail of this short text. The fact it is very clearly titled 'Preface' doesn't mean it is *actually* a *prose* preface. The whole look of the fragment — those one-sentence paragraphs, their uncramped spacing on the page, and their building of expectation through that list of not this's, not that's — strongly suggests to me there is a struggle going on here. Perhaps it's a little like Apollinaire's battle between l'Ordre and l'Aventure, but this time, I'd suggest, it's a struggle between prose and poetry and the outcome is an intriguing and affecting attempted but unresolved merger of the two.

Like 'La Jolie Rousse,' this fragment I'd argue has more than one ending, the first conclusion being the short line 'The Poetry is in the pity.' Really, that's the end of the poetry in this piece; after that, there's the first real prose paragraph. Though I can see why Owen wants to make a further refinement to his statement, to me it comes across as an unfortunate fussing that lessens the power of what had been a very good, direct, last line, the line that is perhaps one of the most remembered in Owen's work. (I must declare a minimalist sensibility so perhaps I am being unfair.) But it is surely a harsh jump-cut that leaps from the appeal to the eloquence of reality's tragedy - 'The Poetry is in the pity' – and lands on the state-of-the-nation reviewer-speak of 'Yet these elegies are to this generation in no sense consolatory.'

Owen recovers directness, though, with the second 'conclusion':

[...] All a poet can do today is warn. That is why true Poets must be truthful.[15]

This is Owen's resumption of an appeal to poets to represent the war honestly. Here, very like Apollinaire, he appears to be defending his work before an audience that implicitly may not want to listen. Finally, however, he adds one further paragraph. This is in another register again, with its opening square bracket. This is a parenthesis that is not closed in the manuscript, though printed versions, seeking a closure the text does not have, either delete the bracket altogether (Sassoon)[16] or make it into a rounded bracket and clamp it down with a further concluding one (Jon Stallworthy's approach in his popular edition — though Stallworthy, I repeat, also presents the manuscript as a frontispiece in that edition where the difference can be plainly seen).

This last paragraph begins as more of a poet's technical note — he is explaining or apologising for the fact that he is not using actual people's names in the poems that the 'preface' was intended to accompany. This is an admission that modifies the reader's understanding of what sort of truth his poetry is actually going to contain: not the realism of journalism, clearly, or confessional poetry. Then he finishes with an expression of the hope that his poems and the spirit of those they commemorate will survive Prussia and Flanders. This is a mention of specifics which is quite separate in tone from the rest of this otherwise abstract text whose

---

[15] Wilfred Owen, edited and introduced by Jon Stallworthy, *The Poems of Wilfred Owen*, (London: Hogarth, 1985), p.192.
[16] Wilfred Owen, with an introduction by Siegfried Sassoon, *Poems* (London: Chatto & Windus, 1920), p.vii. British Library shelfmark: Cup.410.f.490.

focus is on the aesthetics of war poetry. Nevertheless it reminded the reader, if they needed reminding, that there was a reality of horror beyond the Channel that the poems were there to address. Perhaps it's a small thing, but this is why I think it's important to observe the manuscript in its punctuation here: if we were to leave that square bracket open in our printed versions, as Owen did through absent-mindedness, hurriedness or, just perhaps, by design, we would have the benefit of understanding this as a text declaring its own unfinished state and so reflecting on the hopes, stresses and doubts of Owen's declaration.

From a poet who made a fragile uncertain bridge between prose and poetry, I now move to one who for many years was known as a prose writer but who flourished in the last couple of years of his life as a poet: Edward Thomas.

First, though, because Thomas's first poetry collection, *Six Poems*, is printed in a way that emulates a manuscript's handwriting, I think it's worth mentioning the physical format of the work of the three poets' so far discussed. Apollinaire's shaped poems the *Calligrammes* are of course very aware of the space of the page and if you think of the bestiary that he wrote for Raoul Dufy's collection of animal images[17] you can see that, in the simplest terms at least he is a poet who is beginning to imagine the visual territory of the book. For Owen, who did not have a book of poems published in his lifetime, the key first publication was the short, pamphlet-like, posthumous book that his mentor Siegfried Sassoon published in 1920 and which included the fragment I've just been

---

[17] Guillaume Apollinaire, *Le Bestiaire, ou, Cortège Orphée* (Paris, Deplanche, 1911). Victoria and Albert Museum shelfmark: Safe 1 A.4.

discussing. It is a curious facet of the pamphlet form that it should often announce a poet, as it did with Edward Thomas's first book, but also, just occasionally, as with Owen, simultaneously commemorate one. In fact, because Edward Thomas was killed so soon after the publication of his very slim poetry collection I suppose it also had a commemorative role.

With Thomas's book, his friend the artist-printer James Guthrie engraved a handful of his poems for the very slim volume, *Six Poems*. Thomas used a pseudonym, Edward Eastaway. It is quite unlike Owen's publication by Sassoon because the printed words are handwritten, almost giving the impression that it is a manuscript that you are looking at. Although Apollinaire used handwriting as part of his calligrammatic approach, in Thomas's case the direction is not forward towards a new flexibility, a new expansion of poetry but, rather, backwards, in perhaps idealised memory of the lone hand of the artisan or even of the inspired author writing a draft in fair copy.

Although Philip Larkin spoke of the magic of that connection to an individual author as an exclusive value inherent in the literary manuscript, this viewpoint requires some modification I think .[18] Really, such magic is bound up in a version of publication. It is the exposure to the public of the private (of something touched by the author) that is a large part of the 'magic' here. The magic of manuscripts cannot only be in apparent uniqueness or in absolute connection to The Author, nor even in the promise they seem to hold of understanding a writer's process, but in their ability to be

---

[18] See, Philip Larkin, 'A Neglected Responsibility', in *Required Writing: Miscellaneous Pieces 1955-1982* (Faber, 1983), pp.98-108.

'published' on the retinas of those now privileged to view them; their magic is not in intimacy but in intimacy shared. Looked at that way, Larkin's magic inheres in the individual privacy of an artist only in so much as it is observed by visitors to archives and their exhibitions who have in that sense 'published' them.

As such this is at the extreme end of a subset of other acts of publication: the magic is about the individual reader and their relationship with the author's work; the magic is that mystery of wonder and pleasure that a reader has when an artist's text, in whatever phase of creation, is made public to them. By maintaining special collections that represent and honour the range of formats — manuscript, sound recording, print and film, and the digital options upon us — research libraries recognise such publication in its broadest and deepest sense. If archives are not for, at least in this special sense, publication — though such publication may be for a future generation — then it is difficult to know what they are for. There is a paradox at the heart of the archival concept which places immense value on the private, the rare and the unique — the secret, even — yet, in the public realm at least, must and should justify its collections in terms of public access of various kinds. At the individual text-object level, Edward Thomas's book 'understands' this: emerging from an Arts & Crafts sensibility that seems only to faintly remember Blake's more roaring artist's books, *Six Poems* quietly foregrounds the handwritten as if it were such a cacheted manuscript, yet sells the work, albeit in a limited edition, to a wider public.

The Thomas poem I'll focus on is 'A Private'. It is, in a way, about keeping things genuinely private, about keeping silent about that most enigmatic of secrets: a person's inner life. That is a subject that even the most complete of personal archives will never be able to divulge fully. This poem does not have the detail or exhilaration of the witnessing verse written by Apollinaire and Owen. Instead it has a mythic power whose grip is gained through brevity, through understatement. Perhaps this constitutes a partial reversal of the elegiac certainties which ceremonies of mourning normally require: of character remembered, or at least of listing in affection. The tone of elegy is still important however so that a suggestion that the hero of the poem, and he is a kind of hero, is 'sleeping' can be found from Arthurian legend to Bob Dylan's unsettling ballad of the doomed gangster 'Joey' — 'He ain't dead, he's just asleep.' It is a natural and popular wish that the loved who are dead be actually in mystic hibernation but Thomas's handling of 'sleep' has, in my reading, a harder edge. Unlike Apollinaire and Owen, this poem eschews detailed or realistic observation of the Front, and again this quickly contributes to the mythic charge.

A Private

This ploughman dead in battle slept out of doors
Many a frozen night, and merrily
Answered staid drinkers, good bedmen, and all bores:
'At Mrs Greenland's Hawthorn Bush,' said he,
'I slept.' None knew which bush. Above the town,
Beyond 'The Drover', a hundred spot the down
In Wiltshire. And where now at last he sleeps
More sound in France -that, too, he secret keeps.
(Six Poems, p.[7])

From the off, the text is telling us of the private's dual identity — he has two lowly roles as a soldier of the lowest rank and as a mysterious and perhaps itinerant ploughman. From the off we also know he has been killed in the war. The reader may be briefly confused here though because of the temptation to read the immediate reference to sleeping 'out of doors' in the first line as a bitter-edged euphemism for 'death'. Although this is preparatory work for the use of sleep at the end of the poem, Thomas quickly adds more detail and the reader sees that the sleeping is, for the moment, literal and that this man has been practically a force of nature, a joyous one at that, 'merrily' responding to questions from fellow pub-goers.

Thomas contrasts how tough, mysterious, and exciting the ploughman is compared to those 'staid drinkers, good bedmen, and all bores' —what a joie-de-vivre he possessed — and also how private this private was. In contrast to the townspeople's tedious but gossipy curiosity and the transparency of their routines and property, he speaks in a teasing riddle. No-one may know where Mrs Greenland's Hawthorn Bush is but that's because they are taking it all rather literally, and again this is a sign of their failure in imagination. Thinking laterally, Mrs Greenland's Hawthorn Bush is surely like 'Shanks's pony', the joking phrase for walking. The ploughman is making a circumlocutory jest that declares a cold and prickly territory for a bed: the ploughman is simply, or rather, humorously, saying that he sleeps rough. It's a potent phrase, though: the green and pleasant land of fair England is here creatively conflated with the frozen region of the world's largest, coldest island, and perhaps underlying it is a bittersweet understanding of feminised territory, harsh, beautiful mother Earth. If that meaning is available it gives the phrase a planetary perspective and so only adds to the sense of the ploughman's solitariness beneath the night sky.

Finally the heroic tone of sleep is fully activated in what I read as an emotional charge that is more angry than serene. In the closing couplet his noble privacy has become tragic anonymity: 'And now where at last he sleeps / More sound in France — that, too, he secret keeps.'

So, finally to David Bomberg. Here is an extract from one of his poems, 'Unburied', from the war years.

> Unburied
> Wasting misery; venereal disease;
> delirium tremens; courting disaster on a playing card
> are in their killing process all too slow –
> war has learned to do the 'double-quick'
> in half the time.
> (*Poems and Drawings*, p.39)

After this the poem focuses on the remains of the eponymous soldier, a picture, as it were, of the 'sleeping' private who Edward Thomas chose not to depict in realistic detail:

> War [...]
> with a bludgeon crushed the man,
> splattered his brains; -- merged what remained in filth –

The poem then concludes with an observation on the displaced local people who return to what was once farmland:

> Near such a trench – lying in an attitude,
> callous to what went on –
> maggot-eaten, the fatted maggots dead –
> they found him when the refugees came back to cut the corn.

I want to do little more than quote it to show Bomberg was a war poet of interest, not to mention emotional power. There is a sketch-like quality to it – sketch in the sense of speed and flow – the dashes that punctuate this text; sketch in the sense of generalization — the isolated phrases at the beginning that establish in broad brush strokes, to continue the metaphor, the slow ways that soldiers might die if war itself didn't intervene; sketch in the risking of infelicities — some clumsy or unfocussed lines here and there — and, finally, sketch in the sense of making a drawing in real time, from reality. I know that these qualities overlap, but you see the point. It's free verse, utterly different from most of British poetry of this time, though not all. Actually, Bomberg had provided a cover image for a collection of poems by avant-garde poet John Rodker in 1914 and they clearly shared an interest in this mode of expression.[19]

Bomberg's poem 'Russian Ballet' was published in 1919 within a booklet of the same name composed of Bomberg's chromographs, and it is also free in form.[20] As the title suggests, it relates to Sergei Diaghilev's Ballets Russes, the dance company that had arrived in London in 1911 to sensation and success. Richard Cork, whose work I am indebted to for much of the biographical detail here, notes that sketches Bomberg had made before the war were re-worked after the war as prints and then incorporated with the text of this poem, which is then eked carefully out, opening by opening, through the book.[21]

---

[19] John Rodker, *Poems*, London: [Privately Printed], 1914. British Library shelfmark: Cup.403.s.4.
[20] David Bomberg, *Russian Ballet* (London: Hendersons, 1919). British Library shelfmark: RF.2008.b.81.
[21] Richard Cork, *David Bomberg* (New Haven: Yale University Press, 1987). See especially: pp.122-126. Future references to this work are given in the text as 'Cork'.

It is a beautiful book and important in Bomberg's artistic journey because it appears to mark a last farewell to his pre-war abstraction: he would never work in quite this way again. I would suggest it is also one of the earlier starting places for the modern artist's book in Britain. If the Guthrie/Thomas book looks back to a Blakean tradition, however faintly, Russian Ballet looks forward to a conceptual one. Since Bomberg and his then wife Alice Mayes, used it while they were pretending to be programme sellers at a post-war Diaghilev event (Cork p.126), I'd argue that it is also an early contribution to what is now called 'performance art'. Here is the opening of the poem:

Russian Ballet

Methodic discord startles
—Insistent snatchings drag fancy from space
—Fluttering white hands beat—compel. Reason concedes
—

One of the things this isn't, on the face of it, is a work of war poetry. I've included it here, however, because it seems to me to relate in one way to the testimonial urgency I noted in the first poet whose work I started to explore here, Apollinaire.

There are many ways of reading the fact of this publication of course. Psychologically, Bomberg could have been going back to the sensual comforts of dance, of a pre-war idyll of colour, spectacle, and theoretical licence; as Richard Cork points out, even the lithographical process he used for *Russian Ballet* he had learnt years before (Cork, p.126). Like Apollinaire, Bomberg does not seem to repudiate his pre-war experimentalism. He may be saying one last goodbye to it, in elegiac fashion, but that is far from a denial. By publishing this poem and these images in pamphlet fashion, he seems not to accept that the First World War's real unrealities, its large-scale dehumanisations, should silence abstraction or modern forms of expression. Rather, in contemporary ballet, and implicitly in his manner of addressing or describing contemporary ballet, Bomberg suggests that 'Reason concedes' the argument of new artistic complexity. This is an assertion, which is rather like Apollinaire's boast that Time may be commanded — 'exiled or brought back.' For both, the avant-garde is not necessarily about intelligence, be it Order or Reason, but about shared sensation — 'Impressions crowding collide with movement around us' — and sensation which is almost beyond interpretation: 'The mind clamped fast captures only a fragment.' The way that Bomberg spreads this poem out across the book, with vast amounts of white space beneath each line, each accorded its own page and a facing abstract chromograph, is a physical analogue to the poem's near isolation of the fragment. At the same time he uses the delay of turning the page to foreground time as an element in both the reading and the 'being' experience – in the manner of many later artists' books (for example, Ian Hamilton Finlay's use of delay in his canal lock work in the *Canal Stripe* series). As the poem warns, this 'discord' is 'methodic': the book not only broadly describes modern ballet's approach but finds a textual analogue for it in its execution.

Unlike the physical reality of the frank war elegy I read earlier, in which Bomberg focuses on the remains of the 'Unburied''s actual, fatally injured, brain, 'Russian Ballet' is about consciousness, the more nebulous but alive 'mind'. I suppose the word 'brain' carries a stronger sense of death, of physical decapitation or extreme violence, than, strangely, the disembodied concept of 'mind'. I read 'Russian Ballet' as a positive counterpart to the grim elegy of the 'Unburied' and its war poetry companions (I don't mean a literal or deliberate counterpart). In Bomberg's post post-Impressionist blur, the only substantiated nouns appear to be the 'white hands' of the dancers (or, more likely, audience members?) and the venue's falling curtain — the rest is free verse, Bombergian dash, and a stream of abstract nouns such as 'discord,' 'fancy,' 'Reason,', and 'illusion'.

Certainly, Wilfred Owen is a defter user of the abstract noun. Famously in 'Dulce et Decorum est', he describes an 'ecstasy of fumbling' as soldiers try, under attack, to put on their gas-masks, the phrase a brilliant coupling of the intangible with the desperately haptic.[22] Nevertheless 'Russian Ballet' marvels winningly, it seems to me, at the human ability to create —and at least partially experience — what is exciting and beautiful. It even marvels at the beauty of being only able to grasp the whole partially: here the fragmentation is not that of destroyed brain tissue but of fleet, sensual, fully-alive new forms, new carefully-orchestrated 'illusions', and the glorious fragmentation made from our own limitations to fully comprehend them. It is another sketch that is thinking on its feet, trying to explain even as it registers, as it were, its own witnessing.[23] I don't think it is stretching things too

---

[22] Wilfred Owen, 'Dulce et Decorum est', in Owen, edited and introduced by Jon Stallworthy, *The Poems of Wilfred Owen*, (London: Hogarth, 1985), p.117.

[23] Contrast the satire of Pound's approach to a performance of Russian Ballet in his poem 'Les Millwin' in *Lustra* (Elkin Mathews, 1916), p.24. Pound characterises Slade art students in attendance as 'turbulent and undisciplined', in thrall to Russian Ballet, while, with perhaps a homophobic undertone from Pound, a wealthy effete middle- or upper-class observe the students with it seems as much interest as the performance itself. British Library shelfmark: 11651.cc.25.

far to say that in a way Bomberg, following a sketch aesthetics, is self-archiving sensation.

I'd like now to finish with a librarian's plea for the importance of the printed book in the special collection. Three of the four books I've described, Sassoon's important edition of Owen, James Guthrie's Edward Thomas, and the David Bomberg, were purchased by the British Library some time after their initial publication because the Legal Deposit obligation on publishers to deposit with the Library isn't always enough, or hasn't been historically, especially with pamphlets and artist's books; and sometimes catastrophe occurs within the securest archives. The Edward Thomas was only acquired in 1927, more than a decade after its publication; the Owen was only acquired, incredibly, in 1993, some seventy years after its publication (though a later impression the Library had for much longer). *Russian Ballet* is a particularly sad story: the copy in the Library was destroyed by the attacks of a later war — in the Blitz — and so entered that large category known there as 'war damage'. It was only replaced in comparatively recent times.

Luckily, curatorial expertise was able to recover those publications for future research. 'Luckily' because it matters not only that we have what we think is the 'original' text of a historical literary work (a manuscript) but that we have that text in its various manifestations, the authority of the manuscript and, as or more importantly, the authority of the published work as different generations of readers will have received it and so understood it. It may be as critical to understand how the word has been *shared*, in different succeeding ways, as how an author first conceived it before beginning his or her collaboration with editor, publisher and audience. The digital age makes the role of the archive as witness of the pre-digital more important, not less: the best special collections seek to represent manuscript and published works (whether print or digital), within a community in which and for which the archive safeguards the shared word.

His Care for Living English: Ford Madox Ford

Basil Bunting was very briefly sub-editor, personal assistant and factotum for Ford Madox Ford in Paris while the *transatlantic review* was underway. He didn't last long in the post —a matter of weeks, perhaps in late 1923 and early 1924[24] — in any case a period considerably less than the duration of the *transatlantic review* itself, whose period of publication, just the calendar year of 1924, was short enough. The briefest of surviving correspondence suggests they were still in touch in the early 1930s.[25]

Yet nearly fifty years later Bunting remembered Ford both fondly and respectfully. The fondness I'll return to later — perhaps it is more significant than it seems — but first there is the selection Bunting made in 1971 of Ford's poems for the US publisher Pym-Randall and, in particular, his focus on Ford's literary achievement in the preface.[26] Bunting opens that preface:

---

[24] Richard Caddel, 'Bunting, Basil Cheesman (1900–1985)', *Oxford Dictionary of National Biography*, Oxford: Oxford University Press, 2004.

[25] Ford Madox Ford, letter to Basil Bunting, 7th Sept 1932, in Ford Madox Ford Collection, Collection Number 4605, Cornell University Library, Ithaca, New York.

[26] Basil Bunting, in Ford Madox Ford, *Selected Poems*, edited with a preface by Basil Bunting, Cambridge, Mass.: Pym-Randall Press, 1971.

> I dare not maintain that Ford Madox Ford was a great poet or even a very good one; nevertheless in a few years before and after the first German war he did write some excellent poems which had a wider influence than anybody has acknowledged except Ezra Pound, and which might have more. Ford's friends at that time admitted Wordsworth's precept of a vocabulary taken from everyday speech, though they neglected it, and Yeats' further precept of everyday syntax, as much neglected; but Ford did not neglect them. He tried to write as he would speak, informally, and add to conversational diction the rhythms of conversation. That was rare in 1910, almost unknown.[27]

There's quite a lot in that paragraph. I think Bunting is trying to offer a measure of Ford which will convince the reader of the trustworthiness of Bunting's own judgement so that in turn the reader will take Ford seriously — he 'dare not' attest to a greatness in Ford not necessarily because Ford isn't a great poet but because Bunting is adopting a sound rhetorical tactic for the re-introduction of a poet many of the book's readers would not have thought of as a poet at all, if indeed they knew him as a novelist.

Let's not get carried away with ourselves, Bunting is telling us: with the sort of discriminating sensibility I have, I'm certainly not going to and you shouldn't either. At the same time, though, he suggests that not only was Ford interesting in his time, but that his interest has not all been consumed: he 'might have more' influence on the contemporary scene.

For this reason I'm not sure that Max Saunders, in his later, broader selection of Ford's poems, is right to say Bunting is

---

[27] Basil Bunting, op.cit., p.vii.

damning Ford with faint praise in this preface.[28] Yes Bunting does go on to say that his selection is brief because there are a lot of 'lifeless piles of patched rags [in Ford's poetry], sticky with commonplace adjectives, dusty with nouns out of a museum'[29], and that does sound rather negative, but in the context of Bunting's emphasis on good judgement and discrimination I still read his selection of Ford as an unequivocal work of advocacy.

Before getting down to championing Ford on stylistic grounds Bunting first sets a wider literary context, praising Ford's verse for its synthesising and catalytic effects on others, early on in the history of modern poetry. They are 'excellent poems' of far-reaching *influence* which were not only composed of the words of common parlance but the structures of that speech, too.

There is an accusatory undertone in this passage in that only Pound is said to have willingly acknowledged Ford's innovation and, as the preface unfolds, at least one prime suspect is revealed to be not a poet at all but that other famous language hygienist, that ungrateful fosterling of Ford's, Ernest Hemingway. I think I'll have to leave it to others to see how far Hemingway is stylistically in debt to Ford, though he certainly seems to have owed Ford in other ways. Perhaps Bunting is casting his net wider, too — to Eliot, say, who may have been very interested in what Ford was writing in the years immediately before and during the First World War — but this is beyond my scope here.

Bunting states Ford's approach to vocabulary and rhythm 'was rare in 1910, almost unknown' and I suspect he is right, but such re-

---

[28] Max Saunders, in Ford Madox Ford, *Selected Poems,* edited and introduced by Max Saunders, Manchester: Carcanet Press, 1997, p.xii.
[29] Basil Bunting, op.cit., p.viii.

orientation of poetic diction doesn't isolate Ford, even if it gives him special prominence as an early innovator. Paul Skinner, in his article 'Poor Dan Robin: Ford Madox Ford's Poetry', documents and discusses the various aesthetic schools of this period that Ford's poetry anticipates or with which it shares common ground; I won't replay those here.[30] Suffice it to say that, for Bunting, Ford becomes a branch on the bough of the modernist family tree whose authors by and large have faith in the philosophical, sonic, poetical resources of carefully stylised contemporary speech.

That's the family to which William Carlos Williams, Chekhov and D. H. Lawrence in their different ways belong, as does Hemingway, and which, arguably, could claim an uncle in Thomas Hardy and in Joseph Conrad and cousins in Edward Thomas and Charlotte Mew. They deploy common speech (though not, generally speaking, working-class speech) and have confidence in its emotional and intellectual depths and in their own sophisticated use of it.

There is also one thing in this passage that Bunting seems to be saying, by not saying it, which I find particularly interesting. His emphasis would surely lead us to think that Ford's poetry did not belong, taxonomically speaking, to the other quite different modernisms: the modernism, say, of the book or sequence as an attemptive totalising scheme (*The Cantos, A Drunk Man Looks at The Thistle, Finnegans Wake*); the modernism in which top-down views of all human civilisation and history are imposed on what are seen as the sordid disappointments of the present-day, as *The*

---

[30] Paul Skinner, 'Poor Dan Robin: Ford Madox Ford's Poetry', in Robert Hampson and Tony Davenport (eds.), *Ford Madox Ford: A Reappraisal*, Amsterdam: Rodopi, 2002, pp.79-103.

Waste Land, and much of Pound appear to me; the modernism of the continued mobilisation of tales, poems and events from classical Greece and Rome, with perhaps the literature of medieval Europe thrown in for an extra didactic scourge. Bunting also doesn't refer to the collage and recycling effects that you see in, say, Eliot and Blaise Cendrars; and, especially striking for Bunting, he doesn't mention musical concepts as organising principles (or at least organising analogues). I of course simplify and unwind these inter-braided themes — forgive a librarian's tendency towards classification.

The odd thing is that although Ford is characterised by Bunting as a moderniser of poetry for both process (rhythm and syntax) and phenomenon (vocabulary, and therefore subject), both predicated on 'the everyday', that is precisely not the sort of poet Bunting is for large swathes of his own poetry. It is also not the poet Ford often is. Rather, Bunting, perhaps more than Ford, has his Poundian frustrated-professor-with-a-view-on-everything manner (Professor Yaffle as bookend); both Bunting and Ford are very much Europhiles and classicists; and both use sequences that proceed by collage effects. Ford and Bunting are more than all that, too, but those classic modernist elements are there in both their work: yet Bunting chooses not to mention them at all.
In this he is, only to a relative degree, following Ford himself. In Ford's preface to his *Collected Poems* (1914), he goes to some lengths to downplay the necessity of classical and European education, and the use of biblical and Irish myths in poetry. He is liberal and acknowledges poets as 'heirs of all the ages', but in preferring what he calls 'the right appreciation' of the 'facets of our own day' he presents a much richer version of modernist ambition than Bunting's representation, including the challenge to the modern poet of engaging with urban spectacle, class

consciousness, and crowd behaviour — all elements that Bunting does not explicitly highlight as characteristics of Ford's work but are in fact there.[31]

Bunting doesn't mention Ford's championing of juxtaposition either and, as we have said, neglects to mention music as an ordering concept in Ford's work, though he is alert to broadly aural effects of which rhythm is one. This is surprising because Bunting is himself such a musically-attuned poet, as witnessed by a much later work — that exquisite sonic work *Briggflatts*, which is published as one of several 'Sonatas' in his own *Collected Poems* — but is only the culmination of a life interest in classical music.

Specifically, it is in music that Bunting and Ford meet. They are both fascinated by music as a subject and, especially, as an analogue and example by which they organise their own work. The Ford who wrote early poems to be set to music and whose compositional skills did not desert him in later works is the Ford Bunting is especially fond of. Ford is *particularly* interested in music: many poems are labelled as songs, some appearing to aspire to pieces in a classical repertoire, and others, more abstractly, more tenuously, seeming to toggle from a collage (visual) structure to an almost symphonic (aural) one, or hybridise both.

Bunting does include such poems in his selection — perhaps 'On Heaven' and 'Footsloggers' as examples of the latter, but his focus is really on the spoken word. After his assertion of Ford's inspired use of speech patterns Bunting goes on to warn how this is a

---

[31] Ford Madox Hueffer, *Collected Poems*, London: Max Goschen, 1914. p.20.

dangerous tactic — there's the high risk of 'letting the poem sag'. Here Bunting uses a sailing metaphor: to prevent that laxness 'Ford sweated up his halliards like a sailor. He took a fresh purchase and another swig again and again till the sail's last wrinkle was smoothed out.'[32]

What does he mean by this? It looks at first as if Ford is writing and re-writing to get a better expression of things — to achieve, say, the sort of tight, no-flab nonsense that the Imagist anthologies promoted — halliards hoist and then tighten a sail and the smoother the sail the more efficient it is. But it's not a re-drafting process that Bunting is talking about — this isn't honing or, that favourite craft of Bunting's, stone-chiselling. Ford is not emerging as a herald of Imagism: something quite different is happening, something that rather leapfrogs Imagism in the 'Boy's Own' chronology of literary movements and moves forward to something much more like the on-the-move observations of Objectivism. Maybe its meaning is already hinted at in that curious use of the word 'swig'.

When I first read it I thought that Bunting meant 'swing' on a halyard ratchet, an inspired misprint that has it both ways with swinging's hearty lust-for-life tone, and swigging's repeated drinking motion. Bunting, distrustful of footnotes and open to the anarchy of musical effects, might well have enjoyed that misreading. In fact I should have trusted Bunting's lexis: there is no such misprint, 'swig', as a verb, is a precise nautical term for, as the Oxford English Dictionary has it, '[pulling] at the bight of a rope which is fast at one end to a fixed object and at the other to a

---

[32] Basil Bunting, op. cit., p.vii.

movable one'.³³ The word has a literary pedigree, too: as a noun, a swig, it is used in both drinking and marine senses by Melville in *Redburn* (1849) when he describes, perhaps with an additional homo-erotic frisson, shipmates surreptitiously getting together over a brown jug of alcohol 'Every once in a while, the men went into one corner, where the chief mate could not see them, to take a 'swig at the halyards', as they called it.' ³⁴

So in Bunting's use of this little word there is joie-de-vivre, command of a precise technical vocabulary, a sense of movement, and also a tension, embodied in the metaphor, between fixed form and the 'movable' — to swig is to acknowledge a line that is held, controlled, but also to allow its free verse form, all within a structure, a vessel, that is itself, of course, moving on. Imagism's static and mere visual accuracies (in fact, effects) are far from what Ford is doing because there is something much more mobile, cumulative and recurring in his technique, something I would suggest, that is much more Objectivist. As Peter Makin says, when discussing Bunting's aesthetics, '[rhythmic play] has far greater value when the poet can articulate it into a paragraph-long progression of changes, of shifts developed for some deep analogy – or contrast – with changing meaning. [...] This art, for Bunting, is the real thing: it is that for which verse, in English, essentially exists.'³⁵ Bunting continues in his Preface to Ford:

---

³³ 'swig', verb, 3ʳᵈ definition, in *Oxford English Dictionary,* Oxford: Oxford University Press, 1989; online version http://www.oed.com/.
³⁴ The Melville quotation is taken from the dictionary reference.
³⁵ Peter Makin, 'Introduction', in Peter Makin (ed.), *Basil Bunting on Poetry*, Baltimore: Johns Hopkins University Press, 1999, pp.xxxv.

Ford and Conrad talked too much about Flaubert but did not waste much time playing hide-and-seek with the precise word. They surrounded their meaning *with successive approximations instead, and so repeated in the texture of prose* the pattern by which their narrative captured their theme. It is a circuitous technique, prodigal of paper. For sure, Flaubert would not have recognised it: yet nebulosities and imprecisions are much of our landscape without or within, and worth reproducing. In his best years Ford reproduced them in verse.' [36]

In *The Good Soldier*, I can't help thinking of the spiralling use Ford makes of the sentimental and colloquial phrases his narrator deploys in strange centrifugal forms, distancing himself from his own drama. They are a kind of emotional avoidance, vain attempts to push away expressions of passion and culpability, but the reader is drawn to the trail of their heat source and gradually infers the mess at the heart of the emotional vortex (perhaps it is not so out of place that *The Good Soldier* should have been part serialised in *Blast*, the self-proclaimed mouthpiece of the Vorticists).

Maybe this technique is a Chekhovian tactic of saying a series of only small things to get to the depths of something that cannot be said outright or without the purchase of time or perhaps it has its roots in Browning's elliptical dramatic monologues ('My Last Duchess', like Florence in *The Good Soldier*, 'had a heart'): it is certainly reliant on voice, successiveness and on levered silences so is especially suited to the stage — I think of the waves of patterning in Beckett, Pinter, and Mamet — Angus Wrenn has written on Ford and Pinter though doesn't really address affinities

---

[36] Basil Bunting, op.cit., p.vii.

in prosody[37] — and to the novel when it proceeds by stylised rhythmic dramatic monologue: followers of Ford may be surprised to find kin in James Kelman's novels, *The Bus Conductor Hines*, or *How Late it Was, How Late*, where remarkable speech patterning, nebulosities and imprecisions add up to complex texts of great emotional power.

At this point a case study seems appropriate. Bunting was particularly interested in Ford's 'The Starling'. He chose it to open his 1971 selection of Ford's poetry and, in his talk, 'Precursors', from the 1969-70 series of lectures he gave at Newcastle University, it is the poem that Bunting chose to exemplify Ford's work: he praises Ford and then reads the whole poem to the class.[38] As with his role in the American publication of Ford's *Selection*, Bunting's public recognition of Ford within modernist history shows what an unrecognised champion of Ford both sides of the Atlantic he was: Bunting really was an early and discerning critic who never forgot Ford's literary significance and was able to re-ignite interest in his work when he had himself been re-connected to a broader audience of readers.

Nevertheless, at first look 'The Starling' is an odd choice for asserting Ford's modernity — it has a medieval, villagey, aspect to it and so would appear to be precisely the type of poem Ford casts

---

[37] See Angus Wrenn, 'Long letters about Ford Madox Ford: Ford's afterlife in the work of Harold Pinter,' in Paul Skinner (ed.), *Ford Madox Ford's Literary Contacts,* Rodopi, 2007. pp.225-235.

[38] Basil Bunting, 'Precursors', in Peter Makin (ed.), *Basil Bunting on Poetry*, Baltimore: Johns Hopkins University Press, 1999, pp.105-117.

doubt on in his preface to *Collected Poems* (1914)³⁹. However, Ford's own advice elsewhere in the Preface warns the reader not to take a rural mis-en-scene as intrinsically backwards. For example, he justifies his admiration for Hardy and Yeats whatever the location of their poems (which he characterises as rural) and asserts the primacy of 'the genuine love and the faithful rendering of the received impression'⁴⁰ wherever the setting. 'The Starling' is also, as I'll briefly go on to show, a disavowal of a previous village-based life. In that way — and in others — it is actually a portmanteau poem, a manifesto poem, and so surprisingly well-suited as an illustration of Ford's aesthetic. Ford includes 'The Starling' in the *Collected Poems* and, like Bunting in the *Selected*, positions it right at the start of the book. It is also placed at the start of the collection it originally came from, *High Germany*. So Bunting may be paying homage and respect to Ford's sequencing, and perhaps remembering the impact it made as he first began to read Ford. Introducing the poem at Newcastle he said:

> [...]Pound is not merely being loyal to a friend when he insists on the part Ford played in changing English poetry in the earlier years of this century. Ford at his best uses language that is not merely current but conversational. Ford at his best names *things* and lets them evoke the emotion without mentioning it. He had not the gift of monumental brevity, but he uses repetition for a kind of

---

[39] Ford Madox Hueffer, *Collected Poems*, London: Max Goschen, 1914. See for instance: 'Love in country lanes, the song of birds, moonlight – these the poet, playing for safety, and the critic trying to find something safe to praise, will deem the sure cards of the poetic pack.' (p.16).
[40] Ford Maddox Hueffer, op. cit., p.28.

hypnotic effect: uses it quite consciously, without trying to disguise it.[41]

'It's an odd thing how one changes...' Ford begins his poem 'The Starling.' There's a three-dot ellipsis at the end of that sentence, one of those pre-Pinter pauses Ford comically but sincerely codified in *transatlantic review* as an essential part of English speech, something 'by which the Briton — and the American now and then — recovers himself in order to continue a sentence.'[42] Angus Wrenn doesn't mention the connection between this pause and Pinter's prosody but it is surely a mark of significant affinity; it's the hard-wiring they share.[43]

As well as the signalling of an emotional or cerebral breathing space, the pause in the poem alerts us straight away to a time signature, warning us that the text is likely to modulate. The

---

[41] Basil Bunting, 'Precursors' in Peter Makin (ed.), *Basil Bunting on Poetry*, Baltimore: Johns Hopkins University Press, 1999, pp.105-117. Passage quoted, p.111.
[42] Ford Madox Ford, 'Communications', in *the transatlantic review*, 1:1 (Jan. 1924), p.97.
The passage reads:
> For ourselves we limit ourselves to the use of..... to indicate the pauses by which the Briton – and the American now and then – recovers himself in order to continue a sentence. The typographical device is inadequate but how in the world..... how in the world else ? – is one to render the normal English conversation? The last one at which we attended on English soil ran as follows: (We were in our club waiting for the waiter to bring change for a cheque)
> *First Club Member.* What sort of a feller is... er...?
> (*He points with his chin at an individual by the further fireplace.*)
> *Second Ditto* Oh..... He's..... He's a ;;..... Er;;;;;; Er......
> *First Ditto (Briskly)* Ah !;;;..... I always thought so.

[43] Wrenn, op. cit..

rhyming couplets Ford uses for much of the poem make this transmission once or twice rather clumsy, especially when two short lines follow each other as they do soon enough:

> It's an odd thing how one changes...
> Walking along the ranges
> Of this land of plains,
> In this month of rains, [...]

Plains and rains? It sounds as if cranes, drains and Spain will be just around the corner. It is not a serious opening for what is, as it turns out, a relatively serious poem.

Before the rhyme crime though, let's go back to that very first sentence's 'It's an odd thing how one changes...' That's an unpoetic thing to say, too, but it's type of 'unpoetry' is much more interesting than plains and rains. Taken literally it really isn't poetry at all, it's surely seven words of a single sigh, one of those arresting sighs you might make to have a listener turn to you and say, 'come on, what's the matter?' and later you'd feel, when you had unburdened your heart and your interlocutor was now perhaps wishing you hadn't, that you could still declare with some honesty, 'well, you did *ask*...'

So it looks like a low-key and even an inept beginning to a poem, but I think that first line in particular is actually something of a disarming lure. Looked at more closely it gives up a bit more. It's a line about aloneness and pace. That 'one' hovers between an indefinite anybody (so bringing in all readers to sympathise — they are invited to agree, 'Isn't it though?') and a more commanding, authoritative statement — the use of an upper-class third person replacement for a first person pronoun. It is a circumlocution, a class-based sleight of hand, which is very similar to the tactics of emotional avoidance that takes place in *The Good Soldier*.

What then happens in the poem is that several kinds of non-human plurals, groups, are described, contrasting to the speaker's solitariness and to his sense of almost waking to find that he has been overtaken — not just by the feathered friends of the eponymous bird but by changes in his own behaviour over time; he's been overtaken by his consciousness of his own singleness. There are those plural ranges, those plains; even the weather — the rains — is happening severally (and exotically). Then there are the 'the poplars [that] march along' and finally 'With a rush of wings flew down a company, / A multitude, throng upon throng, / Of starlings, / Successive orchestras of song, / Flung, like the babble of surf, / On to the roadside turf.' Not just one bird orchestra but 'successive' ones, a travelator of them!

This contrast, between the silent speaker full of thoughts, and between apparently unthinking groups, now fully and variously vocal, is *the* contrast of the poem. Later in the poem the two shortest lines cut the word 'I' off at the end of the line ,the subjective particularism of 'but I,' and then, later, the phrase repeated, 'but I.' But before these we have another of those improvisational 'nebulosities' that Bunting described as part of Ford's genius — this time the comic attempt to gauge the distance of the moving starling flock 'And so, for a mile, for a mile and a half — a long way, / Flight follows flight'.

It might be a nebulosity but that surely captures something of the difficulty of such a measure – it isn't an inarticulacy, it is a super-articulacy because it is conveying the distance in as far as it can be estimated, conveying the flocks' movement away from the speaker, and conveying the speaker's honesty as he modifies his assessment 'live'. This is something that it's easy to miss if you are not are attuned to Ford's poems as dramatising speech, or thoughts dramatised as speech: they offer a different kind of linguistic density which is not necessarily visual, nor necessarily attractive as savourable vocabulary, but which, perhaps because they are not snagged by those effects, offer a different sort of sequence-of-events sophistication altogether.

The opening sentence then comes back in the third stanza:

> It's an odd thing how one changes...
> And what strikes me now as most strange is:
> After the starlings had flown
> Over the plain and were gone,
> There was one of them stayed on alone
> In the trees; it chattered on high,
> Lifting its bill to the sky,
> Distending its throat,
> Crooning harsh note after note,
> In soliloquy,
> Sitting alone.

Chatter, dandyism, and apparently a fascination with the grating 'note after note': there seems to be self-identification and a manifesto in this, an interest in the solitary being paradoxically all loquaciousness and volubility, an interest even in what might conventionally be regarded as ugly sounds. Ford goes on to describe the starling's ability to mimic (Ford the master of pastiche). However, after dwelling on this Ford's speaker turns away from the starling with a near stutter of the me, myself, I –
> But I,

> Whilst the starling mimicked on high
> Pulsing its throat and its wings,
> I went on my way
> Thinking of things,
> Onwards and over the range
> And that's what is strange.

The reader never gets to know what the speaker is thinking about: as the speaker descends into a village, which is pulsing with a multiplicity of life in anticipation of a wedding party, the reader can only infer that the speaker's rueful avoidance of both bird and then festivities — his avoidance of 'a dance / With the bride in her laces / Or the maids [...] / [...] in the stable...' — has everything to do with his inner thoughts, with what he has done in the past. He is no longer that sort of man, he bumbles, refraining from the starling's display behaviour, refraining from love and passion (while strongly signalling his enduring interest in them), until he is left finally only with himself – 'And I... I stand thinking of things.' — that double 'I' and the long pause within it: dot dot dot.

After all that refraining, it is only his own poetic refrain he has for company: 'And I... I stand thinking of things. / Yes, it's strange how one changes.' Bunting's Preface again stresses the peculiar quality displayed here:

> There are explorations that can never end in discovery, only in willingness to rest content with an unsure glimpse through mists, an uncertain sound of becks we shall never taste: approximations. To this Ford's rhythm and diction in these poems tend steadily; to this their matter is organized with great skill. Ford leaves his hearer with no perfection to contemplate, not even a line that might become a 'familiar quotation,' but rested as though something

lovely had passed, which he cannot quite recall, which yet makes it easier to put up with the day.[44]

that phrase – 'organised with great skill.' The larger structures that Ford builds — his orchestration, an orchestration that can use a mundane phrase like 'it's strange how one changes' with other cumulative effects and build them into larger and deeper works. As Max Saunders suggests, it's the handling of the whole poem in which Ford excels — 'He can express complex ideas in complex forms that unfold effortlessly, as if perfectly improvised'[45] - and it's this that Bunting must have recognised early on. Many years later, when the good cop/ bad cop dynamic of Eliot and Pound's reputations, 'fighting in the Captain's tower' as Bob Dylan so agilely confined them, was in danger of monopolising wider understanding of the complex nature of modernism, Bunting returned to and remembered Ford in these tributes.

Bunting recognises that Ford is simultaneously improvisational, allowing the improvisations their place in the poem or novel, though foregrounding them as character traits, and a consummate structurer of his work. For both of them it is about being subtle over time, about being subtle with unpromising raw materials.

Bunting himself wants more direct yield from each of his lines — either you need a muscular tongue and a dictionary that comes in volumes to read Bunting, you need to be open to collage and jump-cuts, or else you need to suspend precisions and somehow imbibe, swig, the sound and art-cinema images (as Bunting encourages you

---

[44] Basil Bunting, op.cit., p.viii.
[45] Max Saunders, in Ford Madox Ford, *Selected Poems,* edited and introduced by Max Saunders, Manchester: Carcanet Press, 1997, p.xiv.

to do in his various statements of aesthetics). Bunting recognises there are other kinds of value that Ford's poetry can offer when it appears at first to be most prosaic. That value requires a sensitivity to what is actually being said in everyday speech but it also benefits from a broader organisation of the text to release it. Ford delivers that organisation. Ford's attention to speech vocabulary or speech rhythms is probably what Bunting is referring to when, in a letter to Bernard Poli, he describes Ford's 'care for living English' but the compressing high modernist in Bunting isn't so able to follow Ford's example in that — he is much closer to Ford when considering how a poem might be furled by the poet so that it can unfurl for the reader.

There is so much more to say. You can see Bunting's Ford in the 1971 *Selected* but what would Ford's Bunting be? Maybe he would be fond of the poems Bunting was making in his lifetime, working very quickly to adopt the techniques of the milieu that Ford had helped introduce Bunting to. Maybe Ford would have been aware of the making of 'Villon', Bunting's poem of Paris, formed during the early years of Bunting's friendship with Pound and Ford while Pound was working on Villon the Opera. Ford was a particular enthusiast of Villon's[46], particularly for what Ford saw as Villon's modernity, and perhaps both Pound and Bunting owe Ford a debt on that account, too. Ford would have remembered Bunting's own imprisonment in Paris and he knew of his principled stand as a Quaker and conscientious objector which had

---

[46] Ford Maddox Hueffer, Preface, *Collected Poems*, London: Max Goschen, 1914.

led to his first incarceration during the First World War. Maybe, to acknowledge a possible source, he would have republished the 1928 ode in which Bunting uses the word 'buckshee'. Looking down (or across) from Heaven, maybe Ford would have chosen later poems by Bunting which share some of his own work's characteristics and even motifs: Ford's sequence 'Buckshee' (1931) shares quite a few things with *Briggflatts* — that autobiographical look back, of course; a sense of the fragility of intellectual culture; a glimpsed sensitivity to childhood. There is even a shared motif —bees as a marker of time — and both are in that symphonic, or at least sonata-like, form where juxtaposition and recurrence and variation are of such interest.

There is more to say, and these surface affinities would need to be tested quite a bit more before they could be trusted. Less to do with literary criticism and more to do with literary history, there is the curious role each had in relation to younger writers. One of Ford's qualities was his openness to younger writers, editorially and personally — Bunting suggests male writers in particular — and it is this characteristic that Bunting singles out in the closing paragraphs of his Preface:

> What does matter is his kindness to young men and men in distress, his readiness to talk to them at length, without being patronising or pedantic, his willingness to consider everything, the tolerance in his frivolity, his care for living English, his generosity, his fun.

Ford as mentor, protector, taker-in of strays — this is the impression the reader is left with from this account and to Bunting that appears to be exactly what Ford was for him. Perhaps *the transatlantic review* was Ford's last attempt to keep the compact he had earlier made in *The English Review* between the old and the young — the small number of 'discoveries' suggests that it was not so easy post-war to find new young writers of interest — but for Bunting the personal kindness of Ford was important, too.

Curiously, from the viewpoint of the late 1960s and early 1970s, Bunting himself was now in a figurehead or rallying position. Never a group worker in the way that Ford was, Bunting nevertheless identified very much with the energy and urgency of the younger writers who had sought him out. It is striking that he attracted writers from a very broad spectrum — you couldn't get a much greater difference in approach than that found between Jeremy Prynne and Tom Pickard, but both recognised the great interest of his work. There is a significant difference though: to some degree, Bunting, in his sixties synchronised with the years of the century, was again his own stray — in a sense the young rescued him in a way that Ford had helped rescue him fifty or so years before. It was young poets like Pickard and, earlier, Gael Turnbull, who were instrumental in Bunting's own personal renaissance, encouraging him to write again, arranging his publication and giving him a venue to read to astonished audiences. That, perhaps, is another context to his selection of Ford's poetry — Bunting may not have just been thanking Ford but also thanking the young who, with their 'willingness to consider everything', with the 'tolerance in [their] frivolity', their generosity, their fun, had brought Bunting (and indirectly, Ford) back to life.

Making

CAT-scanning the Little Magazine

The Beatles and a Brontosaurus

Computerized axial tomography, 'CT-' or 'CAT-scanning', is a procedure in which multiple X-ray photographs are taken from different positions along a single axis. A composite three-dimensional image is rendered from the results. In medicine it is a particularly powerful diagnostic tool because it allows radiologists to see soft tissues, normally beyond the scope of ordinary X-ray machines. Other branches of sciences use the invention, too: for example, it can be used in the non-destructive investigation of the fossilised embryos in dinosaur eggs.

The first CAT-scanning equipment was invented in the late 1960s when experiments by Godfrey Hounsfield at the EMI Central Research Laboratories in Hayes, Middlesex, enabled the development of a commercially available scanner. A working prototype was used in a hospital as early as October 1971. It is said that EMI were able to fund Hounsfield's research on the back of The Beatles' enormous commercial success. Fittingly, it would appear that this famously idealistic pop group, a product of a complex Fifties and Sixties counterculture of which poetry magazines were such a part, had inadvertently funded this remarkable instrument of public health, spreading the message of 'Love, Love, Love,' in the most practical of ways.

In tribute to that relationship, perhaps the metaphor of CAT-scanning might be applied to the study and appreciation of little magazines. This would certainly involve looking in multiple ways at a single magazine in order to render its complexity in a concentrated, composite form. It would allow readers to see more in retrospect than the basic bone structure represented by a magazine's celebrity authors: all a magazine's authors and all its other contributors, be it illustrator or correspondent on the letters page, all its advertisements, its graphic design, its economics and marketing; the CAT-scan would detect the soft tissue, the living organs, of the magazine.

More than this, in the same way that the data underlying individual CAT-scans can be aggregated to identify material patterns across the particular category under study — be it patients with a particular medical condition or the eggs of a particular species of dinosaur — so the CAT-scanning project would go further than commentary on individual magazines. The project would press on to look across many examples — in the reasonable expectation that this would identify common characteristics, building indeed to a kind of aesthetics, perhaps even demonstrating the little magazine, like the novel, like the artist's book, to be an art form in its own right. Such a project would eschew anecdotal approaches to literary history, which so often perpetuate the folklore surrounding this or that author, this or that movement. Rather, it would take a data approach rooted in indexing, pattern recognition and number; it would observe and aggregate 'behavioural traits' rather than amplify myth.

The Fortnightly, that monthly
One behavioural trait any little magazine must have is what can be termed 'periodicity', the expectation that it will re-appear, that it is indeed a 'periodical'. After all, a magazine is not a magazine if it not intended to go beyond the first issue (there are one or two interesting exceptions to this, but more about that later).
Periodicity is a key aesthetic cue — indeed for all serial literature not just little magazines. Importantly, little magazines as a population exhibit a particularly large range of responses to periodicity, sometimes slavishly observing rules of frequency, sometimes rebelliously flouting them. This is an indicator of the

meta-magazine role that little magazines can have: they are not always simply conveyors of text but can be highly reflexive commentators on the otherwise unacknowledged set of signs that serial publications of all kinds emit.

Periodicity is also one of the aspects of a magazine that can be 'flattened' by traditional forms of literary study and by trends in re-publication. Following the work of a particular author through the paper trail of first publication, it is easy to isolate his or her texts from the environment of their publication. In the 1910s and 1920s misplaced devotion to a single author might miss that one 'magazine' was in fact a newspaper (*The New Age* for instance), another was a monthly (*The English Review*), another was issued only in term-time (many student magazines), and yet another was the erratic creation of an ad-hoc collective (the Vorticists' *Blast*), yet in each of these cases the circumstances of publication, the expectation of audience as a function of publishing frequency, is likely to be different and to have a bearing on either the intention of the author and (more certainly) on the nature of that text's reception. Context may not be entirely everything, but if audience behaviour counts for anything there is a difference between a poem published in a weekly and an annual, even if the poem is the same.

Attuning to this is made more difficult by the reprinting of excerpted materials without proper indication of the nature of their original publication, and even by the levelling of the library catalogue where all kinds of materials are gathered together, creating the distracting conditions in which frequency, which may be faithfully recorded, is not understood as the para-aesthetic data it in fact is.

Like the 'punctum' – Roland Barthes' term for the moment encapsulated in a still photograph for the viewer, precisely when and how a magazine is received is a fundamental aspect of its meaning. Indeed the means of delivery — whether postal or bookshop, whether issued at readings, whether in galleries, pubs, bookshops, seminar rooms or more imaginative venues, all are part of the richer meaning of the magazine. A magazine is not a just a work but one that is issued in a particular way on a particular occasion and in the expectation of a particular sequence.

One example of this is detailed by Mark Morrisson in his discussion of Ford Madox Ford's *The English Review*. As Morrisson explains, this magazine, launched in 1908, adopted a monthly publication frequency, which in so doing asserted genre similarity to the *Mercure de France* and to the confusingly titled *The Fortnightly* which was, apart from a short time at the beginning of its life, also a monthly. The monthly regularity of *The English Review* mirrored certain format considerations of *Mercure de France* and *The Fortnightly*, such as a monthly round-up feature, attuning itself to a particular audience that was not looking for breaking news. (Such structural deployment may actually help to create or at least maintain such an audience.) News it was felt, could be handled by daily and weekly serial publications of one kind or another, a principle which is essentially in force today even if 'twenty-four hour' news has increased the frequency – so *The English Review* could devote itself to longer pieces that reflected on broader issues. It also published more literary content, which might take a month to absorb in the round.

Sometimes the 'event' of a magazine is synchronised with an external event that is so important it becomes a time marker itself. The self-designation of *Blast*'s second issue, its last, the 'War Number', aligned the magazine to the First World War almost as if subject and time had coalesced. This gave the magazine an importance, perhaps a self-importance, that appeared to shadow the appalling rhythm of world events. As Mark Morrisson also demonstrates, the magazine was privately trying to cover the ineptitude of its irregular publication schedule and was arguably taking advantage of the War as a marketing opportunity.

This meeting between an external event and 'magazine event' is related more broadly to special issues — a translation issue, a green issue, etc. — which similarly assert a coherence and importance to their topic and, while appearing to try to move a particular subject up a news agenda, may as likely be attaching the magazine to a topic which has more marketing force than the magazine itself.

As the *Blast* instance shows, the reason for this may not be obvious. Since shareholders as much as actual consumers are the target of advertising (since advertising alone may bolster confidence in the brand), sometimes a funder of a magazine may be the most significant target for a themed issue, for example when a state-sponsored magazine demonstrates through a themed issue that it is publishing work of a kind fostered by that state. Perhaps such practice is gently mocked by Ian Hamilton Finlay in his special issue of the 1960s magazine *Poor. Old. Tired. Horse.* (i.e., *P.O.T.H.* or *POTH*) when for its twenty-third outing he ran a whole number devoted to the humble, lisping 'Teapoth'.

The posthumous life of a magazine attracts journalistic interpretations of frequency, especially focussed on the ending of a magazine, the final note in the sequence of publication. Here the CAT-scanner needs the literary historian to compensate for distortion from the electromagnetic stimulations they may have brought into the lab with them: in the lab it's best to switch the gossipy mobile phone off, or at least switch it to flight-safe mode.

Wyndham Lewis's *Blast*, like Ford Madox Ford's *The English Review*, may be an example where posthumous fame is built on rather Romantic ideas of the nobleness of failure and failure is another aspect of periodicity. How a magazine comes to grief can, of course, say a lot about its nature, including its lack of adaptability, but can easily become too significant a part of its history when read back by later commentators with an aggrieved accusation of the vulgar wider public not being ready for the art of the future. Peter Barry's account of the wrestling for power of the Poetry Society during the 1970s, a conflict in which the editorial role of the *Poetry Review* was a key issue, demonstrates how different models of accessibility and innovation may well be issues at the heart of a magazine's demise, or at least at the heart of radical editorial change. Such models are not straightforward: the simplistic Romantic narrative of positive anarchist collectivists pitted against, say, state control and middle-brow taste is inadequate to explain the complexity of the world of publishing.

Censorship, too, is a much more complicated affair than at first may appear. When censorship brings a magazine to an untimely close, as with *Klaxon* in Ireland in 1923 (following a favourable review of Joyce's *Ulysses*), libertarian impulses are naturally offended and 'the State' identified as the villain. But the State is far from a unitary body, and just because public taste is short-circuited and second-guessed by the usual forces involved — printer, police, funder and advertiser — it doesn't mean that a majority of the public wouldn't indeed have acted in the same way given the chance.

Looking across the whole life of a magazine, one tone encoded by erratic periodicity might be a bumbling amateurism hybridised with connoisseurship. For example, the sound and visual poetry magazine, *And*, edited by Bob Cobbing and others from 1954, achieved only eleven irregularly spaced issues in its first five decades of life. Was that a testament to do-it-yourself poetics outside commercial considerations, eschewing the building and maintaining of an audience by regular publication, or evidence of a high quality threshold, that Cobbing published only when the work was good enough?

Certainly Cobbing's remarkable achievement with the small press *Writers Forum*, running parallel with *And* (if *And* could ever have been said to 'run'), gives the lie to inactivity or bumble. Energy, openness, 'driven-ness', would be better nouns for a publishing programme of hundreds of books, amounting to one of the most significant artistic interventions in contemporary poetry in England in the last century. If the CAT-scanner's variables are fixed in a certain way then the role of *Writers Forum* might be identified as para-periodical in operation so prolific was it and so responsive to topical events — and so keen, too, on periodical-like distribution methods (dating publications by month and tying publication into a regular public workshop schedule).

Across the twentieth century there are fascinating examples where periodicity is deliberately activated aesthetically. Under normal bibliographic conventions the books produced by the Imagists shouldn't fall into the magazine category but after the first volume, *Des Imagistes* (1914) the next two asserted that they were 'an annual anthology' (the 1915 and 1916 volumes). This simple apparently utilitarian phrase suggested at least two things — that this was a winnowed collection taking the best from the last year, and there would now be a reasonable expectation for successive annual volumes (as indeed there were, for a short time): this was a discerning movement that was here for the long term. Additionally this attuned the reader to the Imagists as a group operating within a recently established market of serial publication: anthologies of modern poetry. The annual Georgian poetry volumes which, despite their mixed posthumous reputation for luke-warm innovation, demonstrably trailblazed for the Imagists in genre terms; unlikely as it may seem, they were in one sense the avant-garde's avant-garde.

Activated periodicity could have charm. The last issue of William Nicholson and Robert Graves's *The Owl*, vol. 2, no. 3 issued in November 1923, is marked by a knowing and elegiac change of title to *The Winter Owl* — the time of issue, and the knowledge that it is the last issue, has bubbled over and transformed the magazine's actual name. This is followed through in artistic direction: gone are the warm soft blush-red colours Nicholson had adopted for previous issues and instead here is something bluer, greyer. Reference to the seasonal captures a traditionalist perhaps pastoral aesthetic. It is a dignified, bittersweet farewell.

One much later magazine provides a final example of self-consciousness in periodicity. Strictly speaking Tom Clark's *Once* only had one issue. *Once* had the subtitle a one-shot magazine, and though it was probably issued in 1965 was undated. After all, why would you date what you knew would be a one-off magazine? But the magazine was in fact resurrected, with its next reincarnation called *Twice*, which only appeared once, and that set the pattern for succeeding issues, though various creative flourishes added some teasing permutations: *Thrice, Thrice and a 1/2 , Frice, Vice, Spice, Slice, Ice, Nice, Dice* and, finally, *Lice*.

Success!

Little magazines are traditionally associated with ideas of marginality: political radicalism, support for one minority or another, support for the art form of poetry itself (conceived as a Cinderella art), and for various kinds of aesthetic extremes. This is conventionally cross-referenced to otherworldly economics, an idea that little magazines are necessarily non-commercial. The CAT-scan needs to be careful with this approach, indeed needs to put it to the test.

In assessing 'commercial success', it is of course possible to measure longevity and, though more difficult to evidence, circulation. Little magazine accounts, including subscriber lists (whose addresses can be mapped onto class structure maps of the period, if available) are valuable but rare finds in archives and editors are generally reluctant to disclose figures while the magazine is still being published. I suppose that if there are the data then a magazine that lasts for a long time, has a large circulation, and makes a profit, could be assigned high-scoring values and 'commercial success' confirmed, but the words 'commercial' and 'success' are both fraught. To place this in the relief of a negative example, so-called 'failed' magazines may have a kind of impact not measured by these criteria (Wyndham Lewis's *Blast* is still the subject of wonder, exploration and debate) and this may include long-term economic success for some of the participants.

While there are classic examples of 'successful' magazines which have consistently failed to make little artistic impact — the best-selling long-lasting *Poetry Review* (successfully artistically failing for most of its 100 years) — there are others which are not the commercial enterprises they seem. The most notorious example is probably *Encounter*: it ran from 1953 to 1990, with a circulation of what appears to be tens of thousands of readers per issue. So far so good; but *Encounter* was secretly part-funded by the Central Intelligence Agency (CIA) as a form of soft propaganda during the Cold War. This only came to light in 1967, several authors withdrawing their involvement in disgust (Auden, Betjeman, Creeley, Ted Hughes, Robert Lowell and Christopher Middleton). It would appear that *Encounter* was not, after all, a commercial publication; rather, it was practically a product of a planned economy, a sleight-of-hand planned economy, in this respect not so unlike the one its backers were trying to destroy.

Even so, the state/private dichotomy seems inadequate to the fascinating complexity of literary artefacts, perhaps little magazines especially. As far as *Encounter* is concerned, commerce was arguably still at play, whether or not it was state-funded, because the Cold War was, among many other harder, angrier, deadlier things in part a commercial conflict about literary and art products, all of which are not just caught in a mercantile mesh but, I would argue, part of its fabric. Is 'commercial' a helpful word in a suffusedly material world? The material nature of a magazine CAT-scan does not produce the reductive results a 'follow the money' approach might suggest it would: rather it reveals layers of association between aesthetics, individual participants, and institutions of various kinds.

Ian Hamilton Finlay's magazine of the 1960s, *Poor. Old. Tired. Horse* was commercial enough to survive five years of regular publication until Finlay decided to end its run. For most of its life it didn't send out the conventional cues of 'success': for example, although Finlay's sister press, the Wild Hawthorn Press, produced beautifully realised books with high production values, *Poor. Old. Tired. Horse* has a quaint, type-written quality to many of its issues; many were produced on mimeo stencil. Mercantile ambition doesn't seem to be the right lens through which to view the magazine, but as a means through which Finlay began to position himself (on paper) alongside the American avant-garde poetry milieu he published and then as a means, gradually, to position himself within the visual arts economy, it can indeed be seen as a commercial success. It is a classic example of how a little magazine, however well it does outwardly, can operate very effectively as a networking node, establishing a nub of contact between the editor and his or her contributors, a considerable measure of success which would not be obvious by looking at the magazine through the single dimensions of longevity or circulation (interesting though these elements also are).

Rather, the CAT-scan needs to re-focus, to see more clearly what the nature of funding for a particular magazine was — even photocopied, stapled, magazines — and how this may have contributed to the identity of the magazine itself and, importantly, to the measurable success of its editors and contributors after the demise of the magazine or of their involvement in it: the little magazine is probably not just a node in a network but the creator of networks that have a much longer life beyond the magazine itself.

If the theoretical CAT-scan were lucky enough to detect magazine archives with accounts, it might glean useful references to costs and funding from editor and contributor correspondence held in various collections here and abroad; memoirs are risky because of hindsight but need to be looked at; oral history is another way of getting closer to the money trail. Contextual information can be gathered from any advertisements in the magazine; if it doesn't have any advertisements or fliers then of course someone or something else was funding it, and that is part of what the magazine is: the optimum CAT-scan will detect that funder.

A magazine of any longevity was often funded by an arts council or regional arts board and their broadly regional or culturally nationalist agenda is usually reflected in content (*Chapman* (1970 onwards), for example, funded by the Scottish Arts Council or *South West Review* (1977–1985) published by South West Arts. However, it would be a mistake to see the productions as always social realist regional equivalents of tractor music —the CAT-scan would be able to collect content data and begin to say more about that hypothesis. Educational institutions (a university or university department or university society) appear to be significant funders, too; for example, *Poet & Audience* was funded by the University of Leeds's Student Union from its first issue in

1954. The CAT-scan would see if various kinds of funding association with the university (central official funding, student union, English department, informal student group, for example) influenced, say, the level of didacticism in their texts, the number of translations, adherence to or deviance from curricula, and other aspects which might reasonably be associated with university life. Once measures were established, comparative studies could begin their work to see pattern and pattern difference.

Looking at the wider picture, one hypothesis might be that university-based magazines compete with state-funded territory magazines by asserting either depoliticised texts (they think), or gendered and internationalist political concerns which lack self-consciousness about home regionality and home nationality, and vice versa. An empirical model might test such a research question.

The CAT-scan would triangulate more detailed measures of patronage by seeing that the allegiances between editors and contributors built up in and expressed through magazines continued in the later careers of these participants, within the world of newspaper and broadcast literary journalism, the prize-judging circuit, the prestige anthology, the university department and so on. Little magazines that 'failed' to the casual eye may have been very successful in creating other kinds of value for their participants, with that value continuing to be realised many years after the demise of the magazine. Because a series of artistic alliances that are maintained through the years is a major part of what an intellectual culture is, little magazines are worth testing as an early expression of this culture or set of interlocking cultures and how friendship is expressed and mobilised within literary networks. Where the university is involved, it may also be a way of seeing patterns of behaviour beneath aesthetic differences between and within 'mainstream' and 'avant-garde' forms of poetry, differences which the data already suggest are a playing out of the consequences of the massive over-representation of Oxford and Cambridge agency: in the geographical index of British Poetry Magazines 1914-2000, apart from the special case of London, which far exceeds those of all locations, no other cities beat the productivity of Oxford (83 different titles) and Cambridge (71) in this period; the few that come close are university cities (Dublin, 61; Edinburgh, 53). Poetry 'differences' in this light come over more as a series of high-end turf-wars whose rarefied environment may look like intellectual and aesthetic debates — and of course are, too — but whose result is the perpetuation of widespread adherence to whatever rules are articulated, distributed and controlled (metaphorically speaking, of course) by a tiny number of eminent gangster 'families', whose apparent differences give the false appearance of functional diversity in the poetry system.

Controls

The CAT-scan needs to look at other kinds of magazine, to understand the nature of its subject. In the language of the laboratory, it needs a 'control'. *The Poetry Review* is ideal for this purpose because it has many of the attributes little magazines would be shy to claim but which are key to its self-image: popularity, longevity, and the ability (or desire) to represent the whole of the UK. World significance and intellectual authority are also fundamental, though admittedly some little magazines might claim these also!

Encapsulating its establishment credentials in recent years *The Poetry Review* has begun to call itself the poetry magazine 'of record', a phrase which seems to have jumped the species barrier since it is normally reserved for newspapers — *The Times* was for many years regarded as the newspaper of record, probably because of its then serious tone, apparently broad coverage, relatively large and widespread circulation, London location and even its reporting of the royal calendar.

The Poetry Review uses some of these attributes for a similar claim but, through the woven web of citation, also mobilises the apparent authority of others - to do so. In the words of former editor Fiona Sampson: 'The Poetry Review is a world class publication and Britain's longest-running and most prestigious poetry magazine. Started in 1911, it continues to be 'the magazine of record' (Michael Schmidt in The Guardian) and as well as being the UK's bestselling poetry magazine, is hailed by Sir Andrew Motion as 'required reading''.

In fact, although the act of citation can seem, as it were, to guarantee the guarantee, Sampson is mistaken in seeing Michael Schmidt as endorsing The Poetry Review in the quoted article. He says exactly the opposite: 'The Poetry Review, […] as the organ of the Poetry Society might be thought (erroneously, it seems to me) to have a duty to be a magazine of record.' It is also clear that Schmidt's indefinite article, 'a magazine' — which allows plurality even while entertaining authority — has become a definite article in Sampson's retelling. The Poetry Review might have been one among many by Schmidt but in Sampson's version it is now self-special, the One and Only.

A CAT-scan would go further than face value, however. A study of the authors that The Poetry Review has featured and reviewed in the last ten years say, cross-checked against a range of other magazines operating in the same period, would test the face-value veracity of its claim. A survey of book publication, say, publisher by publisher, would map particular authors that appear in The Poetry Review to particular presses and their editors, which in turn could be analysed for company size, geographical location and column-inch coverage in the general print media (there is a dilemma about the direction of cause and effect here, so such a survey would have to be handled carefully). Because poetry is, of course, a formal art, you could also map formal analytics of poems that appear in the different magazines, and do the same using subject descriptors: is there a correlation between certain presses, print media coverage, and the frequency of their authors' publication in *The Poetry Review*, as opposed to the broader set of other poetry magazines, and, if so, how does that affect the meaning of that authoritative-sounding word 'record'? (There is an innate contradiction in the claim, between representation or witness and quality, which a CAT-scan would theoretically tease out). Such an empirical account would not prevent more detailed nuanced work; it would inform the parameters of later qualitative discussion. Without an empirical underpinning, commentary in this area should find it hard to escape the claim of bias, unconscious or otherwise.

There are wider-ranging comparisons to be made quantitatively. If the posthumous reputation of a single magazine can affect true understanding of it, this can also be the case when particular 'golden ages' (arguably, the British Poetry Revival of the 1960s and '70s) and apparent 'low points' (conventionally, the 1940s) are discussed, or else when concepts of nationality are brought up, for instance, the alleged insularity of the English. Devising empirical ways of testing legends and their varied lives (since legends do wax and wane), can help to understand not only the literary infrastructure of the day but also the extent to which anecdotal observations later become so-called accepted fact. The CAT-scan would be a means of testing today's assumptions, of testing today's claim to authority.

In the case of the British Poetry Revival, the phrase used to describe an apparent surge in poetry experimentation and a concomitant increase in poetry magazines in the '60s and '70s, it is worth stating that there is quantifiable evidence for the scale of this: from 1963 to 1970 tens of new magazines were launched each year (not hundreds, not thousands, as you might have thought, but certainly a sizeable shift from previous decades). However, productivity was not limited to the 1960s. Poetry publication again revived in the late '70s and '80s — at least thirty new titles appeared in most of the years in the period 1976-2000. The CAT-scan doesn't worry that no romantic phrase for this period has appeared to give it the status of the British Poetry Revival, it just notes the facts.

Other myths can be exposed. Did UK post-war interest in American contemporary poetry really begin as late as the 1960s? (*The Poet*, edited by W. Price Turner from 1952 to 1956, and publishing Cid Corman, Robert Creeley, and William Carlos Williams, suggests not). Is England really insular? In the period 1914-2000 the presence of nearly one hundred poetry magazines with a significant translation mission suggests the case is far from proven. The CAT-scan project should also be international, if only to reality-check national assumptions.

Literary criticism tends to deal with individuals — either famous individuals or those the critic argues should be famous. Book history tends to deal with presses, distribution and marketing, which work on impressive but conventional business models, or — for publishing in the literary arena —are associated with the famous individuals beloved of literary academics. This is a form of biography-led story-telling which has its place but sometimes confuses narrative with wider understanding. Today, however, there is no reason why the aggregating energies released by the inspired use of modern technology should not be applied to the history of literature. The vibrant long tail of little magazine (and small press) publication would be a very good place to start: an overarching project is yet to be made that links book history and literary criticism via such empirical analysis, interrogating at survey level what is known about these publications and the literary infrastructure in which they exist. The first steps towards a theory of CAT for little magazines have been made in the last twenty years or so within little magazines research, with some crucial isolated examples going back much further (see the examples in the Bibliography), but the next task is to begin to build some CAT-scan prototypes.

To Shake the Torpid Pool

In the meantime, here is a basic range-finding exercise, an attempt to look at the relationship between little magazines and small press pamphlets, scanning down the century in the hope that patterns might emerge that could be tested in more detail at a later time. Here are ten pamphlets from across the last century: Edward Thomas, *Six Poems* (1916); W. H. Auden, *Poems* (1928); Dylan Thomas, *18 Poems* (1934); Philip Larkin, *The North Ship* (1945); Roy Fisher, *City* (1961); Ian Hamilton Finlay, *Glasgow Beasts*(1961); Bob Cobbing, *Six Sound Poems* (1968); J. H. Prynne, *Fire Lizard* (1970); Denise Riley, *Marxism for Infants* (1977); and Kathleen Jamie, *Black Spiders* (1982). I have chosen them to represent different kinds of poetry, poets, and communities of publication. Being only ten, they can hardly be truly representative, but reflecting on them can form the basis of further more empirical investigation.

Friends

Almost all of these publications were either self-published or published by a friend. The two that appear to be published by someone else — Finlay's *Glasgow Beasts* (The Wild Hawthorn Press) and Bob Cobbing's *Six Sound Poems* (Writers Forum) — were in fact self-published, since the presses concerned were owned by the authors and co-run with friends. Five of the pamphlets were published by friends of the poet in question: in Edward Thomas's case, by the artist-publisher James Guthrie; Auden by Stephen Spender; Roy Fisher by Michael Shayer and Gael Turnbull (Migrant Press); Prynne by friends Barry MacSweeney and Elaine Randell (Blacksuede Boot Press); and Denise Riley by her friend Wendy Mulford (Street Editions).

Two authors appear to be neither self-published nor published by friends: Philip Larkin and Kathleen Jamie. It is interesting that Larkin and Jamie, characterised today as more mainstream poets, appear to have begun their publication history without obvious help from any old-boy or new-girl network. In a romantic history of the avant-garde this is counter-intuitive — perhaps there is an expectation of the little press world bravely operating outside the philosophy of 'it's not what you know but who you know'. That may be a serious misunderstanding of the poetry infrastructure, little press or mainstream. Who you know in the little magazine world is likely to be very significant for initial and later publication, and for whether your work is reviewed or undergoes critical study.

The more empirical survey work to test and quantify this would take in measures of association that went beyond the printed page, including body presence solidarity: for example, the hosting of events to promote friends, those attending those such events, and so on. Class, gender and educational affiliation might also help to understand better the history of little magazines. It's not a surprise that the female poets on this list of pamphlets emerge only later on in the century, but the role women had as editors in little magazines within modernism (Dora Marsden, Harriet Monroe) and as poets themselves (H.D., Mina Loy) is not reflected in such a selection: does this mean that men in this period simply did not reciprocate publishing favours as they clearly did man to man?

A key set of questions revolves around the issue of acts of friendship. How does little magazine publication, and little press publication, itself constitute an initiating act of friendship, that then has active power later on in the participants' lives?

The spectrum of friendship relationships is a key and under-researched concept in little press publishing even though it comes up again and again in critical studies. The circles of friendship around, say, Ezra Pound or Ford Madox Ford; the friendship within the modern Scottish renaissance — Catherine Carswell, Lewis Grassic Gibbon, Edwin Muir, Hugh MacDiarmid and Neil Gunn; the Bloomsbury group, MacSpaunday and so on. All of these work through complex friendship processes that have to varying degrees been studied case by case but not, I think, tested empirically or properly theorised.

I'd suggest that little magazines and little presses initiate, develop and continue lasting or critical acts of friendship. However, did such friendships work within existing power structures, with the aim of advancement and incorporation, or offer a counter to them, with the aim of offering aesthetic and even political alternatives? Did they augment and maintain the pre-eminent cultural capital of high-brand institutions like Oxford or Cambridge, the geographical location of London and the South-East as 'the centre', and the status of the male as the arbiter of taste? Or, could magazines and presses offer opportunities to those outside these zones of power?

One aspect of such a social sciences approach is to go beyond the life of a press or magazine, to track the lives of a magazine's contributors after the publication has seemed to 'fail'. Such tracking would follow authors and editors into other publishing realms — review journalism, the broadcast media, more capitalised presses and so on. Furthermore, scrutiny would extend to the judges and the judged in literary competitions, grants, and to appointments at universities and the arts, and to a network of mapped behaviour.

The controls spoken of earlier would be needed here: in mainstream publishing, 'the old boy network' is friendship plus the power to appoint, to deploy a marketing budget. Both little press and mainstream publishing can quietly infer an objectivity of standards that neither can truthfully meet because microscoping down to a concept of standards in so much moot poetry is a category error. Nor, within certain limits, should any press feel the need to be objective. Friendship in little or large presses is an enabler of publication which, to the outside world at the time, may be unnoticed and so appear, outside a circle of friends, to be more disinterested than it is. Friendship is privately inscribed in the public act of publication: 'between you and me, you are my friend because-and-as-demonstrated by the fact that I am willing to make you and your works better known by publishing them'. Perhaps only when friendship itself can be mobilised as a positive — 'a collaboration', 'a school', 'a movement' — does it announce itself more publically.

It's important to avoid a view of friendship as a negative force in the arts. Artistic and intellectual community is underwritten by the public good of private friendship. Finding a neutral vocabulary which avoids both positive and negative terms might be helpful, perhaps using the concept of an index of association. In the little magazine world analysing a dataset containing, for example, editor, publisher, advertiser and contributor information to establish the relationship between these variables would be one way of understanding its nature, with particular rewards when extended to wider access media.

Since the poet as editor is such a common element in both the little press and the little magazine world it is already safe, if not quite redundant, to say that this a key node of reciprocation.

The Campus Magazine

Another pattern that is obvious in the ten pamphlets, and as we've seen correlates with little magazines too, is the massive over-representation of Oxford and Cambridge in their publication. Of the ten poets, at least half are well-known as having an Oxbridge education. At least four of the ten publishers are Oxbridge educated. Some of the functions that little magazines serve could come into play earlier for these exclusive university attenders, with networks being kick-started through the school magazine. It is safe to say that the schools concerned would be overwhelmingly private. There is also the anomalous position of the student magazine / newspaper, for example Oxford's *The Cherwell* and *Isis*. These types of publication are not generally classified as little magazines but are probably significant within the poetry infrastructure: it's no surprise that one of Larkin's poems in *The North Ship*, 'This was your place of birth', was published in *The Cherwell* for example.

This is an opportune moment to revisit the issue of university publication in more detail, using, as before, the place of publication logged by the British Poetry Magazines 1914-2000 survey. In the period 1914-1939, London dominates with about half the new titles in our survey (117 of 236). Next Dublin is, if anything, slightly more productive than either Oxford or Cambridge, accounting for just over 7% of the new titles, while Oxford and Cambridge account for just under 6% (since we are now looking at very small numbers the difference is probably not significant). The period 1914-1939 is of course a huge swathe of history and more needs to be done to break this down to clarify better publication patterns. In terms of new titles, the 1940s were proportionally quiet for Oxbridge, but the 1950s are more active.

The 1950s saw the average rate of new titles per year increase in these university towns at a time when fewer little magazines overall were being produced across the country. Quite a few other university towns — Belfast, Keele, Hull, Newcastle upon Tyne, Manchester, Liverpool and Edinburgh — produced more new titles per year than they had in the previous decade. This seems to confirm that the 1950s was a time of cultural re-building in poetry, setting the literary foundations that underwrite the 1960s. It's no great shock that the universities were part of this, but it is interesting to see circumstantial evidence of it at least in the pattern of little magazine publication. The overall decline in the 1950s of the little magazine in terms of number (from 152 in the 1940s to 125 in the 1950s) might be better considered as the unsustainability of so many magazines outside a war context (the fraught but substantial leisure time by the military and by those on the homefront was particularly suited to the printed word). The Fifties can be seen as a time when the UK saw a clarifying and founding of poetry networks by those who had been children or young adults during the war and who were now taking advantage of wider access to university education in an environment of cultural as well as physical rebuilding.

At least three little magazines from the 1950s relate in this way to the pamphlets in the list. Bob Cobbing's magazine *And*, which, although it began as the magazine of a north London group called Arts Together, soon became a Writers Forum title, so there is a direct link between the magazine, the press, and the pamphlet portfolio *Six Sound Poems* published in 1968. Cobbing's background, however, was not university education: he was grammar-school taught and then went on to teacher-training college. There is also his dissenting and Quaker background to think of as models of support and artistic procedure: the workshop, say, as a secular Quaker meeting. With this in mind — and thinking of similar non-establishment backgrounds in writers associated with London groupings — some of the apparent animosity between London and Cambridge 'schools' of poetry can perhaps be put down to differences in learnt formal approaches to making, workshopping and disseminating poetry, but also to rivalry between modes of education, at times, as with genteel-seeming Oxford versus Cambridge debates, even a turf war over educational hegemony. From the outside, however, the differentiation has a 'good cop / bad cop' effect: both groups of poets benefit from the interest their apparent conflict generates and a UK perspective is concentrated within the London-Cambridge nexus to the exclusion of the overwhelming majority of the country.

Roy Fisher's *City* emerged from Migrant Press, the imprint of two men who had known each other since they were schoolboy boarders at a Cambridge private school in the 1940s. Michael Shayer and Gael Turnbull set up the magazine *Migrant* in the 1950s, moving into relatively regular pamphlet publication once they closed the magazine in September 1960. Finlay's Wild Hawthorn Press was also directly influenced by *Migrant*, magazine and press, and may have been brought into being directly because of it. For Finlay, the conventional publishing model of progression from little magazine to small press was reversed: only after Wild Hawthorn Press had been established did he set up, in 1962, the classic little magazine *Poor. Old. Tired. Horse*. This may have been because Wild Hawthorn was largely a means of self-publication, whereas *Poor. Old. Tired. Horse.*, with a little help from Gael Turnbull's address book, was a way of continuing and radically widening the poetry network Turnbull and Shayer had built around and through *Migrant*. Unlike the Migrant publishers, Finlay did not have a university education, never mind a Cambridge one. Fisher's education, at Birmingham University, may also mark a post-war difference in relative accessibility to education.

Finally there is J. H. Prynne's *Fire Lizard*, published by Barry MacSweeney and Elaine Randell under their Black Suede Boot Press imprint. Again this can be seen, admittedly very broadly, as a consequence of a chain of events set up in the 1950s by the emergent little magazine and little press infrastructure: Prynne was the final editor of the Cambridge magazine *Prospect*, set up in 1959 by Elaine Feinstein and concluding in 1964. Roger Banister's and Peter Redgrove's *Delta* was also a force in Cambridge in the 1950s and '60s. Prynne went on to co-edit series 3 of the magazine, *The English Intelligencer*, in 1968. Randell, while she was co-running the Black Suede Boot Press, was also editing the magazine *Amazing Grace*. It's obvious, too, that Cambridge University is, if not a protagonist in these publications, an enabling, or provoking, environment. There appears to be a slight quantitative difference, too — in the 1950s Cambridge produced more new little magazines per year than any other location except London — on average, one per year. This rate was sustained in the period 1960-1975 (though Oxford began to publish more) and in arguably the key period 1966-1972 was higher. When that is mapped on to the appearance of presses that published Cambridge-associated poets — Andrew Crozier's Ferry Press and John Riley's *Grosseteste Review* — the suggestion is that there is something like a critical mass being both represented and stoked. More quantitative information a survey of little presses, for example would help build up a better dataset to put the correlation into perspective.

Generators
In the meantime, I'll present a simple comparison of the association between little magazines and presses between two

fascinating periods: the classic modernist period of 1914 to 1939, and modernism refigured in the period 1960-1975. These periods are of a different duration, which makes comparisons difficult, so analysis needs to proceed with caution.

In the first period there were some 236 new magazines, on average about 9 new titles per year. Approximately 23 had an associated book imprint: publishing single author collections, anthologies or in some cases local history: a book press to new magazine ratio of just under 1:10. For every ten new magazines there was a book imprint associated with one of them.

In the second period, 1960-1975, there were 539 new magazines in our survey (on average about 34 new titles per year). Of these, 141 had an associated book imprint, so a book press to new magazines ratio of about 1:4 In other words, not only were there quite simply many more little magazines per year in the 1960s and the first half of the 1970s, a little magazine was much more likely to have a little press associated with it as well.

This may go to the heart of a problem of communication in the 1960s and '70s. Such poetry fecundity would have posed difficulties within a centralised and near-unitary media that had not necessarily moved in the same direction as the little press infrastructure. Even if sympathetic, the established reviewing and publishing organs would have found it physically impossible to accommodate such prodigious diversity. The classic modernist period in the UK, often seen as a model and inspiration for the British Poetry Revival, worked in a quite different way.

Comparatively few magazines, comparatively few presses, meant, arguably, comparative ease of transmission into the reviewing press and beyond. The name of Eliot's journal, *The Criterion*, is a clue to the assumption of authority in the earlier period, a hierarchy-accepting mantle that would be much more problematic for later Revival magazines (even if, among the 'Cambridge' poets, they would passively or actively take advantage of the immense educational authority of their 'brand').

The electric power industry furnishes, hopefully, a useful analogy here. At the moment a very small number of very large power generators produce power distributed through the National Grid. It is possible now for a small number of small power generators to localise energy production by solar power and wind-generation on domestic properties and even to feed that into the National Grid. However, even hundreds of thousands or millions of such small-scale producers would fail to make their political presence felt on the National Grid as a large community of small-scale producers, unless they organised collectively. At least the product, electricity, is already in a communicable form that the National Grid immediately 'understands'. The same could not be said for the different varieties of little press poetry, especially with that community's paucity of reviewing and contextual articles, as demonstrated in Peter Barry's account of the period in the 1970s when *The Poetry Review* was in the control of experimental poets and was particularly uncommunicative about the work it was publishing. The history of twentieth century little presses points to the widespread benefits of constructive anarchy at numerous local levels, and the limits of the influence such constructive anarchy may achieve. Indeed the establishment in the late 1960s of the Association of Little Presses, by Bob Cobbing among others, was a recognition of this, though the CAT-scan would establish if ALP was a way into a more powerful transmitting infrastructure or simply the construction of a parallel but less effective network.

Cross-under
Finally, some of the pamphlets suggest format cross-over with little magazines. *Fire Lizard, Six Sound Poems*, and *City*, all make

a similar statement about the potential of a small press book to be a time-bound event closer to periodical than book publication. Prynne's *Fire Lizard* declares the occasion of its publication, the colophon stating it is 'written in Cambridge, New Year's Day 1970'. Perhaps the presentation copy dedicated to Charles Olson, lodged now in the Ed Dorn archive at the University of Connecticut, was an alternative Christmas card: 'For Charles, across the water, with love, New Year's Day 1970, Jeremy'.

Both Fisher's and Cobbing's work are dated not just with a particular day but with a month: May 1961 says the title page of *City*; September 1968 says the colophon of *Six Sound Poems*. This indicates that Migrant Press and Writers Forum, even when they didn't specifically mention a periodical-like date on their publications (they often did), were functioning as somewhere between a little magazine and a book publisher; they were probably issuing books regularly to a list of subscribers. Their slim, light-weight nature also made them more post-able and again this is a characteristic of magazine culture. Writers Forum's frequently meeting workshop was a further means by which its little press books were sold as the occasion for launches of new work; such regularity strengthened the sense of each Writers Forum being an instalment in an open-ended series of booklets.

This simple, range-finding CAT-scan suggests that little presses and little magazines in the British Poetry Revival period didn't just have a symbiosis but, in some special cases, they were practically the same thing.

Select Bibliography
Brooker, Peter and Thacker, Andrew (eds.). *The Oxford Critical and Cultural History of Modernist Magazines*, Vol. 1: Britain and Ireland 1880-1955 (Oxford: OUP, 2009).

Clyde, Tom. *Irish Literary Magazines: An Outline and Descriptive Bibliography* (Dublin: Irish Academic Press, 2003).

Görtschacher, Wolfgang. *Little Magazine Profiles: The Little Magazines in Great Britain, 1939-1993* (Salzburg: University of Salzburg, 1993).

Hoffman, Frederick J., Allen, Charles, and Ulrich, Carolun F. *The Little Magazine: A History and Bibliography*, 2nd ed. (Princeton: Princeton University Press, 1947).

Miller, David and Price, Richard, *British Poetry Magazines 1914-2000* (London: The British Library, 2006).

Sullivan, Alvin (ed.). *British Literary Magazines: The Modern Age, 1914-1984* (London: Greenwood, 1986).

Sylvia Pankhurst and Germinal

Pankhurst as a literary editor

Sylvia Pankhurst is probably best remembered as one of the major socialist and feminist campaigners of the first four decades of the 20th century. In feminist history, until relatively recently she has been seen as a more marginal figure than her mother Emmeline and sister Christabel. Their leadership is seen as having been more effective in helping to deliver the vote for women and not snagged by the different political perspective that Sylvia's enduring socialism afforded. In labour history, there is probably more variance in the assessment of her achievements, but she is still seen at times as naïve, untheoretical, and too individualistic a figure to be taken entirely seriously in her political work. These are attributes which appear to have a rather sexist aspect to them.

Mary Davis's recovery of Pankhurst in her biography *Sylvia Pankhurst: A Life in Radical Politics* (1999) challenged the way that Pankhurst had fallen through the gaps between labour and feminist history, although even in the *Oxford Critical and Cultural History of Modernist Magazines* all 'the Pankhursts' continue to be treated as if they held the same views: far from it.[47][48]

---

[47] A discursive summary of Pankhurst's achievements is also given in Mary Davis, 'Class, Race and Gender', Sylvia Pankhurst Memorial Lecture 2003, http://sylviapankhurst.gn.apc.org/SPML%202003.pdf, [accessed 3/7/09].

[48] See Jean-Michel Rabaté, 'Gender and Modernism', in Peter Brooker and Andrew Thacker (eds.), *The Oxford Critical and Cultural History of Modernist Magazines, Vol. 1: Britain and Ireland 1880-1955* (OUP,

However, in all the accounts I have read very little attention is paid to Pankhurst's *literary* activity as an editor of political newspapers which had significant literary content. And only very rarely, and almost always in passing, is it mentioned that Pankhurst was an editor of a little magazine devoted to literature (curiously, this hardly occurs in biographical accounts, either, although I'd say a biographical reading of some of the texts would be compelling). This was the magazine *Germinal*, which had two issues, July 1923 and an undated issue in 1924. I drew attention to this in an unpublished paper on *Germinal* at the Feminist / Anti-Feminist Workshop at the Cambridge Centre for Gender Studies in 2003. I also refer you to Morag Shiach's 2004 discussion of Pankhurst's work as a campaigning journalist and artist, in which she briefly cites *Germinal* as a place where Pankhurst's 'interest in the interrelations between political identities and imaginative representations found fuller expression'.[49] It's a brief citation but Shiach recognises the importance of *Germinal* as a place where the overlaps between political and artistic work are explored.

Here I would like therefore to further signpost the interest of the literary editorial work Sylvia Pankhurst carried out, especially through her little magazine *Germinal*, which appeared in the early 1920s. I suggest that political, literary and artistic aspects are not very easy to disentangle in her work and probably should be considered in the round.

2009), pp269-289. This work's index also appears to regard Emmeline and Christabel Pankhurst as 'sisters': they were of course mother and daughter.

[49] See, however, Morag Shiach's discussion of Pankhurst's campaigning journalism and her work as an artist, in 'Sylvia Pankhurst: labour and representation', in Morag Shiach, *Modernism, Labour and Selfhood in British Literature and Culture, 1890-1930*, (CUP, 2004), pp.100-148.

Pankhurst's activity in contemporary literature in the first half of the 1920s, while complex political events twisted and unravelled around her, is probably regarded by various political assessors of this period in her life as a falling away, a diversion or a confusion. It is seen as a mark of a quiescence before a re-emergence of her political campaigning (against fascism) in the 1930s. This view is a familiar one: raising an opposition between politics and artistic engagement, as if they were quite separate things and best kept separate. There is also a suggestion that one was more important than the other: here, that political engagement was the priority rather than the distractions of literature.

If Pankhurst were able to read such accounts I can imagine her uttering a weary sigh, and remembering, years before *Germinal,* the frightened and confused anxiety of the Vorticists in the face of the Suffragettes' attacks on paintings. Famously in the first number of *Blast* (1914) Wyndham Lewis, for all his futurist bravado, has clearly and queasily reached his limits of comfort when he advises Suffragettes to 'stick to what you understand,' warning that they might 'DESTROY A GOOD PICTURE BY ACCIDENT' (which is to say, as if they didn't know what they were doing). 'IF YOU DESTROY A GREAT WORK OF ART,' he informs them, 'you are destroying a greater soul than if you annihilated a whole district of London. LEAVE ART ALONE DEAR COMRADES.'[50] As Alex Houen argues in *Terrorism and Modern Literature*, Lewis saw the Suffragettes as a threat not just literally to works of art but, more fundamentally, to the male prerogative to make and judge art. Although Sylvia Pankhurst was privately opposed to the

---

[50] See also the discussion of this power struggle Alex Houen, in 'Wyndham Lewis: Literary 'Strikes' and Allegorical Assaults', the second chapter in Alex Houen, *Terrorism and modern literature from Joseph Conrad to Ciaran Carson*, Oxford University Press, 2002, pp.93-137.

physical attacks on paintings and to the Suffragette arsonist campaign, it's interesting to note in passing that the fight for *authority* in both politics and aesthetics is played out at the symbolic level of title between Pankhurst's publication of the day and Lewis's. In this very specific sense, Pankhurst's *The Women's Dreadnought* (first appearing in March 1914) and *Blast* (tardily appearing in June 1914) are competitors. Of course I don't mean in market terms by size or by nature — *Blast* wouldn't have stood a chance on those terms. *The Dreadnought* had a readership of tens of thousands, especially working-class women, and was a genuine disseminator of news that other newspapers were not able to cover, while *Blast* was a high art and literary object with little topicality and a fraction of the audience. In fact, if Dora Marsden's *The Freewoman,* which began in late 1911 and collapsed in October 1912, hadn't already been called a 'unique forum for suffragists, feminists, anarchists, and socialists'[51] *The Women's Dreadnought* could be described in that way. Rather, as Lewis's quoted reproval suggests, *Blast* and *Dreadnought* were in a sense fighting in news-conscious aesthetic space where one version of English futurism, the explosion of *Blast,* was pitched against another version of English futurism, the warship of the *Dreadnought* (the title refers to the class of warship, initiated in 1906, whose array of large guns and turbine propulsion gave the British navy a leading edge and the return of a fearful reputation).[52]

Later, when *The Women's Dreadnought* became *The Worker's Dreadnought,* Pankhurst showed in its first issue, of 1917, that mixing politics with the arts rather than trying to police aesthetics

---

[51] Jean-Michel Rabaté, op. cit., p270.
[52] See also, Andrzej Gasiorek, 'The 'Little Magazine' as weapon: *BLAST* (1914-15)', in Peter Brooker and Andrew Thacker (eds.), *The Oxford Critical and Cultural History of Modernist Magazines, Vol. 1: Britain and Ireland 1880-1955,* (Oxford University Press, 2009), pp*290*-313.

could have direct political results: *The Dreadnought* was the first to publish officer and poet Siegfried Sassoon's 'Statement' asserting that the British were now pursuing a 'war of aggression and conquest.'[53] There was real risk involved in such action and, although, Sassoon was classed as mentally ill by the military authorities to isolate and undermine him, the offices of *The Dreadnought* suffered a police raid on the back of it.[54]

There is much more to be said about the intersection of literature and politics in the decade-long history of *The Dreadnought*, but suffice it to say that literary elements to this newspaper shouldn't be written off as something incidental to Pankhurst's editorial practice or her political perspective; on that basis *Germinal* shouldn't really come as a surprise. In the early 1920s it might be fairer to say that *if* Pankhurst was confused so was the world around her. After all in 1920 she had found herself imprisoned for five months for sedition under the Defence of the Realm Act because of work she had published in *The Workers Dreadnought*. Soon after leaving prison, in 1921, the new Communist Party of Great Britain (formed in part from a grouping she had helped bring about) censured her for not allowing the Party to take over the *Dreadnought* and then banned all their members from reading it. Who's confused now?

Germinal in brief

So what was *Germinal*? It was a slender literary magazine that, although describing itself as a monthly, appeared once in July 1923 and once on an unnamed date in 1924. It was edited anonymously,

---

[53] Siegfried Sassoon quoted from John Stuart Roberts, *Siegfried Sassoon*, Metro, 2005, p.104.
[54] Mary Davis, *Sylvia Pankhurst: A Life in Radical Politics* (1999), p.56.

but in fact by Pankhurst, with initialled editorials by her. The advert that appeared in at least five issues of *The Dreadnought* emphasised its working class audience, its literary nature, and that it was for leisure: 'Just the right magazine for all workers. Good Stories [,] Pictures [,] Poetry and Reviews [.] Take a copy on your Holiday! 32 pages — Sixpence.' Because of the advertising in this way it is likely that it was seen, or intended to be seen, as a kind of literary supplement to *The Dreadnought*.

Albeit from a small base, contents-wise it was an extremely international magazine, probably one of the most international literary magazines there has been in the UK (I can think only of Janko Lavrin and Edwin Muir's *The European Quarterly* (1934-1935), Ian Hamilton Finlay's *Poor. Old. Tired. Horse* (1962-67) and Ted Hughes and Daniel Weissbort's *Modern Poetry in Translation* (1966-ongoing) as having that sort of density of foreign literature). I'm quite interested in empirical measures for assessing the character of magazines (as well as qualitative, prosey, ones, of course). One such measure might be a 'ratio of internationalism'.

This would actually be a family of ratios, depending on whether you took, for example, page extent of an identified author's work, the number of individual works, or, say, the number of individual authors. You might then divide the non-UK element by the UK element (of course you could do this with a finer granularity so you could look at, say, non-England content and so on, helping you gauge the different 'home nations' content etc, for example). Clearly there are all kinds of theoretical and practical problems with such a measure, but I'm determined all the same to persevere. In *Germinal's* case I tried this out, looking at the individual authors count (c.8 different foreign authors, c.13 different UK authors, so an author's internationality ratio of about 0.6) and a page extent ratio of text contributions (c.35 pages given over to non-UK texts and about 16 pages given over to UK texts, so a page internationality ratio of about 2.2).

Ideally you'd want to compare this with other magazines of the day but I thought I'd use *Germinal* as a prophet for our own times. To put this in contemporary perspective, an issue of *The Poetry Review* from the first decade of this century (the Dreams of Elsewhere issue of Autumn 2007, designed specifically to be an internationalist issue) has an individual author's ratio lower than *Germinal's* two-issue run (about 11 non-UK authors to 23 UK authors, c.0.5) and a much much lower page extent ratio (about 30 non-UK pages to about 49 UK pages, a ratio of about 0.6), so UK work again dominant. For both cases I've stripped out the reviewing pages — if I'd included them *The Poetry Review* would have come out even worse.[55] Pankhurst's magazine, although its UK poetry is dated even for the time (a subject I'll come back to), was publishing relatively recent foreign literature in translation. Aha you say, but *The Poetry Review* issued a separate contemporary Dutch poets supplement with that issue, with nine Dutch poets in it. Yes, you're right — that does tip the balance for the author ratio, bringing it up to c.0.9 for the special occasion compared to *Germinal*'s 0.5, but on page internationality this still only brings up to c.2.0, failing to match *Germinal*'s 2.2.

Well, I don't want to labour this too much – if you were to adopt such apparently empirical measures you'd need to be careful about thresholds; for example, *Germinal* actually didn't have many pages and you might want to look at categories of size and genre classifications when you do comparative work. That said,

---

[55] Perhaps it's not a fair comparison – *Germinal* was publishing short stories and drama, but then *The Poetry Review* was publishing longer articles and interviews with foreign poets and its ratio had the help of translations of Sophocles and Euripides.

Germinal made no editorial claims to *be* international yet here are translations of Maxim Gorky, Alexander Blok, Anna Akhmatova (one of the earliest translations, Nicholas Gumilev and Ernst Toller (a sixteen page play)), stories in English from New York, India and South Africa (a short story by L. A. Motler about a friendship between a white and a black boy). There are also striking wood-cut portraits of Rabindranath Tagore and of George Bernard Shaw by L-R Pisarro, who also supplies the cover art. Pisarro was the French émigré Ludovic-Rodo Pisarro (b.1878), son of the more famous Camille. He had been a very young contributor to the 1894 anarchist journal *Le Père Peinard*, as well as to the first Fauve exhibition in 1905.

Some meanings of *Germinal*

I now want to dwell a bit on the name and look of *Germinal* because together they capture something of the overlap between literary, artistic, and political concerns that Morag Shiach hinted at in her reference to the magazine's interplay 'between political identities and imaginative representations'. I also think there is something to be said about *Germinal* in terms of a tradition of the little magazine. Although I've just said internationalism isn't explicit editorially, there is a utopian element to the magazine, which I see as one idealistic view of internationalism.

Firstly, that name. *Germinal* is suffused with artistic, literary and political meaning. Artistic because it echoes the name of that which is famously regarded as the first classic little magazine, *The Germ,* the magazine of the Pre-Raphaelite Brotherhood. Pankhurst's artistic education and family background meant that she had been brought up in a household and education system which regarded the Pre-Raphaelites and its Arts and Crafts legacy with admiration. There's a literary meaning within *Germinal*, because it is of course the name of Zola's novel of industrial unrest in the French mines, a novel which Pankhurst was fully aware of, since she had serialised it in translation in the *Workers' Dreadnought*.⁵⁶ Incidentally this appears to have been a significant popularising act: until it was taken up by Dent's Everyman's Library in 1933, only a privately published limited edition of the translation, published in 1895, had been available. As you can imagine, *Germinal* the novel is not merely a literary document but a political one. In France the title has an added political echo because it was the name, under the French Revolution, of one of the newly organised months, roughly corresponding to March.

The little magazine's title, which I think bears all these meanings and holds them in play, also has a face-value or 'pure' meaning: it refers to the capacity of a seed to grow. L-R Pisarro's striking cover for the first issue is of an androgynous figure sowing seeds in a ploughed field. The style is medievalesque, as it were: a woodcut carrying a further pre-Raphaelite (and Arts & Crafts) echo. Pankhurst continues this pastoral focus too: an advert within the magazine for the magazine itself refers punningly to 'a new field being opened up'. The editorial in the first issue repeatedly uses the pastoral imagery of flowering, fruiting and harvest to assert mutual support across humanity and the development of the individual within such a commonwealth. With an anachronistic back glance, today's reader might almost see it as an early hippy text: 'All things we have are but ours for the using; we use them without stint; but we waste them not; for these fruits of the harvest, these treasures of earth and sea, are wrought and gathered and grown by the service of comrades, who render their service with love, the love that we also bear them; countless unknown

---

⁵⁶ Zola's novel had been available in English but for private circulation, in the translation by Havelock Ellis for the Lutetian Society (1895; British Library shelfmark: 1094.k.1).

comrades; numberless, skilful, industrious brains and hands that toil with us.'[57]

The editorial in the second issue also uses imagery of sensual new growth, adopting a Whitmanesque prosody to do so: 'I sing thee, I sing thee, O peace of the peoples; O peace of co-workers; O peace that is fruitful; that blossoms and grows, with a growth ever changing, a growth ever new in its births and its matings; ascending triumphantly; in knowledge ascending.' [Unnumbered page, inside cover]

There are indications, I believe, that this use of natural imagery is not just the use of a much-used and almost worn out poetic trope — though it is certainly that — but marks a political-aesthetic change in Pankhurst which has perhaps not been understood. It seems to me that Pankhurst is moving towards a kind of universalisation of humanity, dependent on a pastoral trope, which also emphases the public celebrations of workers through holidays, art and other aesthetic devices.

'Others have sung of the States; but I sing of the peoples,' Pankhurst begins her editorial in the second issue, and in that I think there is a move away from state-ism to something more utopian: pastoral but futuristic, sexually liberated but also focussed on fertility. The first page, a full-page 'advertorial' for James Leakey's *Introduction to Esperanto*, published by Pankhurst's Dreadnought Press, adds further to this universalising subtext. Pankhurst has been criticised as 'confused' for changing the subtitle of the *Workers' Dreadnought* at this time from

---

[57] Unnumbered page; inside cover of Vol. 1 no. 1.

'International Socialism' to 'Going to the Root'[58] but, whatever one may think of it, this isn't so much a confusion as a determined shift, and it's in line with the imagery Pankhurst adopts in her editorials in *Germinal*.

It is also there in much of the poetry that she self-publishes in the magazine and especially in her libertarian sci-fi allegories. These are 'Utopian Conversations', in the first issue, which could be summarised as exploring some of the problems of free love within a countryside commune; and 'The Pageant' in the second issue.[59] Both of these stories end in the prospect of birth, and both take place in a rural but futuristic idyll. I don't rate this work: it is curiously sentimental as well as progressive and it's neither fluent nor otherwise well-made — I'm only interested here in thematic undercurrents and the fact that *Germinal's* themes bubble up across its pages in a surprisingly single-minded way. Various pieces that are not by Pankhurst —the Gorky short story about an incident in a Russian village, the South African story — also use rural or village life as a way of exploring class, race and work concerns, so Pankhurst is clearly directing the pastoral for both political and aesthetic benefits. To this end, the medieval exterior of the magazine is continued inside the pages with woodcuts and faux-primitive line drawings by a dozen or so other artists.[60]

---

[58] Barbara Winslow; see also www.ibrp.org/en/articles/2000-01-01/sylvia-pankhurst-the-meaning-of-the-revolutionary-years.
[59] Pankhurst adopted the name 'Richard Marsden' for both stories, a reference to her father's first and middle name.
[60] Finally, a contemporary tract, one of the last publications issued by Pankhurst as publisher of *Germinal* and *The Workers' Dreadnought* imagines a Labour Prime minister invoking the ancient fertility festival of May Day for a national holiday: *May Day: The Vision of a Labour Prime Minister* [1925] by Asit Mightbee (surely Panhkurst herself).

Art and Play

Finally I want to say just a few words about *Germinal* as a magazine of leisure. When it was advertised in *The Workers' Dreadnought*, potential readers, identified in the advert and of course by the newspaper as 'Workers', were specifically encouraged to 'Take a Copy on Holiday.' Comparing *Germinal* with other literary magazines of the day, it most resembles those with a residual Arts & Crafts-like ruralist iconography: perhaps *The Apple (of Beauty and Discord)*, which closed in 1922; and *The Owl*, which closed in 1923.[61] Rebecca Beasley has shown that magazines of this kind were designed to widen the audience for contemporary art, in part to sell artworks.

This is clearly the case for *Germinal* too: there is an advert for the sale of 'A small collection of pictures either together or separately' in the first issue and a note in the second issue that 'Prints and originals of the drawings appearing in GERMINAL may in some cases be obtained from the artists.' [Back cover]. It is difficult to assess the intended audience however: there is also a curious note, for example, encouraging 'English holiday-makers who happen to stay in Les Andelys this year' to 'enjoy the beautiful Art Exhibition of the Foyer des Artistes', where works by Monet, Camille Pisarro and others are represented.[62] At first the luxuriousness of this sits oddly with the magazine's role as a kind of supplement to the *Workers' Dreadnought* but a statement on the same page announcing the setting up of 'The Germinal Circle'

---

[61] See Rebecca Beasley's discussion of the Arts and Crafts legacy in early 1920s magazines in Rebecca Beasley, 'Literature and the Visual Arts: *Arts and Letters* (1917-20) and *The Apple* (1920-2)', in Peter Brooker and Andrew Thacker (eds.), *The Oxford Critical and Cultural History of Modernist Magazines, Vol. 1: Britain and Ireland 1880-1955* (OUP, 2009), pp. 485-504.
[62] Unnumbered page, [p.27], in first issue.

may help re-calibrate this. The Germinal Circle it says is 'intended to assist in the artistic expression of current thought, in order to bring art into contact with daily life and to use it as a means of expressing modern ideas and aspirations'.

For Pankhurst it wasn't just that established artistic expression should be made available to the working classes, but that artistic expression itself should be changed by class theory and other ideas. *Germinal* was trying to demonstrate this by striving for coherent pastoral utopianism in its literary content, in its look and its editorial cues. In this way *Germinal* becomes a modest and of course very flawed step towards a high ambition: the placing of artistic expression, defined as field of rest, creativity and play, as part of working life. As Pankhurst said in her *Dreadnought* pamphlet, *Education of the Masses*, 'Communism is a classless order of society in which all shall have leisure and culture [...].'

Migrant the Magnificent

In July 1959 several hundred copies of a magazine emerged from the house of a British doctor, then living in Ventura, California. They were posted to poets across the United States, Canada and the British Isles. With a light blue cover and soft yellow pages, the magazine was unconventional but welcoming in design. The printing, from an unsophisticated second-hand duplicator, had the look of having been typewritten. The homespun atmosphere was also underlined by the text, only appearing on one side of the page. Despite this — or, rather, because of it — Dr Turnbull, later better known as the poet Gael Turnbull, had started one of the most influential poetry magazines of the second half of the last century. It would only run until September 1960, when its eighth issue brought the magazine to a close. Nevertheless, quietly, exploratively, and with the invaluable editing of his old schoolfriend Michael Shayer back in England, *Migrant* heralded the decade of ideas and creativity now thought of as the Sixties.

The Play Way
Born in Edinburgh in 1928, Gael Turnbull was the son of a Scottish minister and an American of Swedish descent. The family lived where his father preached, first in Jarrow and then, from 1934 to 1939, in Blackpool. At the beginning of the Second World War the family emigrated to Winnipeg in Canada. Turnbull returned to England in 1944, where he was a boarder at Perse School, Cambridge. It was here that he met fellow-student Michael Shayer. They were to become life-long friends.
The friends were able science students and each decided to study natural sciences rather than literature at Cambridge (Turnbull at

Christ's College, Shayer at Clare). Shayer, who had joined the student mountaineering club, broke his leg while climbing in the Lake District. His hospitalisation for three months intensified his interest in writing: a friendly hospital orderly lent him James Joyce's *Ulysses* (the official book trolley did not contain it), an experience Shayer regarded as life-changing. On his return to college he asked to be transferred to an English degree but was persuaded to stay with natural sciences. His tutor persuaded him, wisely I think, that great writing did not require the formal study of English.

North America
After Cambridge, Turnbull moved back to North America, successfully completing a medical degree at the University of Pennsylvania, while, back in England, Shayer served two years National Service with Shell. They corresponded and also exchanged 'audio letters' recorded on reel-to-reel tape (extracts from this type of recording would later be transcribed in *Migrant*). Soon Shayer joined Turnbull in Philadelphia, which was enjoying a quietly bohemian arts scene: the two would visit 'The Heel', the Horn and Hardart cafeteria, where classical musicians, actors and poets would meet, and they'd attend plays and poetry readings, one by e.e. cummings.

In 1952 Turnbull married Jonnie Draper, a drama student at Pittsburgh's Carnegie Institute of Technology (which, despite its applied sciences focus, had a celebrated liberal arts programme). However, a new law meant that even non-nationals resident in the United States could and would be called up for the Korean War. The friends sought to avoid this. Shayer boarded the Queen Mary back to England. Turnbull took a 'day trip' bus to Montreal, to be joined by Jonnie travelling on the train: in Canada they made their new home.

After requalifying, Gael was able to practice medicine in Iroquois Falls, Northern Ontario. During this period he corresponded with many Canadian poets, and was especially associated with *Contact*, a magazine and small press edited by Raymond Souster. He co-translated several francophone Quebec poets with Jean Beaupré, including Hector de Saint-Denys-Garneau and Roland Guiguère. These translations were published in very limited editions in association with *Contact*. As Phyllis Webb later recalled, 'Gael had quickly and astutely diagnosed the need for more communication between French-speaking and English-speaking writers in Canada and set out to remedy the situation.'[63]

Crucially, Raymond Souster was in touch with Cid Corman, poet and editor of *Origin*, and with the Black Mountain poets associated with Black Mountain College in North Carolina. It appears that it was Souster who put Gael Turnbull in touch with this milieu.

At this time Black Mountain College, the experimental arts college in North Carolina, was in its last creative phase before its eventual closure in 1956. Charles Olson was its Rector and Creeley was editing *Black Mountain Review* (1954-1957). The magazine featured many of the poets that Corman had been publishing (Paul Blackburn, Denise Levertov, Charles Olson, Robert Duncan, were perhaps the core ,with Louis Zukofsky a slightly older figure from the Objectivist generation of the 1930s). The *Review* also reproduced the work of modern artists such as Philip Guston and Franz Kline. A student of photography at Black Mountain, Jonathan Williams, ran the press Jargon Society, and distributed the *Review* outside of New York (presumably because Paul

---

[63] Phyllis Webb, 'Air, Air' in Peter McCarey (ed.), *A Gathering for Gael Turnbull* (Au Quai, 1998).

Blackburn was able to distribute the magazine there). An energetic correspondent, Turnbull was in touch with most of these figures and began to develop a network of very individual modern poets, soon to be among the contributors to (and select audience of) *Migrant*.

Migrant Books c/o National Provincial Bank

In 1955 Gael Turnbull returned to England from Canada, settling in Worcester from 1956 to 1958. In late 1956, he set up Migrant Books as a UK distributor of books by Divers Press, Origin Press and Jargon Society. These presses published the work of his old poet friends in the American avant-garde: Creeley, Corman, and Olson (Creeley in fact *was* Divers Press and Corman Origin). Their work was very little known in the United Kingdom, though it had appeared in little magazines that Turnbull had read with fascination: John Sankey's *Window* (London) — where Turnbull appears to have first seen Roy Fisher's poetry — Robert Cooper's *Artisan* (Liverpool) and W. Price Turner's *The Poet* (Glasgow). All of these magazines had closed by the end of 1956.

It is noticeable that there had been a strong so-called provincial element to this first wave: the established and centralised conduits appear generally not to have been finely tuned enough to detect, receive or understand the new poetry; or, if they did understand, they did not at all like it. Migrant Books as a distributor was therefore an important way of opening the doors wider in Britain to experimental American work.

Turnbull was helped in this by the poet and editor W. Price Turner, who gave him a copy of *The Poet*'s mailing list. By the same token, the major British writers later associated with Migrant would also be based outside of London, Oxford, or Cambridge: Roy Fisher (Birmingham), Ian Hamilton Finlay (at this period, various locations in Scotland), and Edwin Morgan (Glasgow).

Perhaps most significantly in these early years, Migrant distributed Charles Olson's *Maximus Poems*. Prime examples of what Olson called Projective Verse, a freer poetry that used the space of the page with a sense of exploration and the breath of the voice as a marker of rhythm; they had been published by Jonathan Williams, *1-10* in 1953 and *11-22* in 1956, but with no British distributor. Turnbull sought to correct this: after buying stock, he simply stamped the colophon with Migrant Books c/o National Provincial Bank, Worcester, and began to distribute them using his growing address book as a mailing list. The bank was used effectively as a poste restante address, presumably while he sought a more permanent home. Because so many of Turnbull's correspondents were poets, Migrant Books became an early and key bridge across the Atlantic between British and American avant-garde writers.

It was during this time in England that Turnbull met Roy Fisher and encouraged him to think of himself in the company of the authors Turnbull knew and championed. Almost like a manuscript pre-cursor of *Migrant*, Turnbull kept a notebook into which he would copy interesting poems he liked and would then show this to fellow poets: this was how Roy Fisher first came to know the work of Basil Bunting, later celebrated as the author of the long poem *Briggflatts*. As Roy Fisher would remember: 'I met Gael Turnbull and I was exposed on one day to Olson, Creeley, Bunting, Zukofsky, Duncan, Ginsberg, Corso, Ferlinghetti, Ray Souster and, most of all, William Carlos Williams.'[64]

---

[64] Quoted in Michael Peter Ryan, 'Career Patterns among Contemporary British Poets' unpublished PhD dissertation, University of London, 1980, p.86; itself quoted in Simon Jarvis, 'A Burning Monochrome: Fisher's Block', in Kerrigan and Robinson (eds.), *The Thing About Roy Fisher: Critical Studies*, Liverpool University Press, 2000, p.189.

Migrant's first book appeared in 1957: *The Whip*, by Creeley. This was a three-way publication between Migrant, Jonathan Williams and Contact Press (Toronto), which had published Turnbull's first book in Canada. It was printed in Mallorca, where Creeley lived, and almost certainly under his supervision. However, it would not be until Turnbull took control of the printing process himself that more of Migrant's own publications would appear, and with regularity. This happened after Gael had again been on the move, back to America in 1958.

Migrant *the Magazine*

In Autumn 1958 Turnbull moved to Ventura, California, where he practised as an anaesthetist. He bought a secondhand duplicator, later affectionately referred to as the Monster, and began to publish *Migrant*. Jonnie Turnbull, Gael's first wife, recalls the first attempts:

> When Gael decided to start up a little mag, the first hint of what he intended came when he suddenly appeared one afternoon carrying what looked like a large, very cumbersome piece of junk. It was an old mimeograph machine which he had found downtown in a 'second-hand' shop. My first reaction was, 'You're not serious'; and I tried not to laugh or be too disparaging when he finally, proudly, had it set up. It was ancient — a far cry from the electric machine I had used at secretarial school. 'What're you going to do with it?' I asked. 'Start a magazine,' he replied.[65]

The first issue captured the spirit of *Migrant*: an epigraph taken from Samuel Johnson that emphasised literature that was plain-

---

[65] Jonnie Turnbull, 'Migrant Reminiscences', in *PS* [the Prose Supplement to *Painted, spoken*], No. 1 (2006).

speaking and rooted in everyday speech. There was a charming poem about writing sad books by Gael's French American friend Pierre Delattre (later an editor of the Beat magazine *Beatitudes*), six poems by Edward [Ed] Dorn; poems by Turnbull himself (disguised as Thomas Lundin), French literature in translation (Leon Bloy translated by Michael Shayer); and an extract from an anonymous letter intended to stimulate debate. Extracts from letters were used in this way throughout the run of *Migrant*, producing a questioning, thought-provoking, open collage of texts as counterpoint to the crafted poems. The experiences of the manager of an English launderette were also included, establishing connection to a wider world, playing with literary register, and establishing a sense of social context, in a similar spirit, as Shayer has observed, to the social survey project Mass Observation.

From the start, Turnbull decided that it would not be aimed at the 'general reader', though anyone interested was encouraged to subscribe. It was essentially for poets. Subscription was on a voluntary affair: 'Subscription is by donation, even a few stamps will be of help; or just a postcard to indicate that you would like to receive it regularly.' (When Corman re-started *Origin* in the Sixties he would adopt this approach, too.)

By the second issue, the Canadian poet Ray Souster made an entrance, and the Black Mountain connection hinted at by the inclusion of Dorn in the first issue, was now in full swing: Creeley, Corman, and Duncan all had work included. Later issues would include works by Denise Levertov, Larry Eigner, the Canadian Jay Macpherson, the English poets Charles Tomlinson, Hugh Creighton-Hill, and in the fifth issue, Roy Fisher and Edwin Morgan (translating Mayakovsky into Scots), followed by Alan Brownjohn (comparing Robert Creeley with Philip Larkin in issue 6 (May 1960)), 'The Drama of Utterance' (Hugh Kenner, in issue 7 (July 1960)) [on William Carlos Williams, a presiding spirit of

Migrant]; Ian [Hamilton] Finlay; Henri Michaux, translated by Raymond Federman. Finally in issue 8 (Sept. 1960), there was Edwin Morgan (translating Pasternak), a prose piece by Charles Olson, German translations by Anselm Hollo, the Canadian Louis Dudek, translations of Georg Trakl by Helmut Bonheim; more Duncan and more Fisher.

As well as letters about literature and about the magazine, usually published without their authors' names, *Migrant* also transcribed tape recordings and reproduced diary entries, contributing to the collage. The magazine must have been an extraordinary eye-opener to its readers, welcoming both European and North American poetry in the same breath as it asserted the value of new English and Scottish poetry.

It seems puzzling that it should have closed so quickly. In 1960, however, Turnbull and Shayer began to move Migrant Press more in the direction of book production and in the September of that year the last issue of the magazine was issued. It appears that the magazine had helped some of its authors towards more extensive work, building a collection, say, and certainly becoming more self-conscious — and more internationally aware — in their work. In that year Migrant Press, as a book imprint, published an early appreciation of Charles Olson's poetry, Ed Dorn's *What I See in the Maximus Poems*; Matthew Mead's *A Poem in Nine Parts*; and Ian Hamilton Finlay's *The Dancers Inherit the Party*. The magazine may have closed, but this was because the scene, as it were, had now been set: books themselves were to carry on the *Migrant* idea.

Nineteen sixty-one was characterised by a new Migrant Press booklet every couple of months or so: books by Anselm Hollo, Edwin Morgan, Roy Fisher, Shayer, and Hugh Creighton-Hill. Turnbull and Shayer were especially encouraged by the success of

Finlay's book, his first book of poems, *The Dancers Inherit the Party* (1960), whose first edition of 200 copies had sold so well that a second was produced in 1962; Finlay's work was to be profoundly influenced by the ethos of *Migrant*.

Ian Hamilton Finlay

One of the most significant poets that Michael Shayer, as its British editor, introduced to *Migrant* was Ian Hamilton Finlay. Finlay and Shayer corresponded and soon there were more poems than could be published in the magazine. From this relative abundance came *The Dancers Inherit the Party* (1960). Although Finlay has since acquired a forbidding reputation, these poems are fun, fey, almost musical; they are also often amusingly sly. The elements of whimsy and lightness are arguably part of a more serious questioning about the nature of poetry (and being), with Finlay's work attempting to widen poetry's field to non-traditional areas, with a particular emphasis on play.

Migrant Press circumvented the traditional publishing establishment which may have wondered about putting Finlay in print, but the imprint did much more. Shayer and Turnbull showed Finlay that it was relatively easy to set up a pamphlet imprint (Finlay soon established his own, The Wild Hawthorn Press); and that a magazine was also relatively easy to manage: with Jessie McGuffie and P. Pond [i.e. the blues singer Paul Jones], Finlay set up his magazine *Poor. Old. Tired. Horse.* in 1962. For a poet who wanted to learn from others as much as communicate his own sensibilities, one of the best activities to master is that of magazine editor, as Turnbull and Shayer had, and for five years Finlay's magazine published sound, concrete and minimalist poetry from Brazil, the Soviet Union, Cuba, France, the United States, England and Scotland. Finlay already had European reference points in his aesthetic but *Migrant* appears to have greatly widened his

American knowledge: *The Dancers Inherit the Party* was sent by Turnbull and Shayer to writers such as Robert Creeley, Louis Zukofsky and Lorine Niedecker, the last-mentioned recognising a kindred spirit in Finlay.[66] Finlay greatly expanded the Migrant idea by publishing such a vast international range, and his greater attention to higher production values — for example in his edition of Lorine Niedecker's *My Friend Tree* — made Shayer and Turnbull change their approach, seeing the book's potential as a beautiful artefact in its own right.

By the mid-sixties, Migrant as a publisher was beginning to fade: although the books by Pete Brown and Anselm Hollo showed that the imprint was getting on top of the design challenges of publishing (they were no longer using the Monster), personal complications in the private lives of Turnbull and Shayer diverted their energies. Neither of them had the sensibility in any case for aggressive forms of marketing and distribution. Although there were occasional Migrant pamphlets until Gael Turnbull's death in 2004, the press was essentially a fabulous creature of the '50s and '60s, i.e. it anticipated and laid some of the foundations for everything since.

Shayer and Turnbull were arguably among the key poetry editors of the Fifties who kick-started the creativity of the Sixties small press poetry scene; in Eric Mottram's famous phrase, 'The British Poetry Revival'. While not at all being like them, they prepared the way, for example, for the 'Cambridge School' poets of the Sixties and early Seventies, a grouping, despite the name, as heterogeneous as the spirit of *Migrant*. Migrant Press's support for Edwin Morgan's translations of Russian poetry into Scots, coupled with the Finlay success, also created new space within Scottish

---

[66] See Gael Turnbull, 'Dancing for an hour' in *Chapman* No. 78-79 (1994), and other articles in that issue.

literature, a refreshing exploratory attitude which was as interested in the international as it was in the creative use of common speech. The interest in and friendship with Basil Bunting that Shayer and Turnbull extended were also critical factors in Bunting's triumphant re-emergence.

Enthusiasm for the various American avant-gardes, an interest in translation, an acceptance of a variety of aesthetic approaches, a confidence in the independent voices of the new poetry of England and Scotland, and the command of the means of production by the artistic community itself: these are some of the key lessons that *Migrant*, among a few other select magazines, taught — and which the flourishing British poetry scene in the 1960s avidly learned.

Acknowledgements
I am especially grateful to Jonnie Turnbull, Jill Turnbull, Michael Shayer and Roy Fisher for help in the reconstruction of events. Gael Turnbull's archive is held at the National Library of Scotland: my thanks to Robin Smith at the Department of Manuscripts for access to uncatalogued correspondence there. An account of *Migrant* is given by Gael Turnbull in *Credences*, Vol. 1 no. 2/3 (1981/82). I have also used Nicholas Johnson's obituary of Gael Turnbull which appeared in *The Independent*, 7th July 2004.

I am grateful to Alexandra Sayer, my research assistant on 'Migrant and the Poetry of Possibility', the exhibition at the British Library, sponsored by the Folio Society, that ran from 19th January to 25th March 2007.

Literary Infrastructure in the 1960s

On the face of it, the television pioneer John Logie Baird isn't the first person that comes to mind when thinking about the Scottish literary infrastructure in the 1960s. Baird was long dead by that time — he died in 1946 — and was a scientific experimentalist rather than a literary one. There is the stark question of contrasting scale of achievement, too: he invented a revolutionary medium rather than used a long-established one innovatively. Nevertheless there are various aspects of Baird's life and work that I'd like to draw out to look across the literary landscape of the 1960s, which was remarkable.

As a Situationist approach is to overlay a tracing of one city's map upon that of another, offering a curious but surprisingly fruitful guide to the semi-submerged metropolis and its 'hidden' landmarks, so I propose a further anti-intuitive approach: to superimpose elements of the popular biography of Baird over another systemised, simplified, area of knowledge — here, the conduits and transformer nodes of Scottish literature, especially as witnessed through its little magazines. The emphasis is on poetry, but other forms will be brought in as appropriate, especially where there is a significant feed into other genres.

London is one of Scotland's other capital cities

Baird was the first in the world to conduct a long-distance television transmission. This took place in 1927 and covered the 438 miles from London to Glasgow's Central Hotel. Baird's act of connecting back to Scotland from a London base is the first of my guiding headings, which will allow the broader UK infrastructure to be taken into account when issues of Scottish literature are discussed. Curiously, the elements of 'sound and vision', so important to TV, have their counterpart in the emphasis placed in the 1960s on the visual and in the aural in literature. The perhaps surprising importance of Glasgow is another point of query (*another* kind of capital city), which I'll go into in due course.

Scotland is European, Scotland is Pan-American (Scotland is Scottish) Baird also made the first *transatlantic* television transmission in the world, to New York State (in 1928). Later, he worked with the French to set up their first television broadcasting company. The internationalism of sixties Scottish literature, and how far it looked to the US, Canada and Latin America or to Europe, is an aspect I'd like to signpost, here even if we may not have time for much further reflection on that topic.

A popular avant-garde? In thinking about Baird you probably have to think about mass communication itself, television being a device which came into its own in the '50s and '60s — though sadly not with Baird's proposed colour system. If the world *had* adopted Baird's system we would probably have been receiving a granularity of high definition fifty years ago, comparable with that which is only just being achieved in the most recent generation of television. (In the spirit of this mass communication, all my references to Baird and the history of television's invention are taken from *Wikipedia*, which I gratefully acknowledge.)

The idea of unmediated works that, as it were, can't properly transmit because they are too complex for the mass communication system of the day is something I've talked about before in terms of

UK literary magazines as a whole,[67] widening the example of Peter Barry's analysis of the Poetry Society in the 1970s,[68] but it is no less relevant for the current Scottish literary scene. This is a debate within the earlier literary forms of Modernism, between — to be simplistic, and to take some American examples — on the one hand allusive complexity (necessarily backward-looking (Pound and Eliot) and usually figured on ideas of past 'European' 'high culture') and, on the other, the complexity of contemporary speech, technology and social history (William Carlos Williams), a not uncritical discourse but a necessarily forward-looking art.

Adaptive Modernism and Other Forms of Response

Finally, the fact that Baird's scientific practice naturally stands Newton-like on the shoulders of predecessors is another transferable point for understanding the practice of literary editors in the 1960s. I bragged earlier that Baird had invented an actual

---

[67] Richard Price, 'To Shake the Torpid Pool: exploring the relationship between poetry pamphlets and little magazines', in *PS (the Prose Supplement of Painted, Spoken) 6 (2009)*, unnumbered pages. Based on a paper given at 'Interaction, Symbiosis, Overlap: Little Magazines and Small Presses', English Research Symposium, Nottingham Trent University, 7/3/09. Downloadable from www.hydrohotel.net/PamphletsLittleMagazines.htm.

[68] Peter Barry, *Poetry Wars: British Poetry of the 1970s and the Battle of Earls Court*, Salt, 2006. In particular Barry's condemnation of the decision by the editor of *Poetry Review*, Eric Mottram, to offer no critical framework for the contemporary poetry he published: 'the 'training' mission that Mottram believed in so strongly could far better have been forwarded by judicious and informative reviewing of at least a few of the kinds of work he favoured. Increasingly, the foregoing of this opportunity to put the case for the 'BPR' [British Poetry Revival] to the wider readership of *Poetry Review* was emerging as a serious tactical error.' (p. 44).

medium but how far can any one scientist actually invent solo? After all, the German Paul Nipkow had conceived and patented a television system several years before Baird was born (Baird was born in 1888). In the same way that Scottish Renaissance writers of the interwar years can be seen, generally speaking, as 'adaptive modernists' rather than radical inventors in their own right — though their adaptations can produce astonishing results — essentially the best Scottish writers of the 1960s were immensely talented modifiers of techniques from elsewhere to which they responded remarkably early.

This can also be thought of in a periodised way. While Wolfgang Görtschacher emphasises the importance of 1959 for the creation of literary magazines that set the foundations for the '60s in the UK, I'll push the timing back into that decade for Scotland in particular.[69] I'll stress that what took place in the '50s is important for understanding the 1960s and I'll conclude by mentioning one or two magazines from that previous decade that might repay revisiting.

With Baird in mind, the first point about the Scottish literary culture of the sixties to note is how important England was in various ways: as a nurturing framework for émigré Scots, and as a bridge into a much freer zone of non-literary political and cultural spaces.

The nurturing framework can be seen straight away in the work of one of the key editors of the last fifty years, Duncan Glen. Glen's working life in London and, after a brief stint in Glasgow,

---

[69] Wolfgang Görtschacher, *Little Magazine Profiles: The Little Magazines in Great Britain, 1939-1993* (University of Salzburg, 1993), pp.122-3.

especially at Preston Polytechnic, gave him the base and I would suggest distance from which to establish *Akros*, the magazine and imprint. *Akros* ran from 1965 to 1983 and its reviews, debate and publication of new poetry make it one of the cornerstones of the Scottish literary culture in that period.

Glen's championing of Hugh MacDiarmid's work in *Akros* and elsewhere should also be seen in the context of a totemic identification within the contemporary avant-garde with modernists from a bygone era, in England's case the enthusiasm, developed from bases in London, Cambridge and Newcastle, for Basil Bunting. My understanding is that it was through the readings series built up as part of this newfound enthusiasm in the '60s that Bunting and MacDiarmid actually came to meet: though they are perhaps spoken of together in terms of their Poundian modernism it appears that it was the sixties that actually created their fellowship.

The re-discovery of modernist predecessors was by no means rigorous or wholesale in the 1960s. It's true that there probably aren't *that* many highly innovative poets from the inter-war years in the UK to re-discover but the neglected example of the Anglo-Scottish Joseph Macleod, who also wrote as Adam Drinan, shows that the editors on both sides of the border weren't thorough in their looking back for experimental predecessors, and they may have gravitated towards 'ethnically solid' poets to champion. Andrew Duncan's recent advocacy for Macleod, the author of fascinating linguistic experiments from the '30s to the '50s, including a significant importing of Gaelic language rules into Anglophone poetry, has to some extent corrected this in England, even if the dissemination hasn't been thorough in Scotland yet.[70] Here's a brief example of Macleod's poetry, the opening lines from his 1946 poem, 'Enterprise Scotland':

> Her bairns stare at twisted tin,
> nylon ropes, cultured colours,
> fibre glass, gleg things,
> in the mirror of their mother:
> > the love of a good maker for a good matter
> > the love of creative seller for thing created.[71]

Lines Review did publish Macleod from the 1950s to the 1980s, and Macdonald, its publisher, also issued Macleod's last poetry collection, *An Old Olive Tree* (1971).

Another experimental Scottish poet, Helen Adam, who began writing in the inter-war years was welcomed by the San Francisco scenes of Robert Duncan and Jack Spicer, anthologised in Donald Allen's landmark *The New American Poetry* (1960), but not accepted within Official Scottish Literature until decades later, at the suggestion of Edwin Morgan in 1999.[72] She remains a figure who is probably still just out of the ken of standard Scottish literary criticism, and wrongly I think. A similar situation is true of the poet and film-maker Margaret Tait, whose poetry and short stories from the late '50s and early '60s are of interest: it is only in recent years, partly through the advocacy of Ali Smith, that she has been invited back into the Scottish literary family.

---

[70] Macleod's works included *The Ecliptic* (Faber, 1930) and, as Adam Drinan, *Women of the Happy Island* (MacLellan, 1944). See also Joseph Macleod, ed. Andrew Duncan, *Cyclic Serial Zeniths from the Flux: Selected Poems* (Waterloo Press, 2009).

[71] Collected in *Cyclic Serial Zeniths from the Flux*, Waterloo Press, 2009.

[72] Edwin Morgan, 'Scotland and the World,' in *PN Review* 130, Volume 26 Number 2, November - December 1999.

Duncan Glen is a key example of a Scottish literary editor working in England at that time, concerning himself very much with archetypically 'Scottish' literary issues, e.g. the publishing and reviewing of Scottish writing and debates about the use of Scots as a literary language, but also with questions of interest on both sides of the border, namely the latent energies of inter-war modernism. It is one of the problems of Michael Gardiner's account of literary theory during this period, *From Trocchi to Trainspotting* (2006) that Glen and *Akros* are barely and grudgingly mentioned. When Glen is given some credit, he seems to be criticised for what is valorised in other contexts —for example, for Gardiner the visual is to be especially praised as innovative in contemporary poetry but an interview with MacDiarmid appears to be criticised as 'largely pictorial'[73]; if I'm right in seeing the spin on that phrase, that is to mistake the value of what is actually a *photo*-essay on MacDiarmid. To recognise it as such would help contextualise it in other image-based approaches to MacDiarmid at this time, such as Margaret Tait's remarkably off-centre film, *Hugh MacDiarmid: A Portrait* (1964). Who else but Tait could have persuaded the elderly MacDiarmid to walk spritely along the top of a low wall, a rich poetic, 'filmic', image if ever there was one. Looked at visually, Glen's story-in-pictures are attempting a similar feat.

In fact, reading back-issues of *Akros* it becomes clear that Glen's editing practice was remarkably liberal, and open to and actively encouraging of modernity; his editorials are literary theory of a kind, addressing absolutely contemporary issues; they are not Barthes or Derrida, but they offer expert witness to the specifics of their time with that expertise being an in-depth knowledge of Scottish literary history. Gardiner's argument, if I understand him

---

[73] Michael Gardiner, *From Trocchi to Trainspotting* (Edinburgh, 2006), p.36.

correctly, that there wasn't really any Scottish literary theory in the 1960s except for that implicit in poems and other creative writing itself, might be true in an academic sense but needs something of an adjustment I think and it needs much further excavational work. Glen's example suggests that it is there if we look hard enough.

To take one example: in one of his editorials Glen rightly observes that the opening of the mass media does not necessarily further centralise linguistic authority in London-approved English but offers powerful decentralised opportunities as well.[74] That is a visionary thing to say: its amplification, after all, has been born out in the radical decentring offered by the Net. It suggests to me that failing to find Scottish literary theory in the 1960s may simply be a practical problem, one that scholars of the earlier period of Scottish modernism will recognise. Much important literary theory is likely to be distributed across the newspaper and periodical literature of the times; it doesn't need inferring from primary creative texts in the face of the scale of that task but it does need patient archaeological work. What is needed is gathering, republishing and re-thinking.

Glen was a very gifted editor in another way. He was a great chooser: he could select poems that turned out to be classics of their kind. This is measured by several now canonical texts that appear to have had their first appearance in *Akros* — for example 'Glasgow Green' by Edwin Morgan and Norman MacCaig's 'A Man from Assynt'.

---

[74] See for example Glen's engagement with Marshall McLuhan in Glen's 'The Unfathomable Ground of Scottish Poetry', in *Akros*, Vol. 3 no. 7 (March 1968), pp.2-10. Glen rightly asserts that modern Scots is a living language and that the new mass media can rise to the challenge of delivering Scots-language programming to Scots communities.

Finally, there is another element to Glen's practice that has a *zeitgeist* component to it: *Akros* is a superbly and idiosyncratically designed magazine, obviously emerging from Glen's experience working as a typographer in England and then teaching graphic design there. Production-wise *Akros* balances a typewritten stencil interior with the offset litho of its often striking covers (by no means always by Glen himself). Different pastel-range coloured paper is used within the text block of each issue to zone content — with a different colour sometimes meaning a discrete sequence, as in Giles Gordon's *Twelve poems for Callum* (No. 11, August 1969) or for an essay, as in Tom Scott's *A Review of Robert Fergusson's Poems* (Vol. 2 no. 6, Dec. 1967).

This is helpfully functional (I think of Lissitsky's use of thumbable index letters in his artist's books almost half a century earlier) but it also gives the reader a sense of the editor's care, his attentiveness to the magazine's design as *more* than the utility of the words it contains. This provides an extra-reading pleasure: the little magazine as artform. Since, in the broadest terms, the foregrounding of the visual in poetry is a key aspect of UK, US and European avant-garde poetry at this time, this tending to the 'artefactual' in *Akros*, despite some aesthetically conservative undercurrents in some of the work published, is another marker of Glen's wider engagement.

However, you could also look at England-based literary magazines headed by Scots who were not so interested in national identity politics at all. Thomas A. Clark, for instance, now celebrated as a poet in the minimalist tradition, was editor in 1967-68 of the magazine *Bo Heem E Um*, based in Sherborne, although its first issue was published in Greenock. Three cheers for Renfrewshire! (Forgive my solidarity – the first literary magazine I edited, *Gairfish*, bore a Renfrewshire place of publication, too: Bridge of Weir.) *Bo Heem E Um* appears to have been produced via typewritten stencil or perhaps solely by typewriter; it is physically insubstantial but pleasingly delicate in production. This was the era of the typewriter poem as a genre and *Bo Heem E Um* is clearly working within the form. It did publish Scottish writers — in the fourth issue for example, Robin Fulton, Edwin Morgan and Clark himself make an appearance — but together with its imprint, South Street, it was arguably more interested in the aesthetic issues to do with the visual aspects of poetry.

This was a key Scottish theme of course, though not exclusively Scottish: perhaps looking generally across formal considerations is as useful in understanding Scottish literature at this time as looking for Scots on Scots. In *Bo Heem E Um's* anonymously edited sister publication, *Arlington,* also published by South Street, Scottish poets particularly concerned with the page as a conceptual space were naturally featured — Morgan, Finlay, Clark — but this was alongside an international field of pioneers and practitioners, including Tom Phillips, Bob Cobbing, Ian Breakwell, Charles Verey, Lilian Lijn, Simon Cutts, John Sharkey, Ken Cox (see for example *Arlington* [issue 4]: Quadlog, where all of these appear). *Arlington* always accompanied an exhibition of concrete poetry, held at Arlington Mill in Gloucestershire. This leads to questions about built space for presenting literature, questions with which Scots of the day appear to have been particularly engaged. Later, in 1983, Clark and his wife Laurie moved these questions from page to gallery, founding the Cairn Gallery in Gloucestershire, a space for minimalist text-based art and for land art. It has now has reopened in Pittenweem.

It's important to emphasise that this international engagement with concrete poetry included it appearing alongside English text-based artists such as John Furnival (and the Channel Islands's Dom Sylvester Houédard), while England's literary infrastructure in the 1960s showcased and presented far more concrete poetry from around the world than Scotland did. It would have been parochial for Scottish concrete poets, of which Morgan and Finlay are the best known, not to appear there.

It was after all the *Times Literary Supplement,* not I believe a Scottish title, which published E. M. de Melo Castro's incendiary letter on concrete poetry in 1962. This was the letter that Edwin Morgan, wired into contemporary English literary developments among others around the world, so eagerly responded to, passing the information on to Finlay. Arguably, it was also the English, Scottish and North American contacts made by *Migrant* editors Gael Turnbull and Michael Shayer in the late 1950s which, when shared with Finlay, allowed the latter to launch his iconic magazine *Poor. Old. Tired. Horse* in 1962. Only later did it modify its Black Mountain influences to incorporate concrete poetry, building on the base that *Migrant* had to some degree helped build. When you look at the number of conferences, festivals and exhibitions on concrete poetry held in England and note the number of England-based magazines and anthologies featuring concrete poetry in the 1960s you find considerable take up. This wasn't just a London phenomenon — Brighton, the central and west Midlands, the north-east of England — were all places of display, discussion, performance or publication. Although many of these occurred within avant-garde environments, concrete poetry was so accepted within the broader life of England that a talk was broadcast on it on the Third Programme in January 1965,[75] a feature on it published in *The Daily Telegraph*'s colour supplement in August 1968[76] and by 1969 the Puffin Club had organised at least one children's competition which accepted entries in this

---

[75] For example the twenty-minute programme at 6.05 pm that took place on the Third Programme on Jan 24th 1965, according to the listing in *The Guardian*, 23 Jan 1965.
[76] Elizabeth Glazebrook, The Last Word in Poetry, in *Daily Telegraph Magazine*, 202 (16 August 1968), pp.21-23.

form.[77] This hardly sounds like avant-garde any more. Rather, like the Russian Futurists' dream of an art that is both intelligent and loved (and adopted) across class divides, it sounds as if a major artistic experiment has found fertile ground on a hegemonic scale, mostly in England, which is where most of the UK readership resides. Görtschacher notes Bob Cobbing as 'one of the major exponents of the international concrete poetry movement' and his publishing from 1963 of concrete poetry. (Görtschacher op.cit. p.142). He further remarks: 'Magazines devoted to furthering the cause of concrete and visual poetry included Michael Gibbs's Kontexts (1969-77), Philip Steadman's Image, Tarasque (1965-71), edited by Stuart Mills and Simon Cutts, John Hall and Ian Breakwell's Exit (1967-73), and Nicholas Zurbrugg's Stereo Headphones (1969-1982). According to Görtschacher (op.cit. p.143), conferences on concrete poetry were often accompanied by exhibitions and associated readings embraced sound poetry aesthetics. Mary Ellen Solt commented in *Concrete Poetry: A World View* (Indiana University Press, 1968): 'Although England cannot lay claim to having been in on the laying of the foundations of the concrete poetry movement, important exhibitions have been held there. We have noted the First International Exhibition of Concrete and Kinetic Poetry in Cambridge in 1964, organized by Mike Weaver. Another important comprehensive exhibition, Between Poetry and Painting, organized by Jasia Reichardt, was held at the Institute of Contemporary Art, London, in 1968. The *Times Literary Supplement* put out two special numbers on international avant-garde poetry on 6 August and 3 September 1964.'[78]

---

[77] See the preview of one such exhibition in the anonymous 'Ego Briefing', *The Observer*, 23 March 1969, p.34.
[78] Downloaded from http://www.ubu.com/papers/solt/england.html, 22nd Jan 2010.

In fact this underestimates the number of exhibitions and conferences. Of course, there are Scottish examples. Finlay's magazine *Poor. Old. Tired. Horse* became a major shop window, or gallery space, for the form, though it did not start out as a concrete poetry magazine. There were other important but isolated instances of Scottish promulgation, too, such as Richard Demarco's Gallery, which displayed concrete poetry later on in the decade. Nevertheless, the contrast between the countries appears so marked it could be argued that there was at that time a widespread cultural antipathy in Scotland to the visual, to the graven image perhaps, or simply to literary experiment itself. I have looked in what comparable sources there are but I've yet to find anything that shows such an interest never mind integration of concrete poetry into the cultural life of Scotland.

As you can see I've moved further and further away from a notional core idea of Scottish literature — not to suggest 'progress' but rather to suggest the danger of missing things if Scottishness is the only or initial filter; and also the need to use England as an experimental control, to fact-check claims about Scottish supremacy in this or that form (not a helpful concept, supremacy, I feel).

I'd like to pause here and draw attention to the work of the gifted arts activist Tom McGrath, a poet, playwright and director. As a literary figure within counterculture, McGrath's example suggests that pigeon-holing won't work for this period.

Features editor from 1964 to 1966 for the anti-war newspaper *Peace News*, McGrath was a musician-poet informed by jazz. In this way he can be grouped with others in the UK at the time, such as Jeff Nuttall, Roy Fisher and, for that matter the Glaswegian, Ivor Cutler. McGrath took part, as both a journalist and a poet, in the famous Albert Hall 'happening' of 1965, arguably a catalytic moment for 1960s counter-culture. He was then the original editor of one of the key counter-cultural titles *The International Times*, which started life in 1966.

His example illustrates how much of a shame it would be if Scottish literary studies or the history of Scottish publishing were to withdraw into an unrealistic definition of 'Scottishness' that proposed a quite separate Scottish literary and publishing infrastructure, of fantastical fidelity to itself, when no such thing existed. It is noticeable that the English avant-garde didn't forget McGrath — although the only substantial book on McGrath that I've been able to identify is a 300-page collection of interviews with him, a work of advocacy by the experimental English poet Gavin Selerie.[79] To assess Scottish contributions only in terms of inward investment or outward influence you have to imagine a society that, against a Bairdian worldview, neither sends nor receives, that somehow is immune to larger historic structures which have actually joined and mingled with it.

As it happens, you *could* play that blind-fold game later on in McGrath's remarkable life: on his return to Scotland he was founding director of Glasgow's Third Eye Centre, was one of the forces behind the Tron Theatre's establishment, and was an innovative playwright in his own right. There are many other achievements to his name but I highlight these to corroborate my earlier suggestion that the 1960s may have been very important to Scottish culture as the beginnings of art-space experimentation, from the intimate scale of the page as canvas to the larger scale of theatrical space. Indeed, this could be extended to the visual arts if we think about the London-based conceptual artists now known as

---

[79] Tom McGrath, ed. Gavin Selerie, *Tom McGrath*, (Riverside Interviews no. 6), London: Binnacle Press, 1983.

Boyle Family, initially the Glaswegian Mark Boyle and Yorkshire artist Joan Hills: their work exploring the surface of the world, and, as lighting engineers for musical performers (for example, Pink Floyd), creating remarkable light effects to accompany futuristic sounds, further suggests the immense *dimensional curiosity* of the times, a curiosity Scots and English enthusiastically shared.

In McGrath's first editorial for *The International Times* he urges poets, theatre directors and others to avoid the misdirection entailed in the state funding of the arts and suggests housing of the homeless and the unilateral re-painting of urban space as examples of *artistic* projects beyond the capability of the current arts infrastructure. (This, incidentally, *is* in contrast to the editorial line in *Akros*, which urged Scottish authorities to produce a similar arts and education infrastructure to that produced by any self-governing state, with England/UK the usual model).[80] Conceding with a wry smile that the Traverse is 'the nearest thing we have to an avant-garde theatre in London at the moment' (the Traverse was and is, of course, Edinburgh-based) McGrath still regards it as 'only succeeding in fulfilling a sacred traditional theatre function' and he proceeds to nothing less than a revolutionary conclusion: 'if you decide you want to change things at base, you are deciding to be your own government.'[81]

---

[80] See for instance, Duncan Glen, 'Editorial' in *Akros* Vol. 3 no. 8 (August 1968), pp.2-5. For example: 'The position at present is that Scottish studies are subsidiary to English studies. We are not suggesting the closing or curtailing of English departments; we require independent Scottish departments in addition to the English departments.' (p. 4).
[81] Tom McGrath, writing anonymously, *International Times*,[No. 1], Oct. 14-27 1966, p.1 & p.8. Downloaded from http://www.internationaltimes.it/, 25th Jan 2010.

As you can see it would be a travesty if the point of McGrath's appearance on the ScotLit radar was simply when he returned to Scotland: it is surely right to say that his explorations of public performance crucially began in London at the height of the counter-cultural uproar to which he was a significant contributor.

This is important because by polarising Scotland and England it may mean that neither Scotland's nor England's people are given their due when working together or when Scottish contributions are of considerable interest within a UK or international framework. Furthermore, when participants are actively working against each other, Scottishness appears on some English critical radars and is forcefully loaded onto what a more objective observer may see as the complex action of a single individual rather than that of a representative of a nation. What this may mean is a double bind: that Scottish academics mistakenly isolate themselves, while others beyond Scotland use such isolation to downplay the positive Scottish contribution to the wider commonwealth of ideas and, worse, to emphasise any Scottish agency as destructive.

I'd like to take the fact of Baird's association with Glasgow and point to what may be a special phenomenon in the literary '60s. Did Glasgow change the rules of the Scottish literary game in the 1960s? If so, why Glasgow?

Here's a roll-call of sixties authors and editors who either spent a substantial part of their upbringing in greater Glasgow or who lived in Glasgow as young adults. The list begins with Rutherglenians Tom McGrath and Edwin Morgan, moves to Duncan Glen, born in Cambuslang and educated at Rutherglen Academy and who worked in Glasgow as a young adult, then there's Alexander Trocchi and Kenneth White, both born in Glasgow and both educated at Glasgow University, where White also taught from 1963 to 1967. If you regard Glaswegian R. D. Laing's 1970s book *Knots* as literature, and I do, then you'd need to include his 1960s work in a broad brush-stroke look at the 60s — in any case it's a commonplace that his psychiatric work *The Divided Self* (1960) fits in with the ScotLit doubles trope. Finally, at the end of the decade, there is Tom Leonard's *Six Glasgow Poems,* appearing in 1969. That physically small collection of poems asserts the resources of Glasgow speech, especially non-realistic treatment of realistic Glasgow speech. In a way it also links back to one of the key figures of Scotland in the Sixties: Ian Hamilton Finlay (who has a tenuous link to Glasgow, as he studied at the Glasgow School of Art). Finlay's *Glasgow Beasts...* (1961) is a beautifully designed bestiary that imagined Glasgow animals speaking in Glaswegian and, through the paper cuts of the young English artist John Picking, created charming icons of each animal.

It's not just conventional genres of literature which suggest the link to Glasgow. I've mentioned Ivor Cutler, but Donovan, born in Glasgow and brought up in Ayrshire, could be enlisted for the wider culture, an international singer-songwriter of (I believe) continuing interest, and in terms of the 1960s an example of an artist who made the huge transition from an intimate folk-based practice to the aesthetics of global mass communication.

However strong the Glasgow link is — and I need to be careful about pleading too much for my home city — the authors I've mentioned expanded Scottish literature quite radically in several ways, and often in opposite directions. First of all, there is the emphasis on poetry as a visual medium not only a linear linguistic carrier. Glen is not typographically experimental but he is typographically self-conscious: it is probably more accurate to say he works in a highly self-conscious typographic tradition within which modernism is an important but far from sole element (this may even make him a post-modernist). Morgan and Finlay are major exponents of concrete poetry.

Secondly, and to some extent conceptually separate from concrete poetry, there is the rise of minimalism: Finlay, like Thomas Clark, and to some degree Kenneth White, put particular value on the concentration and ramification of minimal utterance as did Tom Leonard. But we need a fact-check: you can see this in Norman MacCaig's work, too, and of course in that of some English poets, for example those associated with the magazine *Tarasque* (1966-1972); arguably there are orientalist aspects to this which are Poundian and even Gunnian; Cid Corman may also be a point of reference here.

Thirdly, there is sound poetry: Morgan is a playful but palpable exponent of sound poetry, as Leonard would be in the 1970s, though I am not sure if either pursue it to the lengths that the doyen of English sound poetry, Bob Cobbing, does. Their openness to it, however, may be something to do with the burgeoning of recordings, TV and film, even if they didn't themselves work in all those forms; it could also be to do with a growing emphasis on poetry as live performance. Might there also be a youth aspect to this as youth culture begins to gain hegemonic force? A blurring of the edges between what is for children and what is for adults?

Fourthly, there is membership of international movements: Trocchi belonging to Lettrist International and Situationist International in the 1950s; Morgan and Finlay participating in the international concrete poetry movement in the '60s; McGrath editing *The International Times,* clearly an international countercultural newspaper. 'International' is an important word at this time: *Scottish International* (1968-1974) is the name of the cultural review that Edwin Morgan and Robert Garioch edited, arguably seeking to effect a cultural secession that might be the means to a political one. To be 'international' in the sense of these activities is about collective representation and so recognition within an international framework; this is not the same as responding to foreign influence; for example, translating foreign literature or publishing it, which is a more passive and individual internationalism and more likely to be unreciprocated at scale. The latter did of course go on: Morgan exemplifies it and excelled in it, and you can see this as a UK pattern in the work of *Modern Poetry in Translation*, edited by Ted Hughes and Daniel Weissbort.

The import business in the '60s was an Edinburgh one as far as the place where magazines were published: the Beats came in, for example, via the Edinburgh magazines *Sidewalk* and its '50s predecessor *Jabberwock*; Black Mountain, European and Brazilian poetry came into Scotland via Finlay's *Poor. Old. Tired. Horse* after the *TLS* and Edwin Morgan and *Migrant* had given him a major helping hand; Robin Fulton's editorship of *Lines Review*, from 1967 to 1977 was particularly strong in European poetry in translation; and *Cleft* published American heavyweights of various generations: Henry Miller, Norman Mailer, William Burroughs and Louis Zukofsky. All these were Edinburgh titles.

Edinburgh, a publishing centre for hundreds of years, may have remained in that service-city role at this time, marketing the wares of initial producers of literary art who came from elsewhere (though also from itself, but its own literary productions are likely, the hypothesis would go, to be more conciliating, more popularising). Perhaps like all distributing or retail nodes, Edinburgh is a cautious, filtering, mediating element in the product schema: the expansion of subject range and the stylised and later hegemonic use of urban Scots in this hypothetical model was produced by Glasgow, especially allied and alloyed with the *Dustie-fute* travelling temperament that the Glaswegians I've mentioned seemed to have had. In contrast, Edinburgh selectively imported, reviewed, and, eventually, adapted the prosodic models of those imports. It is in this sense that *Trainspotting* is the end of a line that feasibly goes way back to Trocchi, the Morgan of Mayakovsky in Scots, Finlay's *Glasgow Beasts*, Leonard and Kelman, while of course being influenced by myriad others, too.

If experiment in Scottish fiction before the 1950s were characterised, broadly speaking, by the dominance of rural mis en scène and isolated cases of experimentation with small-town collective registers (Gibbon's *Scots Quair* community voice being the standout example, probably influenced by Nan Shepherd's work and English and Irish modernism), the latter half of the 20th century sees a shift, namely Scottish fiction as urban in subject and individualistic (non-collective) in voice. Forgive the appalling short-hand of that summary but with all caveats active it is striking that poetry and the use of Scots appears to have been an originator in this process — Morgan, Finlay and Leonard are key here. Because fiction is not meant to be influenced by anything but itself, perhaps this understanding of the Kelman and Irvine Welsh phenomenon has in the past been underplayed, though Cairns Craig does make a similar, not quite identical, point in his study *The Modern Scottish Novel* when he discusses 'Typographic Muse'.[82] John Logie Baird produced work that was understood by too few to make an immediate impact but his legacy has been long-term: perhaps that is the case for key examples of Scottish literature in the 1960s.

There is so much more to say about the complex framework within which Scottish literature operated in the 1960s. Some of it is evidenced in Ross Birrell and Alec Finlay's *Justified Sinners: an archaeology of Scottish counterculture (1960-2000)* (2002),

---

[82] Cairns Craig, 'The Typographic Muse' in *The Modern Scottish Novel: Narrative and the National Imagination* (Edinburgh University Press, 1999), pp.167-199.

though it was not meant to be literary criticism and it doesn't function as such. I think of the American Jim Haynes running his Paperback Bookshop in Edinburgh as a shop and as a readings venue. I think of mass communication: Finlay Macdonald's technically modest but significant Poets Places television series that ran in 1966 on BBC Scotland's predecessor, in contrast to Donovan's international successes in both folk and psychedelia. Is Andrew Duncan right when he makes the provocative argument that folk music and cultural nationalism in this period were a distraction, threatening Scottish poetry's ability to innovate?[83] Scots were clearly interested in the burgeoning mass media but, Donovan aside, were they able to break through into it (rather than just write about it within minority forms like poetry)?

I'd like to finish with a simple reminder about some key magazines of the '50s, on which the '60s in my view clearly build. *Gairm* began publishing Gaelic creative writing and criticism from 1952 and became a bedrock for the Gaelic literary community. W. Price Turner's *The Poet* began in Glasgow, also in 1952 and, while it did not last more than four years, its publication of Black Mountain poets alongside modern Scottish and English poets was a close and acknowledged model for *Migrant*. *Migrant*, in turn, ran as a magazine only from 1959 to 1960 (though catalytically), so making *The Poet* influential by proxy. Trocchi's *Merlin*, which ran from 1952 to 1955, was as friendly to contemporary European literature as it was to American. From Edinburgh, beginning in 1952, *Lines Review* was a steady force in Scottish literature for decades. It might be that the beat literature that appeared in Edinburgh's *Jabberwock* in 1959 was just as influential on Scottish

---

[83] Andrew Duncan, 'Peripheral nationalism and collective disloyalty' in Duncan, *Origins of the Underground: British Poetry between Apocryphon and Incident Light 1933-79* (Salt, 2008), pp.254-261.

sensibilities, so big was the shift in aesthetics it was proposing. Like *Migrant* perhaps *Jabberwock* was a brilliant mistake... which allows me to return once more to Baird and his willingness to risk marvellous failures. If Baird hadn't persevered with experiment after experiment perhaps he would only be known for one vain episode: superheating carbon in an attempt to create diamonds — the only consequence of which was to bring down Glasgow's entire electrical supply.

Poetry Pamphlets as Public Private Space

The pamphlet is a special form of communication with a long and rich history as an agent of expression, and the many held at the British Library represent various high-points in its continuing life. The pamphlet is of course not necessarily a poetry-form, though I believe poetry and pamphlet are natural partners. The astonishing range of opinions in the Library's English Civil War collections, for example, witness a nation awakening to its own emotional and philosophical complexity and doing so through what appears at first to be the most modest of physical forms. In the thought and fervour of the French Revolutionary tracts you can witness France daring to think aloud. Pamphlets are also about curiosity, comedy, and pleasure. In the parcelled pages of the 18th and 19th century chapbook, which I would class as part of the pamphlet family, there was news, satire, poetry and song. Travelling from market town to market town, the chapbook sellers made no apology for bundling information and delight into their backpacks.

Politics and religion: the pamphlet is in a way the party guest bent on talking about subjects traditionally thought best avoided. I think poetry is a little like that, too. Actually, though, the modern poetry pamphlet is more often an intimate object than an especially public one, or rather, like the best poetry itself, it thrives in the ambiguous territory between the individual life and social intervention. The pamphlet's special intimate quality is probably a function of its small format. Think of its name – the pamphlet – it sounds like a little thing – and when you think of some of its other family members, the booklets and the leaflets, that's true for them, too. To my mind the sound of the '-let' suffix also has an affection to it, as if the pamphlet is something you cannot fail to love. Of course, it would be fatal to patronise the pamphlet — a poppet it is not — and you should never underestimate the power of its compact universe. Leaflets and booklets — and so perhaps pamphlets — are forces of public information, too, so once again you have that curious and powerful ability of the pamphlet and of poetry to appeal to many by appearing to be directed to only one.

The formal similarities that the pamphlet has with other important printed objects give it a force that can only come from it seeming to be a personal object; seeming to be but never quite. At one end of its immense expressive spectrum it gives pleasure, as if it were somewhere between a well-chosen birthday card and an inspired birthday present; in other cases it can be as sombre and moving as an order of service but of course the pamphlet is enacting all of the commemoration itself; it can be a souvenir programme where the event is the language of its own poetry; and when the poetry pamphlet engages with the visual arts it becomes exhibition and exhibition catalogue in one, a seemingly private memento of the sensation you are holding within your hands.

The only collection published by Edward Thomas in his lifetime was a pamphlet, *Six Poems*, in 1916. It is a glimpse of the lyric poetry which only fully emerged posthumously, following Thomas's death in the First World War. W. H. Auden's first book, *Poems*, was printed by his friend Stephen Spender, on the sort of press normally reserved for medicine labels. Inspired amateurism can be part of pamphlet life. Dylan Thomas's *18 Poems* was published in 1934 when Thomas was barely out of his teens, the very short book being one of the first places poets can begin to develop their talent. Philip Larkin's *The North Ship* published by Fortune Press in 1945 was in a way a false start — in later books Larkin rejected the influences of Auden and Yeats he displays here — but his lonely melancholy is already present, and the opportunity to make false starts, to do 'research and development', is one of the great qualities pamphlets afford.

Triumphantly, the sixties saw the emergence of artists who would stretch and mature the pamphlet form. Bob Cobbing, Ted Hughes and J. H. Prynne each used it to provide very different kinds of experimental work. All united, however, in their understanding that the pamphlet had qualities that longer, commercially produced books, could not hope to match. The modern roll of honour can go on – Laura Riding, Philip Larkin, Linton Kwesi Johnson, Seamus Heaney, Paul Muldoon, Penelope Shuttle, Tom Leonard, Edwin Morgan, Denise Riley have all made important interventions with their poetry pamphlets. It is no surprise that when the current poet laureate, Carol Ann Duffy, published her first book, nearly forty years ago, it was... a pamphlet. It is not always about a pamphlet's higher production qualities or about a short book being a stepping stone to what is called mainstream publication. A poetry sequence need not be crowded out by other poems if it stands alone in a pamphlet. In a way, the pamphlet is actually a variation of the liquid concentrate with which Spender's chemist's press was more familiar. Roy Fisher's 1961 collection *City* has homespun elements to its printing — friends were involved in its making —but its evocation of an English city is matchless and makes a new start in modern English poetry's approach to urban life. It's with Fisher that I'll conclude because although the following quotation refers to *City* perhaps we can take it to refer to the fertile overlap of printing technologies and poetry of the highest order, captured in the pamphlet form. Fisher says with a wry nod to anthropological language: 'The society of singing birds and the society of mechanical hammers inhabit the world together.'

Vennel Press: The Autobiography of a Poetry Press

Vennel Press, which ran for over fifteen years, was initially created as a one-off publishing venture to publish a new book, *Second Cities*, by Donny O'Rourke. In July 1990, O'Rourke, a TV arts producer as well as a poet, was in the United States to research a programme about the 'second' city, Chicago. At the turn of the nineteenth century Chicago had sent a fact-finding team to Glasgow for civic inspiration. At that time Glasgow one of the most advanced cities in the world, providing a high standard of education, libraries and public utilities to its citizens: the burghers of Chicago wanted to know how running a successful city was done. O'Rourke was there to report and reflect on the contrasts in the 1990s.

O'Rourke was heavily involved in transforming the cultural infrastructure in Scotland. The weekly magazine format of his arts programme *NB*, whose design was to be repeated many times in the wider context of British TV, was demonstrating Scotland's cultural wealth to Scotland. It also showcased visiting international shows, writers, and musicians: with friendly wit and not a little panache NB was helping Scottish artists and audience alike view themselves within a worldwide continuum of artistic exploration, expression and engagement. Grabbing the mass medium that the Scot John Logie Baird had invented, these programmes were tonally diverse and featured elements from the reflective to the adrenaline-fuelled. Produced for the commercial channel STV, they were light-touch rather than dumbed-down, delivering the arts and their contextualisation to hundreds of thousands of viewers in a way that print media (and rival broadcasts) could not equal.

Alongside this was O'Rourke's *In Verse* programmes in which many contemporary Scottish poets read their work in the TV studio. A wider, deeper, precursor to his groundbreaking anthology of Scottish poetry, *Dream State: The New Scottish Poets* (published 1994), *In Verse* is one of the treasures of Scottish archival film and, to my knowledge, still has no equivalent elsewhere in the British Isles.

O'Rourke was a cultural activist outside TV. His reading series in Glasgow's Babbity Bowster inn, where poets shared a platform with invited musicians, emphasised the importance of live performance and, because he paired younger writers with more established ones, effected introductions and cross-fertilisation. I first met O'Rourke in 1988 when, as a final-year student at Strathclyde University, my poetry won an all-Glasgow universities competition: he was the judge. We became friends, or rather, he became a mentor to me; his influence would be critical to the framing and direction of Vennel Press, as would the remarkable Glasgow efflorescence that was taking place.

At that time, Glasgow's ability to 'punch above its weight' was demonstrable. Alasdair Gray's novel *Lanark*, Janice Galloway's *The Trick Is To Keep Breathing*, several books by James Kelman and Alan Spence, and the poetry of Tom Leonard and Edwin Morgan and newcomer Robert Crawford, the poetry and drama of Liz Lochhead, were there in astounding plenitude and depth. Graduates of the Glasgow Art School were making international inroads, too. Most of the writers had a political or philosophical edge (though not necessarily a nationalist one) and their intellectual and artistic challenge was contagious. Inequalities and injustice accentuated by preparations for Glasgow's International

Year of Culture (in 1990) made the city seem as if it was a place where writing was more than usually a political act.

This is the background to O'Rourke's visit to Chicago, and to the first stirrings of a new press which took many of its bearings from Glasgow. Poetry and its recalibration for modern times were certainly on O'Rourke's mind in Chicago and, as he recalled, 'Over the next few days, in which I slept hardly at all, I found myself keeping a verse journal of the trip.' Within only a few months of Donny sending me the typescript, that verse journal became the first collection of Vennel Press.

London and the Poetry Workshop
In the summer of 1988 I had moved to London to work at the British Library. Also new there was the poet, former craft bookbinder and (like me) recently qualified librarian, Leona Medlin. Leona, originally from Michigan, had been living in London for over ten years. She invited me to join a group that didn't have an official name; its members simply called it the 'poetry workshop', considering it an activity rather than an entity. The term was put into initial capitals only when the group needed to be more formally defined on an application form for an Arts Council small groups National Lottery grant (awarded for creating a CD-ROM, then website, demonstrating the work and process of the group). Its membership in the late '80s and '90s included Chris Hedley-Dent, C. L. Dallat, Hugh Epstein, Elizabeth James, Duncan McGibbon, the playwright Kim Morrissey, Leona and myself.
Perhaps inevitably in London this was a gathering of nationalities: English, Scottish, Irish, Welsh, Canadian, and American. These writers had quite different social and educational backgrounds and sometimes very different aesthetics. A private group, we met monthly in a room at the Poetry Society's premises in Earls Court Square until the Society sold the property, after which we would

meet in each other's houses. The format encouraged the presentation of a single poet's work in progress for the evening in question, often a sequence or longer poem, though by no means always. Because we wrote in different ways, the workshop became a means of attuning our reading to different contexts and rules. For Leona and me workshop attentiveness and (I hope) openness to thinking beyond initial instincts were crucial to our editorial practice. By the end of 1990, in fact very quickly after we had decided to set up Vennel Press to publish Donny O'Rourke's collection *Second Cities* as a 'one-off', we had determined that other books would follow and that the imprint, as far as sales and self-funding would allow (we would remain independent of the Arts Council secretariats), would have aesthetic range.

From the workshop itself, Vennel published two poets in what had quickly become our standard A5 format: Leona's book of lyrical poems, *The Tilted Mirror*, and an early book of minimalist poems, *1:50,000*, by Elizabeth, later better known for her avant-garde work, including *Base to Carry* (Barque, 2004) and her collaboration with Frances Presley, *Neither the One Nor the Other* (Form Books, 1999). When we began to produce a series of A6 booklets on the broad theme Brief Pleasures, the workshop's emphasis on grouped and longer poems found an appropriate published form. The fairly loose topic of the series also meant that we could accommodate different styles and concerns within a single series: there are many pleasures to be explored. Vennel published Duncan McGibbon's beautiful evocation of English rivers, *Channel*, Elizabeth James's disconcerting interior decorating text, *The World of Interiors*, Chris Hedley-Dent's frightening *mittel*-European circus sequence *Mirror Talk*, and Kim Morrissey's non-smoker's homage to the 'coughy' art, *Smoking*. In the same series was also Donny O'Rourke's *Modern Music*, Peter Snowden's *Plat du Jour*, Hamish Whyte's *Christmasses* and (the most oblique pleasure) Peter Daniels's *Lucynski's Blue Mice*.

Artists

Before qualifying as a librarian, Leona Medlin had been a fine press book-binder with Morrell's Bookbinders and Nottingham Court Press, where she also had editing responsibilities. A highlight had been working on the Rainbow Press edition of *Remains of Elmet* by Ted Hughes and the photographer Fay Goodwin, which had a Morrell binding. At Nottingham Court, Leona worked on a limited edition facsimile of Walton's *Compleat Angler* and *An Intimate Landscape*, the latter a collaboration between Leonard Clark and the wood engraver Miriam Macgregor. Leona brought to Vennel the appreciation of the book as an art object in its own right, and the ability to realise that goal.

Donny O'Rourke's friendship with Scottish and Scottish-based artists meant that, from the first book, we were able to commission special illustrations for our publications: *Second Cities* carried work from Dominic Snyder and Gwyneth Leech, very much in keeping with the urban observations of the sequence. Donny pointed us in the direction of the jacketed paperbacks that the Irish imprint Gallery had developed and we were influenced by this inexpensive but surprisingly elegant design. I had originally thought of calling the press Cloch Point Press, after the Cloch Point lighthouse in the Firth of Clyde (and the way it evoked 'clock', too — perhaps the press would be both a beacon and a measurer of change). Vennel, however, came to me somehow. It's a Scots word, like the English ginnel, meaning a lane or alley. Leona and I both liked the retro-futurist urban atmosphere it had, too, and there would, of course, be a significant Scottish element to the books we published. At one time we used a tagline on our adverts to link the urban connotations to a visceral or vital symbolism, 'Vennel Press: A Gutter, An Alley, An Artery'. I liked the idea of us being a 'Gutter Press'.

C. L. Dallat volunteered to use a computer from his construction industry software company to typeset *Second Cities*, after which it was printed by Blackmatch Litho, a small printing concern on Little Russell Street a few doors down from the offices of *The London Review of Books*. This connection of art to text was important to Vennel: all our larger books and several of the smaller ones, had a special connection between the poet and artist. Elizabeth James's book had drawings by her friend Irene Gunston; Peter Robinson, an artist who worked at the British Library, collaborated with Leona and me on our respective books, absorbing them and talking over our ideas before providing the artwork. Peter McCarey's friendship with the artist Clara Brasca, based in northern Italy, proved especially rewarding, first in Brasca's remarkable re-interpretation of Filonov's The Magi for the cover of *The Devil in the Driving Mirror* and then in her hologram-like cover work for *In the Metaforest*. Chris Hedley-Dent, known more as an artist than a poet, meant that his *Mirror Talk* had particularly eerie illustrations of circus clowns. Occasionally, as with C. L. Dallat's typesetting assistance on the first book (after which Leona set the books), poets we knew would turn their hands to non-poetry activity, as when W. N. Herbert illustrated David Kinloch's *Dustie-fute*.

We were learners but that could be turned to our advantage: with Leona's *The Tilted Mirror*, for example, we made a positive out of forgetting to include no less than the title poem! A special enveloped illustrated insert of it was produced, making I think a well-matched physical analogy to the layers of intimacy in the book. Similarly, when Vennel published the Festschrift for *A Gathering for Gael Turnbull* I was a little surprised to find that the Paris-based artist Jean-Pierre Leray had sent the actual lino blocks rather than camera-ready copy for the cover. Because it was only days away from Gael's seventieth birthday celebration, I had to manically experiment with hastily bought inks and roller but the collection was delivered just in time to be there at Gael's breakfast table on the day in question. I hope the rough and ready look conveys not so much slapdashery but the result of hastily but sincerely assembled celebration.

Pragmatics and Practicalities

Our improvisation skills were one thing but it took us much longer to get to grips with the bookselling and promotion side of the publishing business. It was, after all, not our day job. In fact we were both knuckling down to full-time jobs within a profession which, as new recruits from library school, was familiar to us only in theory. As we soon found out, the British Library was strongly target-led: the days when a library post was seen as the perfect sinecure for a poet were firmly over, if they ever really did exist.

Nevertheless, Donny O'Rourke's book, launched in Glasgow's Athenaeum with Michael Hulse's *Eating Strawberries in the Necropolis* (Collins Harvill), sold quickly. This was largely through personal sales at his outstanding and numerous readings. We developed a list for encouraging pre-publication subscription, in part based on the lists kept by the magazines I co-edited, and we may have been helped by what appeared to be a greater interest in poetry in Scotland.

We were able to secure orders for the next books in some bookshops, we rented tables at book fairs, organised some (but not enough) readings, made sure that our books were sent to commercial and little magazines alike, and entered for prizes. Bernard Stone at Turret Bookshop in London bought multiples of all our books and was our most consistent supporter in that respect; he also generously allowed us to give readings at his Lamb's Conduit Street shop and, later, at the Great Queen Street premises, too.

Frankly, Leona and I are both shy people and it was not easy for us to talk to booksellers, but we did our best. Perhaps this is the curse of poetry imprints — they are often run solely by poets who, like most people I suppose only more so, are often uncomfortable in face-to-face situations, never mind those which require the hard sell. Poetry presses need to have strong marketing talent, too: we weren't against it, it just didn't come naturally to us.

Nevertheless, we did have campaigning zeal. I wrote to the organisers of the New Generation promotion to remonstrate against the in-built bias the project had against small presses: in the end one Vennel author, W. N. Herbert, was one of the twenty poets but the high qualifying sum needed for promotion meant that it wasn't a Vennel book that was promoted. By this time Bill had moved on to Bloodaxe, in any case, but we shrugged and took it as a measure of Vennel's success in advocacy.

In any case, the Vennel wraparound covers proved fragile on the shelf and, as bookshops withdrew from carrying much poetry at all, the cover gave a shop an easy excuse not to stock Vennel books. We did not feel we could invest in full-colour and commercial paperback binding (which would have meant publishing fewer books) so we emphasised the mail order aspect of the imprint. In the end, though, we were forced to concede: our last major book, Peter McCarey's, *In the Metaforest* (2000) was published in this way.

Au Quai
An offshoot was Au Quai, an imprint within the Vennel stable, so to speak. This was set up by myself and Donny O'Rourke in 1996 to publish poems in Scots and English inspired by the Francophone lyrical modernists, Blaise Cendrars, Robert Desnos, Valery Larbaud, Philippe Soupault and Guillaume Apollinaire. A work by

the Francophile artist William Crosbie was featured on the cover. We published it in July, on Bastille Day, at a party in Glasgow where we drank fine champagne, listened to French songs, and heard recitations of French poetry (as well as our own). This was to answer a need in Scotland and further afield, as we thought, for stronger engagement with poetry from overseas, especially with modernism outside the Anglo-American usual suspects. Daniel Weissbort and Leona translated poems by the Russian Yunna Morits and these were issued as A4 sheets in the Au Quai imprint.

Au Quai was also used for the Festschrift of the internationalist poet Gael Turnbull, edited by Peter McCarey (*A Gathering for Gael Turnbull*, 1998); and *César Vallejo: Translations, Transformations, Tributes* (1998), edited by myself and Stephen Watts. The latter book we bundled as a supplement issued with the magazine *Southfields*, guaranteeing a new audience of perhaps a couple of hundred for this extraordinary Peruvian poet. Because of that cross-publication the Scottish Arts Council inadvertently sponsored the Vallejo book since they gave an annual grant to Southfields magazine; I believe this was the only state sponsorship we ever had for Vennel.

Gairfish, Verse, Southfields and Informationism
A further context informed Vennel Press and this emerged from the little magazine world in which I was involved. I have been involved in magazines since my early teens. I was one of the editors of my school magazine back in Houston, Renfrewshire, then sole editor of the course newspaper when I was a journalism student at Napier College, Edinburgh. Soon after starting at the British Library in 1988, I became the compiler of a trade union current awareness newssheet. I renewed my creative editorial interest in 1989 when I contacted the Oxford-based Scot W. N.

Herbert and we decided to relaunch his old student magazine, *Gairfish*.

The new *Gairfish* was a Scottish-focused magazine, publishing contemporary Scottish writing and contextualising it within the history of Scottish modernism. A few years after *Gairfish* was up and running I was approached by Robert Crawford and David Kinloch, founding editors of the magazine *Verse*, and asked to join their magazine as a co-editor, while remaining with *Gairfish*. *Verse* had strong Scottish elements but it was more involved in pan-British poetry: many of the New Generation poets were published early on in it, for instance. *Verse* was interested in all kinds of modern poetry and was remarkably internationalist: it would publish a L=A=N=G=U=A=G=E special issue one quarter, a New Formalist issue another; and European poetry in translation also featured strongly.

I worked as co-editor there for several years but I had come in towards the end of its life, in Britain at least (it was revived and became a US-based journal). Following the closure of *Verse*'s British side and my decision to leave *Gairfish*, I set up the magazine *Southfields* with the poet Raymond Friel. Friel had already published one of my first collections *Tube Shelter Perspective* (1993) in the Southfields Press imprint and, two people from Renfrewshire living in London, we were already firm friends. *Southfields* was to some degree a synthesis of *Verse* and *Gairfish* but added an interest in contemporary visual arts and higher production values. There was less of an academic tone and a steadying perspective which took neither the mainstream nor the avant-garde at their word, but published both.

The common element in *Gairfish* and *Verse*, and later in *Southfields*, was a group of poets mostly brought up within greater Glasgow and who had gone to university in the city. In 1991 in an article in Michael Gardiner's magazine *Interference*, I called them The Informationists. They were Robert Crawford, W. N. Herbert, David Kinloch, Peter McCarey, Alan Riach, and myself. I came to know their work and ideas, and they mine, mainly through reading the work in these magazines and through editorial and personal correspondence with them. At this time, W. N. Herbert and I would meet regularly to discuss and plan issues of *Gairfish* and ideas about the connections between these authors quickly began to emerge. It was a gang of boys, of course — 'brag, sweet tenor bull' might have been a motto — but there was a seriousness of intent among the laddish get-togethers (virtual get-togethers — I don't think we ever all met at once).

All, I argued, were involved in Informationism, a self-conscious engagement with and problematisation of the production, selection, presentation and transmission of information, particularly in authority-asserting media. Government and commercial communication in the print, broadcast and fast-emerging digital media were of especial interest, but so were popular (folk and 'common sense') discourses. Importantly, academic and theoretical modes and register were not beyond analysis or play and poetic form itself had to be used — transformed — to effect Informationist scrutiny. Occupying a mercurial space between avant-garde forms and mainstream ones, the Informationists were shape shifters who seemed to occupy several modes of communication at the same time, their comic and serious registers concurrent with each other, ambivalence and engagement flickering and coterminous.

Robert Crawford and Alan Riach were already published by established imprints but the others were not. If *Gairfish*, *Verse*, and, later, *Southfields* were the main journals of Informationism, Vennel Press ensured that individual collections of their work also appeared: Vennel was as near to an official imprint for

Informationism as possible (though 'official' was not a term any Informationist would accept). With the confidence that Donny O'Rourke's *Second Cities* had given Leona and myself, we started to publish the Informationists who had yet to secure a steady contract. By the mid-90s, books by W. N. Herbert, David Kinloch, Peter McCarey and myself had appeared in the Vennel imprint. These collections more than backed-up the observation made in O'Rourke's *Dream State* anthology (where all the Informationists were represented), that the Informationists had rapidly become a significant force in Scottish poetry: a force in terms of the infrastructure (intervening in the editorial and publishing networks) and in the modernity of their poetry. In the same year that Bill Herbert and I solicited poems and manifestos for the Informationist 'primer' *Contraflow on the Superhighway* (Gairfish/ Southfields, 1994): with this and the individual collections, the Informationists now had a body of work for all to see.

The reaction was almost immediate, and contradictory. In Scotland, there was traditionalist disquiet. The poet George Gunn, reviewing *Dream State* in the magazine *Spectrum*, railed at what he regarded as the academic obscurantism of the Informationists and at their lack of a straightforward political stance. 'The main grouping in *Dream State* call themselves the "Scottish Informationists". But their poetry does not inform, it obscures. Because information is power. With power you can control. & with control you can edit. & with editing goes publishing. With publishing goes status & so it goes on. Missing from all this is real lyric talent & that wild ability to create.'

Paying an unwitting compliment to Vennel Press and the magazines with which it was associated, Gunn expressed horror that the Informationists had set up their own alternative publishing network. He expressed this as a passive occurrence, suggesting, quite wrongly I think, that publishing had somehow landed in their laps: 'Let us call a spade a spade: the means of production of contemporary Scottish poetry has fallen into the hands of a few ambitious academics whose terms of reference will kill off poetry in Scotland, if we let them. They are just another kind of English Department imperialism. A lot of nothing is said in these 231 pages [of *Dream State*]. So much for the Informationists.' I believe the negativity towards both an entrepreneurial spirit of innovation and small anarcho-syndacalist groups like the Informationists, was and is a major Scottish problem (and, to a lesser degree, an English one), and it is not confined to the arts. The causes, if I could fully understand them myself, would be too complex to go into here, but part of the hostility Vennel came up against was simply because it was a new press with new names and new kinds of poetry.

In England, the avant-garde poet and critic Andrew Duncan, editor of *Angel Exhaust* and later author of *The Failure of Conservatism in Modern British Poetry*, took on the face of it another view, but in fact with significant areas of overlap. In the short essay on the Informationists, 'Is this the sound of today' he declared: 'This school is on the map, and I may add that they are the only modern British school sophisticated and self-conscious enough to set down their intentions in manifesti.' Duncan, regarding the group as important enough for him to offer constructive advice ('It is time to get past the outright actions of praise'), then proceeded to identify areas for future development that the group should think about. Like Gunn, Duncan suggested that the Informationists were not political enough; unlike Gunn (who was perhaps appealing to a more romantic concept of political solidarity in the same way that Duncan was appealing to a romantic concept of the Marxist intellectual), this was because they had not developed their poetry fully enough within the direction of political theory. They had as yet failed to 'go on to dissect the logic of capitalism. Moreover, the Scottish audience wants exactly this.'

Singling out Robert Crawford's work in particular, another problem was that the Informationists were too conventional in their treatment of love and family: 'it's difficult to write radical poetry if you are going to freeze the analytical process before it reaches personal relations'. A third problem, rather in contradiction to this, was perhaps one that Gunn was also hinting at, a criticism that has also been levelled at John Ashbery and, say, Bruce Andrews. This is the deadening effect that prodigious, detailed flattening of the hierarchies all information is contained within can have on real human connection: 'There is a kind of hollow defamilarisation, a pointless abundance which severs representations from real social relations and lacks critical charge.' Again, in unknowing agreement with George Gunn, Duncan suggested that the Informationists needed to be more Scottish, so that (apparently a priority) they can be better distinguished from similar English poets and, more importantly, because 'Disorientation threatens to be the radical's relativisation and practical abandonment of his own politics.' Finally, Duncan is as suspicious of the Informationists' careerism as Gunn: are they 'going to continue the materialist analysis of language and prestige [...] or are they going to freeze it and become cultural managers'.

The challenge to the poets, that they were selectively radical and instead harboured ambitions to be gate-keepers and kingmakers in education and the arts, was on the face of it a well-founded one. Robert Crawford, W. N. Herbert, David Kinloch, and Alan Riach all were or became academics within English Studies departments (Scottish Literature in the case of Alan Riach). They continue to take on editorial roles of one kind or another within that subset of the cultural infrastructure. However, 'cultural manager' or 'academic' sounds more negative than 'lecturer', 'professor', 'teacher', 'champion', 'mentor', or even 'intellectual', words and functions which are surely not without honour, as Duncan, who went on to work for Ofsted, may have come to realise. At a stretch, even I, a librarian at the British Library, could be seen as a kind of arts administrator but, although I am sure there have been counter-examples, librarianship is hardly a sinister profession. George Gunn's suggestion, in his catch-all accusation, that an employee of an international organisation devoted to raising public health standards across the world (Peter McCarey at the World Health Organization) is an English Literature imperialist is surely going too far.

In any case these criticisms seem to miss the insider/outsider ambiguities played with in the Informationists' texts themselves and the flickering between all the Boolean imperative categories, so that Informationism can be about 'and', 'or' and 'not' simultaneously, while it is also *littérature engagé* at critical points (I think of McCarey's analyses of armed globalisation and Kinloch's gay radicalism). Perhaps it is the problematising techniques of the Informationists' poetry that is the target here, but that suggests that they have been successful in unsettling their audience and in beginning to move the poetry agenda on from simple identity-politics reassurances. In fact, looking at the remarkable work of avant-garde Scots who were also emerging at this time, such as Drew Milne and Peter Manson, it could be argued that, if anything, the Informationists' practice of de-stabilising mainstream discourses did not go far enough (even if one strand in Informationism sought to identify and destabilise hackneyed avant-garde techniques, too).

Nevertheless, I believe that the significant political and aesthetic questions raised by Gunn and Duncan and others could be answered to differing degrees in the work of these poets at the time these criticisms were raised. Since the mid-90s, however, with the Informationist moment firmly in the past, the group's individuals now have a substantial body of work. The kind of engagement and sophistication that both Gunn and Duncan in their different ways were calling for has been developed more fully, building on the foundation that, with its associated presses and magazines, Vennel Press set down.

Legacy

Vennel was more than Informationism however. Its championing of modern contemporary poetry produced within Scotland and London has been affirmed by the artistic success of its individual authors in and outside Informationism.

If need be, Vennel's success can be measured by poetry's public benchmarks. Most though not all of its authors have achieved publication in more capitalised presses as well as recognition within the creative writing academy to the level of professorship. They have received public art commissions, participated in media-friendly poetry campaigns, and won various awards. One or two have become more associated with the avant-garde support network of poetics conferences, reading series and new little presses. Though these are all fine so far as they go, the poetry honours system is an institution it is best not to take too seriously (which is to say, it should be taken very seriously for its power of influence, not always for its quality of judgement).

Perhaps most importantly, with only a very small number of other left-of-field presses at that time (long gone were the days of the British Poetry Revival when small presses were numerous), Vennel Press kept the door open in the UK to a range of emerging aesthetic responses within an otherwise highly conservative backward-looking poetry network.

Arc Editions

Arc Editions is a partnership between three individuals whose works share a focus on the mercurial, wayward nature of language. Victoria Bean, Karen Bleitz and Sam Winston first came together as artists working at Ronald King's Circle Press during its Notting Hill days. As well as working with King on Circle projects they made their own book objects under the Circle Press imprint. Accordingly, these artists have an openness to both traditional and modern techniques in the book arts and are steeped in the history of the British and American artist's book. This chapter takes stock of their work to date.

At the heart of the artist's book is a three-way relationship between the language of its text (if it has one), the book's visual manifestation and its physical elements. The Arc artists are attentive to all three but perhaps what links them most is their worrying away at, and sometimes glorying in, language's tricksiness. By this I mean both its deceptiveness — language says one thing but may mean another —and, a slightly different quality, its shifting, moving, elusive, restlessness. Language, after all, is fuzzier and richer than it first appears to be and, despite grand projects to codify it, is always on the move — provisional, improvisational, shifting. Almost as much as light and heat, language is a kind of energy.

Bean and Bleitz in particular have an edgy sensitivity to broadly political themes which they find implicit in everyday phrases or, through inspired recasting, redirect polemically. Perhaps unusually in the book arts, they have been willing to address topical, public and political issues (don't look to Arc for personal diaries, I-went-here's and I-saw-that's; nor for pure abstraction).

In Bean's *When Bush Meets Blair*, the artist makes play with the surnames of 'Bush' and 'Blair': under Bean's direction they cross-fertilise to produce 'Blush' and, page-by-page, more serious incriminations. A poet and a copywriter for an agency which specialises in advertising for environmental and ethical issues, Bean is especially concerned with media discourse and how easily fragile, complex truths are warped out of recognition by the pre-existing expectations of newspaper and broadcast stories. *When Bush Meets Blair* reminds me of the Oulipo experiments in French literature where a rules-based procedure (here, the decision to use the leaders' names for permutations) is tied to chance (the accident of their names) and then guided by the creative artist (Bean's choice of combinations). A similar cross-matching of language rules onto emotional states is encountered in *Faction*, a book which uses concrete poetry's transformational rules to start with 'Fact' and, after incremental shifts as each page turned, ends, by close, with 'Fiction'.

Perhaps the most delicate of Bean's books to date is *Ten Poems for Pandora*. The book is cut and folded in such a way as to produce an interlocking suite of pages with a physical fissure in the centre of each page. The poems are printed close to the edge of the 'fault line', recent escapees, perhaps, beginning their first words of free speech: 'the evils rush: they barge without apology' one poem begins. The largish square pages are slightly floppy and with the need to be careful in disconnecting the top layer from the one underneath it, the reader is perhaps anxious about holding the book and moving from one page to another. I see this nervousness as about opening the series of almost locked-down pages appropriate to the Pandora myth in the face of now jubilant and exhilarated (and sometimes anxious) lives and ideas that move out from each box once it has been opened: 'maps a night of illicit handbrake turns / & accelerated joy'. It is a dizzy, precarious, risky world now — for all concerned.

Karen Bleitz's books can also have a distinctly feminist turn. This is most apparent in *The Appeal of Pornography*, a book which follows pornography's photographic dehumanisations to a further stage, mixing meat market and fairground kiosk in mocking explicit fashion. Bleitz's rapid response to the birth of the first cloned mammal, the box-like book *Dolly: Edition Unlimited*, is one of her most remarkable works. Named after the sheep 'developed' in a laboratory in Scotland, *Dolly: Edition Unlimited* samples the article published in *Nature* which first announced the breakthrough as well as early newspaper responses, juxtaposing them before the reader lights on the core of the book: a cut-out image of Dolly which clones herself upon opening as it slides out of a hole in the case-like right-hand page. The sheep is arguably beleaguered, besieged, encased and concealed by the stories of her birth. Reduced with touching simplicity to a blank piece of multiply folded stiff paper, it doesn't matter to her, the reader imagines, whether what she is incarcerated by its scientific description or journalistic reportage; Bleitz's contrast of text saturation with the spotless, wordless sheep itself is inspired. The multiple cut-out, too, is not only a clever physical analogy for the cloning process worthy of Ian Hamilton Finlay's moving part books, but, rendered as an object traditionally reserved for play, it is a poignant reminder of a lost childhood (Dolly, as clone of an adult, was already born several years old so never had a normal 'lambhood').

In a sense I've collaborated twice with Bleitz — *gifthorse*, the blind embossed slow-mo animated book that Ron King and I made in 1999 had its letterpress text set by Bleitz — but the work on which we more creatively meshed is *The Mechanical Word* series of five books. This begins with the notion of a grammar manual's simple sentences whose elements (subject, object and so on) are given particular symbols to help the learner understand the instructed concept. Bleitz writes each panel of instruction using sentences that would be avoided in class: they have the strong undercurrents of sexual politics. The kinetic elements of the book — cogs and cams and other interacting parts set against a field of bright colour — are on the one hand abstract shapes of pure tone, and on the other symbols of the fraught power relationships more than hinted at in the book. Finally a text of mine concludes four of the five pieces, giving voice to the people schematised by the animation. Again, the presentation is not straightforward (this is no poem here, picture there, livre d'artiste) — each poem is laid across the opening in relation to the moving parts of the book and was written to pulse and flicker across the whole screen of the page. For me, Dom Sylvester Houédard, book artist and concrete poet, is a presence behind this element of *The Mechanical Word*. Perhaps it is also related to *Roller*, the book by Roy Fisher and Ian Tyson, in which phrases seem to be emitted as much as written; like *gifthorse* this was typeset by Bleitz and both *Roller* and *The Mechanical Word* series deliberately have an industrial structure and finish to them.

Sam Winston's work is not political in the way that Victoria Bean's and Karen Bleitz's is (though, as I hope I've suggested, they are subtle, unprogrammatic artists who are in danger of giving the word politics a good name). He is, however, as fascinated by words in process. His most immediately striking work, a full folded dictionary (2004), took a set of the twenty-one volume *Oxford English Dictionary*, stood each volume on its side and, through some 80,000 folds (no glue! many assistants!) produced a remarkable set of polyhedra. They have considerable sculptural appeal — they're like huge crystals of knowledge, and their curious white stripes, a consequence of the dictionary's column spacing, seem like rock striations shot through a word-peppered paper mineral. Textural sensitivity to 'hard' and 'soft' is played through the inside-outing of stiff binding and more pliable page. When pages are folded on to each other the comprehension of individual word-by-word detail is almost impossible: in close-up, largely fragments of words can be seen; at normal standing distance, it is a work of soft grey tones. Few would leave the work without feeling awe in the face of its indicated complexity: with breath-taking simplicity, the scale of the English language is laid anew before its observer.

I think this is one of the key tensions within Winston's work, and is one its key attractions: the tension between the astonishing detail of work that proceeds from his interest in language's organisation and the sculptural and visual qualities of the overall product. He is actually a painstaking typographer — in a *dictionary story* (2001), for instance, hundreds if not thousands of individually made text cells, typeset in QuarkXPress, are composed to bestow individual letters with a kind of mobility across the page, while the narrative imagines words from the dictionary becoming independent 'characters'. The latter is the licence for various antics and puns: Lawless and Lawful, for example, are 'neighbours' in the sense of being close together in the dictionary but also because, in Winston's world, they are alive and so share the same 'neighbourhood' (Lawful, inevitably is 'such a boring neighbour'). However, the relative simplicity of the narrative, and the work required to read it down the page, is in stark contrast to the complex beauty of the shapes that other dictionary words are making collectively as they stretch and fall and braid across the tall white column of the page, not illustrating but enacting the story and together producing beautiful organic-like patterns of lines.

As with Winston's *O.E.D.*, which is physically folded in on itself words-wise but folded out book structure-wise, a dictionary story works in at least two ways at once and in each of Winston's works the reader sees this striving between the visual or sculptural and the linguistic. The large posters of *a made up / true story* (2005), in which the rules of different genre (timetables, newspaper stories, fairy stories) are deliberately confused with each other, can feasibly be read as texts — if the reader can stand very close to the wall for a considerable amount of time — but are most striking for the organic shapes Winston has made by mapping the different registers of language onto each other. They are as much about comprehending the conceit of each piece, perhaps reading selected elements as one might 'read' elements of a painting in detail, but then standing back and looking —and marvelling — at the overall composition.

Poets, Artists, Lyricists

Generosity

So while you've this passion for leek vinaigrette,
you know what it means - no French kissing yet.
                          Martial, Book XIII (*Xenia*) xviii [84]

'Xenia' derives from an ancient Greek word that some dictionaries translate as 'strange' and some as 'hospitality'. The Romans borrowed the term: it refers to little poems attached to objects that guests were given to take away with them, probably after a dinner party. It's a tradition similar to the practice today of party bags, those little bags containing sweets and perhaps an inexpensive toy given to children as they leave at the close of a celebration. The singular is xenion, the xenion above referring to a gift of leeks.

The same source is most encountered in English, perhaps typically, within a negative compound, 'xenophobia'. Although xenophobia is usually described as the fear and hatred of foreigners and the foreign, its etymology suggests something more complex, something meaner, something rather more close to home than that. Its modern-day usage is surely conditioned by an aversion to hospitality as much as the foreign, an aversion to active goodwill, to trust, an inversion to the risk that any act of generosity must always entail.

---

[84] From *Martial Mottoes*, translated by Hamish Whyte, Galdragon Press, 1998.

I think immediately of *The Daily Mail* when I think of English xenophobia. Wrongly, because I know that *Daily Mail* readers — people like anyone else, if I may risk condescension in so saying — should not have their identities circumscribed by an easy interpretation of any one behavioural trait, at least not the profoundly ambiguous act of reading one publication.

And, after all, no British newspaper is immune to a tone at odds with civil discourse. *The Independent* and *The Guardian,* which are sometimes, however rashly, taken to represent ground on the middle or even the left of the political spectrum (producing stories that are coterminous with a rational presentation of information) aren't above the constraints of their form. They have more information, and they have more sophisticated ways of being responsive to their own mistakes, but many readers will find these papers, too, read at times discordantly: in their case, like the mouthpiece of any loyal subject born and bred in the ancient villages of Tolduceaux or Tooclever-by-Half.

The larger audiences for the broadcast media make theirs, if anything, a more serious case. The BBC may claim to be unbiased, but anyone who has watched their '24-hour news' TV channel and seen the same half-dozen pat stories recycled like bad air across the hour and throughout the day, will know that they are far from being comprehensive, especially at the point when they claim most to be. The gaps themselves point to a structural prejudice. The world is full of content, but BBC 'Worldwide' appears to exist in a near-vacuum. Why is this? And why raise it in an essay about poetry, about generosity?

It's a question of informational form, of having to add half-story to half-story, while leaving so many full stories completely out. Because it's actually very difficult to write news within the rules of what news must be — a particular kind of brevity is only one constraint, a particular kind of prosody, 'topicality', 'an angle' and 'public interest' are others —without failing the spirit of truth, if not its letter. Often, its letter, too.

Many readers of poetry, though not exclusively readers of poetry (let's not get carried away with ourselves, here), will recognise this immediately. Poetry, by and large, won't actually tell a reader much that is factually new. Pound was saying this when he seemed not to be saying it in his phrase 'Poetry is news that stays news'. A formal knowledge of such a rich and technically nuanced text-type as poetry, will, all the same, develop a sensitivity to the technical limitations of any text, how words serve the characteristics of each particular genre, and what a slave truth is to the conventions of each and every mode of communication.

This doesn't mean that 'everything is relative' or that 'there's no such thing as truth', phrases which are typical of taking the worst-case scenario as if it were the norm. That's a way of thinking, by the way, that will eventually paralyse any culture, an over-insurance that leads to bankruptcy, moral or otherwise. It does mean, though, that one or two steps have to be taken to get round the particular kind of pre-processing of information the print and broadcast media represent.

Of course, readers may always have to turn to newspapers and the online and broadcast services for some recent information, but if they are alive to the formal qualities of the news story (which means being alive to the formal deficiencies, too), they will know they will have to look in other places as well. This is exactly the same as not accepting the four or five well-known poetry imprints as *necessarily* hallmarks of quality: no reader of poetry could seriously believe that these are guarantors of the best, even though the reader knows he or she may have to work harder to find other work.

In the world of news, to correct, re-orientate, and downgrade such mainstream sources, readers will need to read single-issue sites, say, and tap in to information networks not so directly mediated by what is taken to be commercial and state imperative; at times they'll have to consult genuine (as opposed to cuttings) libraries whose careful memories often contradict the instant histories used by the media; and, perhaps as important as anything else, they'll have to enjoy the conversation of friends good enough to refine the arguments of each other and contradict each other's prejudices.

Friends aren't always easy to find, but more formalised circles, be it book groups, poetry workshops, or support or action groups, all of which in themselves may have nothing to do with ideas of a more generalised engagement with the mediators of power, may all provide the grounds for developing a means of social scrutiny that can be transferred and bring life back to the larger power structures and institutions, if they are found worth saving.

Animated discussion with those you love is one of the great pleasures and 'xenia' are surely in that spirit. Open conversation may not always have been possible at the parties where xenia were presented, but I like to think that some meetings would have been among trusted friends only, and then relaxed conversation would have gone on for hours. To folk who prefer the noun 'crony' to the noun 'friend', it is easy to traduce talk like that as 'chattering', but, political insider trading notwithstanding, everyone, I hope, can rise above such jagged naming words. The generosity of relaxed conversation is one of humanity's great 'gifts', and I see xenia as symbolising a more intimate variation on the evening's group conviviality, a host's letting each guest know that they have thought of them individually, too.

Each poem would be epigrammatic in character and ideally say something witty about the gift and the host's relationship to the guest. It might affectionately refer to one of the guest's traits. Martial's *Apophoreta*, strictly speaking a more impersonal form of label, since the term refers to inscriptions for gifts that might well be drawn by lots at the party, seem occasionally to have this sense of intimacy, too:

> So take this torch to light your way at night
> It's shockproof, like my heart, and weathertight.
> Martial, Book XIV (*Apophoreta*), lxi.[85]

Here, perhaps the guest had talked on a previous occasion about the long unlit pathway to his or her villa; perhaps they had said they'd been having nightmares in their new house, or mentioned how dark the rooms were, even in summer. The torch, modernised by Whyte to suggest actual and emotional electricity, has therefore become an attentive kindness and a joke between them, and there is clearly some romantic 'charge' between giver and receiver, too. In other words there is some contextual secrecy in this poem, the sort inherent in any intimacy, romantic or otherwise. That privacy is not a danger to the poem once it has been accepted as an element of it, and, as with any poem, especially those that are far more opaque than this one, readers should not feel excluded by something they think they don't immediately understand. The reader has to be generous to the poem so that it can be generous to the reader.

By having these apparently private poems published, Martial allowed them a public role. He gifted them beyond the

---

[85] *Op.cit..*

individualism normally implied by the idea of the gift: he encouraged their enjoyment and interpretation beyond the specifics of their occasion. Xenia and apophoreta were witty, even edgy at times, and Martial is seldom remembered without a mention of his sharp tongue. I hope I don't overstate the case for his work's gregariousness, although accusatory wit is also an acceptance of a social world where satire has force. If the giver acts indiscriminately, showering gifts on one person, say, or giving to all, generosity must be devalued. As long as mean-spiritedness is not involved, generosity actually needs a critical intelligence, even a kind of hardness, to keep its worth.

At xenia parties, maybe gift and poem were used ostentatiously: you can imagine the tagged presents stacked in a specially prepared corner in the room the host had chosen for the party. They could even be presented one-by-one to those in attendance as part of the proceedings, with a reading of each poem; rustle, tear (if wrapped or boxed), gasp or laugh, thank-you, and applause. Martial structures his book of *Xenia* to correspond to the courses of the Roman dinner, so a variation on the reading of Christmas cracker mottoes comes to mind, with or without the groans at awful jokes. Performance, banter and fun: all the senses and the near-perfection of the best parties. (Yet some hosts, I'm sure, would have preferred to be more discreet, maybe keeping the treats out of sight until the end of the evening when they'd be handed to each guest as good-byes and a special word or two said.)
When Whyte offers two of his translations as a gift in itself, in a Festschrift to the poet Gael Turnbull on the occasion of his seventieth birthday, this complex private/public package of the epigram tradition is picked up and passed on, pass-the-parcel style, as much to new readers of Turnbull as to the esteemed poet himself. The first, in particular, is a kind of non-gift gift. It names something of which Gael Turnbull had better *not* be the recipient,

dumb-bells. Metonymic 'vineyards' (bearing poetic fruit) are appropriately to the fore:

> **Dumb-bells**
> Leave the dumb dumb-bells to the chaps at the gym –
> trenching vineyards will keep you in better trim.
> (Martial, Book XIV (*Apophoreta*), xlix.[86]

Martial has been put to much denser use, too. Arkadii Dragomoschenko's long poem, called 'Xenia', in the translation by Lyn Hejinian and Elena Balashova, remembers a probably childhood present as a means of making a momentary ascent through an unbreathable medium that might be memory itself — 'You rip off the gift's waxed string and you follow the ascent / of the oxygen bubbles'. I think of Orson Welles's sledge Rosebud here, a present that joins childhood to the dying hero's last moments, and I think of the way Eugenio Montale modernises the epigram tradition, too, in the 'Xenia' sequences in his late work *Satura*. Here there is less comfort: the 'gifts' are actually the last points of contact between the dead and the living. Material ephemera, the individual objects of all our clutter offer surprisingly plangent effects: a little thing like the label on a bottle of wine or a now much diminished phone bill, turns unexpectedly into the elegiac mode, a remembrance of Montale's late wife. What the gift, what generosity is, shifts and almost evades us: presents always end up conventionally useless, they become, ideally, tags to the real gifts, the memories to which they, and we, have become so attached.

Xenia have a distant relative in Anglo-Saxon riddles, where, a millennium before the great language change in English language

---

[86] Taken from *A Gathering for Gael Turnbull*, ed. Peter McCarey, Au Quai, 1998).

poetry, which is to say a millennium before Edward Thomas and William Carlos Williams, the focus was again on the beauty and mystery of humble and familiar objects. Riddles, however, defer pleasure: they tease and puzzle, and they make very strange the familiar. The familiar can be made so strange in fact that some of the riddles in the main repository of Anglo-Saxon riddles, the *Exeter Book*, have today no secure solution.

For instance there's Riddle 90, which begins, 'A strange thing it seemed to me / a wolf captured by a lamb'. 'The lamb lay down by a rock, / and pull[ed] out the wolf's bowels' it goes on (they had a rather closer relationship to animals these Anglo-Saxons than most in the West have now), before ending 'I saw a great marvel, / two wolves standing tormenting a third; / they had four feet, they saw with seven eyes.'[87]

Any answers?
A table and some points of light? Candles, jewels? The lamb might suggest Christian resonances since, though most are secular, one or two of the riddles are biblical. I'm afraid I can offer nothing better than that, but the idea of such a long unsolved riddle makes me smile. I guess it was solved at a point closer to the time it was written, only to be forgotten later on.

Sometimes a poem that works in a way with which the reader is not immediately familiar is accused of being like a crossword puzzle. I think it was Norman MacCaig who recalled that one of the readers of his early New Apocalypse verse wrote to him in perplexity, expressing the hope that the poet would one day

---

[87] John Porter, translator, *Anglo-Saxon Riddles*, Anglo-Saxon Books, 1995.

publish the answers. Yet even with the enigma of Riddle 90, where there really is a particular subject that has been deliberately disguised, the poem does not need that meaning to show a good deal of its beauty. It's almost shocking, but it's beauty nevertheless, and the poem has a skilled musicality: it is alliterated in the original in the convention that after centuries only Chaucer's example made minor. These are the 'gift' elements of a poem that was likely intended more as a challenge, and as a piece of public virtuosity, but whose rhythmic, structural, visual and nuanced sound qualities cannot help but foreground its worked-for and so pleasurable elements, the innate generosity of this genre of concealment.

For trying to understand 'difficult poems', some of which really aren't about decoding one text into a clearer shorter one, into some 'real message' or 'solution' (imagine listening to songs that way! — What would be the point!), such a riddle offers an oblique lesson. The 'poemy' parts of a poem, what a poem is doing when it's doing the poem, can be the most of what opaque poems are. Not, as sometimes they're taken to be, 'a private world'. Not, in fact, 'too personal' to be understood, not 'too academic'. Rather, poems experienced by readers or listeners, almost, though not quite, as they might experience a piece of music or a painting they can't wholly accommodate within the sense-making world of their previous experience. People find one or two points that they can fix on, perhaps they like the rhythm or the hook in a song without really knowing what it's all about, the balance of colour in a painting, and then they live with it, hear it again, take another look, never thinking for a moment that they will understand it all or, just as importantly, that there is necessarily a single overarching thing to be understood. They are already relaxed enough to begin to enjoy themselves (taking 'enjoyment' to include a range of emotions, contemplation, much smiling, pretending to be appalled etc).

Some of my most important reading experiences have been through being encouraged to relax with a poet's work in this way. Friends' recommendations that I read, say, Denise Riley, or, Kelvin Corcoran, or, more recently, Karlien van den Beukel, have modified my whole reading and writing practice, have simply allowed me to be in the company of kinds of text-pleasure and articulacy that, good literary criticism notwithstanding, I might well not have met otherwise.

I don't deny that there may be some 'health-giving' corporal punishment in the minds of some 'difficult poets', but instead of treating their poems as an ordeal that the poet hopes will be good for its reader in the long run, it's maybe better, whatever it is felt the poet's intentions are, to see such work as a gift to the reader, as an act of generosity, as something which can be domesticated in whatever way the reader and the text can agree on, and lived with in that way, if they so wish. I'm not expressing an attitude of 'anything goes', rather I'm suggesting an evidence-based faith ('evidence-based faith' is, after all, one definition of science) in the ability of the 'poemy' cues in a poem to offer up pleasure and other shades of feeling, as well as the other points of interest that more straightforward, if less 'poemy', poems offer.

Generosity is always a difficult thing — once you begin to think about it. Biological case studies show powerful gift-giving urges in many species, often but not exclusively associated with sexual impulses. For the recipient, gifts can be very mysterious things indeed. I think of the track 'A hymn for the postal service' on Hefner's album *Breaking God's heart*. Hefner are in the post-punk tradition of Buzzcocks, whose 'Ever fallen in love with someone you shouldn't have fallen in love?' still resonates, to me, as one of the simplest and best songs of this last quarter century.

In 'A hymn' there is that familiar sense of being in the throes of enslaving emotions but the pace is slower, the narrative more complicated. The singer's object of desire, Lydia Pond, has moved to Paris to get away from British politics. There she sends back a passport photo of herself in pigtails and, to the singer's frustration and puzzlement, her letters 'used the f-word / when she never ever spoke it'. Here the gift — a letter between friends, not to mention lovers, is always a gift — becomes a sexual and social mystery. Is Lydia Pond teasing the singer? Does her swearing on paper suggest a new intimacy — either a lover's intimacy where next to nothing is barred, or, to the singer, merely a friend's intimacy (since some kinds of lovers' relationships may force each to be on their swearless best behaviour). Do the swear words suggest the promise of desire's ultimate closeness or friendship's ultimate distance? She promises him 'they'll be creasing sheets' but a strong tone within the song is one of unluckiness, of the singer's failure and bewilderment. In the end the singer describes becoming faithful, not to Lydia, but to her letters: gift has become not intermediary but object of desire.

What is so ambiguous and tension-making about gifts actually contributes to their definition. The doubts and hints and selectivity, the half-obligations, the danger of giving too little, 'being cheap', of giving too much: the impurities of the gift transaction, its snaggish social qualities, are critical to the sense of what gift is.

A gift given to a hoped-for lover, for instance, takes the risk that the loved one may not at all like this *particular* thing. Except for ironic purposes, it mustn't be an anodyne, generic gift that anyone would think 'nice' or 'dutiful'. It must be specific to the person and so well-thought-out (but preferably not agonised over, preferably *as if* spontaneous), and it must, to some degree, confirm the receiver's own self-image without duplicating an item the receiver already has. How far from that self-image the gift may be is a fine judgement, and a judgement made in different ways for different lovers, since a gift ideally should represent something of what the giver takes to be important to him or herself: there is development and movement and progress in that, and again it is in this field of risky generosity where poems, those special gifts, best belong.

Edwin Morgan: Is this a Poem?

Early in 2006 I received a brief letter from Edwin Morgan. It consisted almost entirely of a twenty-line poem, 'The Ropemaker's Bride'. This was initialled with the three short horizontal lines of the poet's proud seal, Ξ, dated – 12-1-2006 – and appended with the shortest of notes:

> Dear R:
> Is this a poem?
> Do not lose it – an only copy!
> Best
> Eddie

This was confusing. It was unlike any other letter I had received in an unbroken correspondence of nearly twenty years. Eddie had been, for want of a better word, my mentor all that time. Here is my transcription of the poem:

The Ropemaker's Bride

My friends, I was going to slip the ring on —
Seventeen, and there must be no slip
(Just as at night there must be no sleep!)
Burghers, all men at thirty are not bad husbands.
I've heard of brides counting the strands
To please their lord, each his chequerwork —
& only after he had checked his lattices —
To please their lord — ivory. What use is ivory,
Well-honed banker's booty, says click, says clack
And you may be free — well, where the servant's darker
Who says you're made to be
Anything like a servant, that's what's free

> Isn't it?
> What a mort of manuscripts we are carrying
> And then we are free.
> My husband is bound to ask me to play
> Some day,
> Such strings and strands,
> More than ropes, more than hopes,
> More than best instruments in gleggest of hands.

'Is this a poem?' On the face of it, this was an absurd question coming from 'Professor Morgan', 'Scotland's Makar', holder of the 'Queen's Medal for Poetry', and so on. While no one should take such honours entirely seriously, Morgan's exceptional abilities were never in doubt. And after all Eddie, as he usually asked friends to call him, had opened up so much of poetry's possibility to so many, he could hardly be asking about the acceptability of a particular form.

In genre terms this poem is in any case a dramatic monologue, a favourite mode of his which warranted no query. Formally speaking, the poem is free but internally rhymed, with the jazz-like energy of his later work. There is nothing here that would make anyone think this was struggling to be a poem. I love its energy. It plays longer lines off against short ones; knotted erudite meanings against impassioned address; and it gently mutates its own creative repetitions. It displays those shuffling alliterations which propelled Morgan's poetry throughout his writing life, as if the exhilarating 'shuh' and spine-honey bass of 'Come Together' belonged to him as much as to his favourite band The Beatles.

'Is this a poem?' One of the things that confused me was that until relatively recently Eddie had never asked my advice and this was his most serious question to date. He shared news with me, told me what he was working on, where he was about to read, and, occasionally, he shared new poems. He quietly, as if casually, introduced me to all manner of poetry, fiction, art, history and politics. In return he hardly got the better of the bargain: I think most of my own correspondence was humdrum commentary on the English news of the day, reactions to his suggestions and enthusiasms, domestic ups and downs, and irritable 'poetry biz' squawks. We shared some things of course — a technological imagination, for example, a fascination with outer space (and a feeling that humankind should urgently step up space exploration). Although he cautioned patience over my frustrations with UK publishing he also had experienced its establishment retardants, the peculiarity of his breakthrough book, *The Second Life,* only being published when he was in his forties. Like my collection *Lucky Day* it is probably still mistaken as a 'debut' though it followed years of publication.

'Is this a poem?' Eddie was proud of his knowledge, of his quickness; of his ability to write with a catholicity of technical accomplishment. That little monogram of his, like Dürer's, was a quality stamp. I think I first came across the EM mark on the full-colour abstracts he made from warped Polaroids. I collected and published four of them as *Colour Supplement* (he gave them to me for an issue of the cultural review *Southfields* in 1994). Usually this 'brand' had three parallel vertical lines following the 3 horizontal, an abstraction of EM of course; in this present letter it was simply reduced to the personal name's initial, a friend in haste, perhaps.

The flowing serifs of his handwriting are another aspect of that quiet confidence of his — they moved across the page with an enlivening zest, gentle flourish after flourish. 'The Ropemaker's Bride' has an underline beneath its title which is clearly written with a zooming lightness of touch. The manuscript poem was completed by a writerly-painterly gesture, too — another fluid long line, as if an S has stretched itself out to take flight.

So in what sense could Eddie be asking me if 'The Ropemaker's Bride' was a poem? I think those little signs of confidence were actually residual — learned behaviour which now lacked total conviction — because he was at a very low point in his life. He really was asking for my opinion of the poem. For at least the last six months his cancer, 'the crab' as he called it, had been ratcheting up the pain as it grew and spread, and it could suddenly 'attack': 'My crab has stuck its claws into me in the last few days with fearsome intensity in the right hip and leg — so debilitating that I can settle to do nothing at the moment. I will come back, I promise, if allowed to. But please don't let me stop you from writing, as I can rely on your letters to cheer me up enormously, and that truly is needed.' (EM to RP, 20-10-2005). The drugs regime was also disorientating, and in the last few months of 2005 I received only occasional very short cards. The stabs of darkness, nightmares, that Eddie appears to have suffered intermittently from all his life and had so brilliantly kept in check, had taken on another form, a waking dread, a constant anxiety: 'Another little non-letter from your queasy drugged-up correspondent. One of these days there will be something proper — I hope. At the moment I am on tranquilisers because I had become so nervous and jingly that — that what? I was in terror of the telephone, put it that way.' (EM to RP, 14-12-2005).

However, right at the end of 2005 some of Eddie's strength returned. 'Is this a letter?' he said in an undated Christmas card, asking a question which again spoke to a range of existential doubts. It was. 'Can you read this I wonder?' Yes, though with some difficulty. Next, in January, within another Christmas card there was even a tone of good cheer, as if the message of the festive season had finally got through the pain and pharmaceuticals and could still be delivered, loud and clear, weeks later — 'One should always use up old Christmas cards, should one not?' he chirped. He had used an unsent card for a new poem, topping and tailing the printed Christmas greetings from around the world with lines of his own:

> O many a muse
> And many a muse
> And merry a muse and all
>
> Season's Greetings
> [in six languages]
>
> And wherever is heaven
> A hookah is leaven
> And Christ receive thy soule

This is a bright piece of fun on one level, on another it's a jolly dance around what is a knot of Morgan's traumas. There is the worry over inspiration (the 'muse'), especially not being able to transfer the products of a still fertile imagination to the page because of the barriers of physical frailty and failing concentration: there is frustration and sorrow in the sheer abundance of those merry muses, rather than the traditional fear of 'writer's block'. There are thoughts, clearly, of death, 'heaven' and 'soule'; and a reflection which once might have been an anti-establishment delight in hedonistic pleasure — the intoxication of the hookah — but which has now become a mark of the routine of medicated, institutionalised tranquillity, drugs to 'leaven' pain.

' — Now there's a piece of something or other,' Morgan writes after the poem, and then asks that question I'll read in a later letter, too: 'Is it poetry.' He adds 'Is it pastichoramic? Morgan, you must stop this! Give it its time. Medieval or not it will come when it has to, 'on extended wings' (like a poem I've been immersed in the last few days).'

Worries of commanding the right register were clearly there even in this spontaneous jeu d'esprit; perhaps he was also worried about repeating himself (though for very different poems, Morgan has very strong associations with Christmas). Though I am not sure if 'The Ropemaker's Bride' was the poem to which he refers — there is evidence in the letter that the mise-en-scène for the poem he had been mulling over was Turkey rather than France — but the next poem that I saw would indeed fly with its own 'extended wings'.

When Morgan sent me 'The Ropemaker's Bride' and asked me that chill question, was it a poem? I wrote back quickly, saying simply I thought that indeed it was. I also said that were some words which I couldn't read: would he annotate a copy of the poem so I could be sure? No palaeographer, I had thought the safest way of resolving various mysteries was to send a copy back to him, marked with my queries — Eddie's now tiny, frail handwriting did not benefit from his naturally calligraphic style, attractive though it was in all other circumstances.

My writing to Eddie in this way, to my great regret, led to a final break in our correspondence, as such, although I still received a card at Christmas, that sort of occasion. This was not because he was offended but because my response suggested to him that all means of communicating clearly had now become too difficult (his typewriter had long ceased to be used, and Eddie was never an e-mailer). He wrote back, replying to some of my queries, but in a very dark mood, saying he was sorry that he simply couldn't keep on writing and so effectively closed the reciprocating correspondence between us. He encouraged me to continue to write to him even so. I am not sure whether, faced with a weekly letter of Price's Choice Reflections, he later regretted that suggestion, but I certainly didn't regret it. Writing, usually in the intermedial state of a Saturday morning, became a way of life for me, half reflective diary, half blether about topical subjects (we both liked, in Tom Leonard's phrase, 'a news'). I wrote to him in that 'Letter from London' way for nearly four years, until his death in August 2010. As it happens I was at the Edinburgh Festival on the morning he died, talking about my recent novel: when a member of the audience asked me where the link between poetry and fiction in my case came from I said, 'Through Edwin Morgan: there is so much and so many ways of trying to tell it.' He really was often in my thoughts. After all this time, Saturday mornings can still catch me not knowing quite what to do with myself now that my letter-writing days to Eddie are over.

The gestation of 'The Ropemaker's Bride' can be traced back to at least our correspondence in the preceding year, when we were discussing the sixteenth century poet Louise Labé. Eddie had suggested I read her work as an accompaniment to a visit I was planning to Lyon, which had been Labé's city. He held her poems in high regard and had intended, he told me, to translate her poems for his *Fifty Renascence Love-Poems* (Whiteknights Press, 1975). Perhaps he had lighted on her too far into the project for her to be included.

There are layers of contextual detail in the poem's association with Labé. Labé is said to have married a rope manufacturer and indeed may herself have come from a well-to-do ropemaking family. Her bridegroom is reputed to have been a much older man and this potential 'mismatch' is an element in the poem which Morgan reads with a characteristic challenge of conventions: the teenage bride tells her gathering that 'all men at thirty are not bad husbands.' Lyon was a major industrial town at this time, with rope a central product — there is surely a read-across here from Lyon to Morgan's beloved industrial giant Glasgow. Lyon was also a publishing and freethinking centre, a read-across to what Glasgow *might* some day be.

Several of Labé's sonnets refer to the lute, which becomes the companion to the speaking voice of her poems, especially when unrequited or stormy love leaves her otherwise alone. There is a wit to these poems which complicates the longing in them, building a response to love which is both emotional and intellectual, as if the speaker is feeling the pangs of love at the same time as she is distancing herself from them. In this way they develop the sonnet, bringing a warmth to the Petrarchan form without losing its self-conscious rhetorical approach. Again, one thinks — very generally, of course — of Morgan's own development of the sonnet, redrawing the rules in *Glasgow Sonnets* and other sequences where a 'watcher approach' allows *overview* — a longitudinal survey approach in effect — giving the sonnet a sociological role which traditionalists are likely to have found hard to take: a leap from apparent intimacy to asserted history. There is the urban element, too, but contrast Morgan's middle- and long-distance viewpoints in his sonnet sequences (I am talking spatially, not temporally) with, say, Belli and Garioch, where the focus is closer, on actual situations and actual characters in the city). Although 'The Ropemaker's Bride' is not a sonnet; it is a salute to and identification with an innovating sonneteer.

The rope and lute motifs are, to adopt loosely the metaphor of the strings they share, 'braided' in Morgan's poem. At times the braiding in the poem presents either an interpretive difficulty or a deliberate layering of meaning (or both). Lutes not only have strings but they can have a latticed aperture, for their resonating chamber, which may be inlaid with ivory and other high-value materials for decoration. Ropes are composites of threads or strings, perhaps laid out initially in lattices as part of the manufacturing process. The erotics of ties, of pluckable strings, of sensuous curves and gently guarded chambers hardly needs exposition: this is a teasing, sexy poem. At least, it is so to begin with. Soon enough, there is concern with the dynamic between man and wife, master and servant, which shifts the initially playful tone of the bride's address (no sleeping tonight, etc) into a much more political landscape. The bride seems to have been diverted by her own contemplation of ivory (the final uncovering of ivory-white skin) to an extempore outburst against the arid pointlessness of high finance and its life-denying qualities — 'what use is ivory, / Well-honed banker's booty.' Perhaps, in this mercurial poem, the click and clack are ivory counters, or beads in an abacus, used for calculations, but they also double as talking 'clique' and 'claque', suggesting to the reader a gossipy but powerful group, the Establishment in action.

La Belle Cordière, as Labé came to be known, appears to challenge the Burghers of Lyon not just on the equality of the sexes — lines 5-10 suggest that women have no time of their own until they have done their ropework — but on racism. Ivory's colour, simply speaking, is of course white and this leads by association to a further flash of anger as the Ropemaker's Bride exclaims — 'where the servant's darker / Who says you're made to be / Anything like a servant.'

Freedom is, briefly, the theme, or kinds of freedom. To be 'free': the poem moves from the governance of a wife's time by her husband, passes through the issue of servants and liberty, and stops at the thought of being free of a 'mort of manuscripts'. This is rather condensed — it is a very condensed poem. The manuscripts in question can be taken as the marriage licence and the husband's will (older and more likely to die before his wife), and there are also the commercial contracts of the successful magnate. The sigh, the weary but exclamatory tone, suggests these are a weight, a burden; they are life-impeding in contrast to the life of love the speech's occasion suggests should be the chief point of celebration.

Again there is a particular context in the production of the poem itself: Morgan's own estate, literary or otherwise, was surely in his thoughts as he wrote these lines. There is a feeling that transient life always trumps literature ('a mort of manuscripts'), a view diametrically opposed to Shakespeare's sonnets and their papery offer of 'immortality' through writing; Morgan doesn't appear to have been so arid or so naïve, and so there is another flash of difference in the kinds of sonnets, the kinds of poetry, Morgan makes — so different from the norm.

The final five lines perform another mood shift in this complex, beautiful poem: if the bride had felt she was lucky not to have married a 'bad husband' she predicts the time, nevertheless, when her husband will be beholden to her, 'bound' in the sense of 'certain' but with a re-directed frisson of the compelling 'binding' we have already witnessed acting on servant and/or bride. Her 'lord', too, is not as free as he thinks he is since he will be tied to her through the greatest bond of all. He will surely request his wife (not compel – remember, this is the *guid* husband) to... to...but to do what?

Neither bride nor Morgan explicitly say, but a wedding poem is usually in the business of preparing its reader for this particular mystery: that bond will be beyond rope or lute, and yet there will be strands, music, vivacity, virtuosity. The word 'gleggest' is key here. In fact one of my transcription queries to Morgan concerned that word. I had actually transcribed it correctly but, because my understanding of Scots is limited, I hadn't recognised it for the Scots word it is and wanted him to make it a recognisable word. This speaks volumes about my grasp of Scots of course, but I should say that the whole poem is in otherwise standard English and it is quite risky to make that 'furrener' 'gleggest' emphatically cap the poem.

It means most skilled, most lively and in this poem emphasises the superlative event or quality that bride and poet place above industrial or creative energies: life itself. The confidence of using a Scots word at that point! The Scottish praise poetry of that line! And so the poem finishes with the bride's acknowledgement of her immense power, her ability, all going well, to harbour life. The bridegroom is to ask her, in time, to bear their child. What was certainly one of Edwin Morgan's last poems finishes with this tremendous yes to the risk and gift of a woman bringing new life. 'Is this a poem? Do not lose it.'

Margaret Tait: Film-maker and Poet

> It's a mistake to write a poem that seems more certain
> of a policy or a belief or anything than you really are.
> Express the doubt too.
>
> *from* 'It's a mistake...', *origins and elements* (1959), p.4

Margaret Tait was a remarkable film-maker whose often short pieces are intense, beautiful works of art. She was born in 1918 and died in 1991. Rightly, she is known as one of the UK's finest film directors — known, but not well-known. What even fewer know, however, is that she wrote short stories and was an accomplished poet —and a provocative one.

My first encounter with her work was in 1993 when her only feature-length film, *Blue Black Permanent*, was released. I was very taken by this film and very soon after wrote two poems inspired by it. I am hardly ever moved to poetry by cinema but Tait's detached handling of an intimate family mystery and her exceptional attention to natural detail (in this case, the sea edge) were catalysts for writing within an area of a particular kind of sound sensitivity, as well as to a certain kind of domestic atmospherics: the protection of being in a good family as a beautiful soap bubble against a hard social world and perhaps a harder natural one.

Much later I learnt about her other films. These include *Portrait of Ga* (1952), a quietly loving tribute to her mother; *Colour Poems* (1974), which uses the animation technique of direct painting onto the film stock; *Tailpiece* (1976), a meditation on an abandoned house; and *Hugh MacDiarmid, A Portrait* (1964), a cleverly indirect film about one of the giants of modern Scottish literature.

Hugh MacDiarmid had published her work in *Voice of Scotland* in the 1950s, and she herself self-published several poetry books in the late '50s and early '60s, Antonia Fraser included her poetry in *Scottish Love Poems* (1975) and Ali Smith championed Tait's poetry in an essay in Peter Todd and Benjamin Cook's *Subjects and Sequences: A Margaret Tait Reader* (Lux, 2004). I'm afraid Tait's significance as a poet escaped my attention until 2009. Talking with others, I find I'm not alone. By chance it was a routine enquiry at my place of work, the British Library, that led me to look more closely at what I now think of as a fascinating figure in modern Scottish poetry, and a truly great film-maker.

Tait's short story collections (*The Grassy Stories* and *Lane Furniture*) were both published in 1959. There is much to say about these two books but it's the poetry I'm concerned with here. Together with the stories, the poems appeared within a relatively short period of literary activity. Tait published three collections: *origins and elements* (1959), *Subjects and Sequences* (1960) and *The Hen and the Bees: legends and lyrics* (1960).

Once you've read these poems, perhaps the first aspect that strikes you is how *fresh* they are, how lithe (though not, I should say, 'primitive'). They are, generally speaking, in a supple free verse. They have clearly learned from the later poems of D. H. Lawrence, the spiky rhythms of opinion in *Pansies* and *Nettles* and, especially, from the poems of the natural world in *Birds, Beasts and Flowers*. Some poems, which are still 'free', use a jazz-like rhyme, others are more formally rhymed ballads. Many have an improvisational rhythm and sometimes a sense of testifying urgency. Like a classic artist's sketch, they risk immediate witness, declaring themselves as approximating or querying something they can only outline as yet. Paradoxically, the inscribing and making public of such tentativeness does, though, assert a certain confidence and draws attention to itself as art. These poems are laid before you by a reporter from the thinking, feeling emotional front whose quick reactions, their publication implies, are those you should trust.

This complexity is also signalled by the idiosyncratic bibliographic designation that Tait gives to each of these self-published poetry collections: each is an 'interim edition'. In the book world such an editorial state barely exists. What these collections would normally be called is, simply, *first editions*, but Tait imagines something more intangible and more individual (to my knowledge no other edition was ever published, no 'final report'). Their self-published nature confirms their personalisation-as-testimony and, with the 'interim' label, that curious and fascinating zone between the private and the public, a zone within which her films live and breathe.

Perhaps there is also something more about that phrase 'interim edition'. Of the many millions of books in the British Library, which must constitute a fair sample, a catalogue search reveals that barely thirty have such a designation; when you look at their kind of publication a pattern emerges. They are typically reports, statistical tables, surveys, and planning documents, the genre known in librarianship as 'grey literature'. Seen in that light, Tait's poems appear to be coming from a social policy environment: they are not just poems, they are best-guess ideas, pressing questions; initial data. Incidentally, this intersection of the emotional with the factual is further alluded to by another bibliographic code: the logo Tait uses for all her self-published books is the heartbeat trace of a hospital monitor, a nod to Tait's profession (she was a doctor), and another suggestion that her work will be a detached but earnest investigation into matters of the heart.

The subject range of Tait's poetry is wide and the individual architecture of her poems is nuanced: they have a knowing naivety and play but also a subtle intertextuality, and a kind of scientific distance. Tait has an acute interest in environmental and sexual politics, but occasionally will go straight to very personal topics, such as 'Alex' from *Subjects and Sequences*, which appears to be about her life-long partner Alex Pirie ('I think nothing of your thought-out thought, / But value you for thinking it'), or the poem, 'Allison' from the same volume, which is addressed to her sister-in-law, her friend and 'my sad sweet sister'. It's an elegy, Allison having died as she miscarried:

>All she did is as alive as all we did.
>In her house I feel her presence.
>Essential child girl and woman affect us and will do so.
>In her little son who cannot remember her I see her.
>And in her bigger boy who remembers her well I see her too
>And hear her.
>Unbroken survival of the germ makes of brief being a heritage.

Textually this poem braids the utterance of profound personal sorrow with a high, epic, register of lament, a prosody that sounds in several sections like Ecclesiastes and Whitman (to me, at least) and meditates on the genetic continuation of her sister-in-law's life-loving qualities. Finally it touchingly incorporates the anonymous medieval poem 'Alysoun' to conclude the poem, Tait having told the reader earlier that Allison loved medieval poetry:

>And so she laughed her life away,
>As she dismissed all weary cares,
>And so she sang and so she told us
>Happy hopeful genial airs,
>Until the day the blood came pouring,
>Tore placenta from the wall,

> And Death leapt out from his lair in the dark,
> Bytuene Mershe and Averil,
> And lyht on Alysoun.

There's only a little room in this article to describe other kinds of Tait poem and though I'm loath to force Tait into being 'only' an eco-poet or a feminist poet, those aspects are worth registering for those as yet unaware of her work. Here's an extract from 'Hooray, Hooray, Hoo Ray Ray Ray,' from *origins and elements*. Tait was an Orcadian and this poem was probably prompted by the recently constructed Dounreay nuclear power station in Sutherland, facing the Orkneys. The play in the title is more to do with the rays of radiation than the sonic qualities of the word for the locale, 'Dounreay', but the occasion for the poem surely still stands. Actually, the title is more typical of the poetry Tait uses in her films than she collects in her books (her page poems being more conversational; her film poems a kind of sound and concrete poetry). There is a scrupulous attention to the sound of apparently ordinary words in her films (witness if you can the veer Tait manages to elicit from the word 'Aha' in the short film of the same name) and a remarkable fecundity of meaning within a minimalist aesthetic. In 'Hooray, Hooray, Hoo Ray Ray Ray,' the first word, 'Hooray' announces the celebration Tait will go on to describe in this poem as the initial response to the wonder energy source of nuclear power as it is first exploited for peaceful means.

But 'Hooray' is also a childish word — the sort of word children are taught to use 'spontaneously'. By the end of the poem's title the naivety of the celebration has decomposed into the lower forms of the substance that constitutes it — Hoo and Ray, as, indeed, radioactive material decomposes into lower elements in the periodic table (achieved giving out its dangerous radiation). The chain of accountability in setting up the nuclear power stations — 'Hoo' homophonically is 'Who?' with a hint of the classroom chill of 'Who Killed Cock Robin?' — but the title moves on from political cause to leave only the radiation of rays, rays, rays, as bleak 'echo'.

The following *is* an extract, so you have to know that this almost prosey tone has emerged from a more generalised discussion in the poem about the strange unexplainability of science's explanations. The poem has opened with the lines 'I think the satisfaction / I have got from Science / All my life / Is the realisation / That it's all completely beyond us'. What we as readers find out is that Tait doesn't just mean science is beyond the layperson but it is, at a fundamental level, beyond scientists themselves. No-one can really understand the most fundamental aspects of existence. But here is the more political ending of the poem, transmitted in that beguilingly informal delivery:

> It's not so easy to get rid of your empty tin cans and
> your waste radiation.
> There's something deadly about ragged sardine tins
> under all the house windows
> And about clots of radiation in the sea.
>
> Maybe we think we can change all the atoms of the
> world, including ourselves,
> Into radiation, helium and lead,
> With a few bright photons
> For an aurora at the poles
> - We can put the poles in a different place, too, if we
> want to –
> And maybe we're right
> But maybe we are thinking through our hats.

Tait's feminism is noticeable and, in UK poetry of that decade, extremely unusual. In 'The Maiden's future', from *origins and elements,* Tait accuses the Church of sanctifying what she regards as the prostitution of 'respectable' marriage. In another key poem, 'Secrets' she takes issue with Lawrence relishing the 'secrecy' of women, a reference to his erotic poem 'Figs' in *Birds, Beasts and Flowers!* (1923) in which he asserts:

> That's how it should be, the female should always be secret.
> [...]
> Folded upon itself, and secret unutterable,
> And milky-sapped, sap that curdles milk and makes *ricotta*,
> Sap that smells so strange on your fingers, that even goats won't
>   taste it;
> Folded upon itself, enclosed like any Mohammedan woman,
> Its nakedness all within-walls, its flowering forever unseen,
> One small way of access only, and this close-curtained from
>   the light;
> Fig, fruit of the female mystery, covert and inward,
> Mediterranean fruit, with your covert nakedness,
> Where everything happens invisible, flowering and fertilisation,
>   and fruiting
> In the inwardness of your you, that eye will never see
> Till it's finished, and you're over-ripe, and you burst to give
>   up your ghost.
>
> Till the drop of ripeness exudes,
> And the year is over. [...]

This is a rich, sensual, strange poem that, as you can see, emphatically confines women to a sexual, sticky, physical, 'natural' (but also alien and exoticised) role, and, above, all, a life of concealment.

As Lawrence works through what figs / women mean to him — the equivalence itself is of course as scandalous as the rhetoric is accomplished — something even more disturbing emerges. For all his dwelling on the fig's qualities — that is, he slows down to marvel — that line 'Till it's finished, and you're over-ripe, and you burst to give up your ghost', Lawrence seems also to be imagining women as mere intermediaries fulfilling a suicidal aspect in the cycle of life, with men the unspoken but obvious centre and beneficiaries; women, for Lawrence, seem to be agents of mere delivery. Perhaps this is being unfair to Lawrence, being too literal — Lawrence's psalmist lyric is a shapeshifter that may well resist such reductive analogies and perhaps this sort of improvisation is supposed to open a dialogue, even with a confident assertion, not shut it down — but I find it disquieting all the same.

Later in the poem, the language thins and, as so often in Lawrence's free verse, meanings have slightly shifted or arguments moved on (this is one of the valuable formal characteristics that I think Tait takes from Lawrence and runs with). Here, the ending of the poem, the women are now alive but, as it were, over-ripe:
>Ripe figs won't keep, won't keep in any clime.
>What then, when women the world over have all bursten into self-assertion?
>And bursten figs won't keep?

Well, there is a question-mark at the end of that poem, as if Lawrence is about to come to his senses himself, but that's hardly enough to turn around the powerful rhetorical assertions he has been making. Tait's answer to this, 'Secrets', uses animal analogies rather than botanical. The animal is the dog, clearly an object of disgust for Tait:

>Why does Lawrence want us to be secret?
>Why does he say that women's secret mustn't be told?
>It isn't a secret really, it's only a mock secret
>Kept secret on purpose for some purpose of man's,
>Kept secret to keep women under covers,

> Hidden so that men can hide women away for themselves,
> Each what he can get for himself,
> Like a dog burying a bone.

Elsewhere for Tait, the dog is a symbol of servility — in another poem she says 'I hate dogs. / Disgusting caricatures of human and of animal life, / Neither one thing nor the other, / Pets / Made to function for human diversion – / to divert people. [...] No wonder they give people asthma!'). ('Dogs', in *The Hen and the Bees*, p.1) – but in 'Secrets' men aren't slaves. Rather, they 'invented the idea that woman is sin', they 'go to the African tribes and tell them to cover up and consider themselves sinful,' and 'They hand them hideous calico garments sewn reluctantly by unhappy schoolgirls / And say to put them on and hide themselves.' Tait continues: 'The Bible says batter the women, / Hide the bones of your women in a corner of the garden, / 'Your' women, / Keep them secret, all happed up in the idea of sin, / Then you'll be safe, old man.'

Well, Tait does not accept Lawrence's 'secrecy' — 'Ah yes, Mr. Lawrence, you are wrong' she says in the closing lines of the poem — and in the same way that she offers the possibility of a radically open society in the poem 'Locklessness' (in *The Hen and the Bees*, p.5) she looks forward, in the very near future to a world where women, contra Lawrence, do indeed self-affirm: 'Because the time of women is at hand / And the good will come of the secret not being secret any more.'

'Hooray, Hooray, Hoo Ray Ray Ray,' and 'Secrets' are explicitly political poems: their subject is clear and, with the exception of 'Hooray''s compressed-meanings title, their delivery relies on the lower frequencies of rhetorical rhythm to maintain that clarity. That rhetoric is of course in part borrowed from preacher-patterning, even when it is anti-religious. In this Tait is not only like the apparently straight-talking, satirical Lawrence of his later poems, of *Pansies* say, but also like the Beats. Lawrence, Tait and the Beats are in these poems 'prophets'.

As far as palpable connection between Tait and the Beats is concerned this is probably more a sign of the times than a real link between contemporaries, though I'd suggest that they are all in Lawrence's debt. While the Scottish poet Helen Adam was literally among the Beats in California at this time, a friend of Robert Duncan, Jack Spicer and Allen Ginsberg, I'm not sure that Tait ever had such a direct connection. True, Edinburgh, where Tait had her home at this time, was one of the first places in which the Beats were published in the UK — Burroughs, Ginsberg, Kerouac, Corso and Gary Snyder appeared in an unnumbered issue of the Edinburgh University magazine *Jabberwock* in 1959 — but Tait's poetry books are collecting poems which, according to dates on them, are clustered round the 1955-58 period and go at least as far back as 1952. One or two of these had already been published by Hugh MacDiarmid in his *Voice of Scotland* magazine, a fact which causes pause for thought in view of the later polarising furore between MacDiarmid and Ian Hamilton Finlay (Finlay and, by association, the Beats, became trivialised by the grand old man of Scottish letters but this somewhat backfired on MacDiarmid, painting him into a reactionary old guard corner). MacDiarmid's publication of Tait suggests that there was more to it than either subject or formal considerations.

I suppose what is striking about this formal aspect of these discursive, arguing poems is that they are so unlike the films, which are indirect, subtly rhythmic, focussed not on large structures but supposedly incidental ones (the texture of the sea-edge, close-ups of moor grasses being blown by the wind, the legs of men walking in a commemorative march; the tops of walls and the patterning of pavements and roads). I'm afraid I don't know my art film well enough to give a context for these films, though note here that Tait had studied experimental film in Rome from 1950 to 1952. I do see certain images in later Scottish cinema — Bill Douglas's child immersed in smoke on a bridge, Lynn Ramsay's child playing with the net curtains in a Glasgow tenement — that seem to follow the intensity of Tait's camera. It's actually in fiction I see one affinity with Tait's films — the novels of Neil Gunn, especially those of the 1930s, and particularly those envisaged from a child's point of view: think of the sensual opening paragraphs of *Morning Tide* (1931) when the young boy Hugh walks gathering seaweed along the shore. Gunn, from Caithness, was also a lyrical experimental artist, whose work, like Tait's, explores childhood and old age together.

Tait's films are characterised by the spare use of spoken or sung words; one characteristic is that though the language use is minimalist it is not usually 'haiku-minimalist' but rather a concentration of word play (not always humorous). So far, most of the poems I've discussed aren't really like that but how about this, an extract from 'Water', from *origins & elements*:

> Hydrogen,
> Light and explosive.
> And oxygen.
> Business-like, useful oxygen,
> Combustible,
> Ready to combine with anything.
> I've always liked oxygen.
> Oxygen.
> Orkney.
> Ozone.
> The air we breathe,
> Oxyhaemoglobin,
> Life-blood

Now this is unlike the overtly political poems: there is microlinguistic attentiveness here. Actually it seems to me this is closer to the animations that Tait made when she painted directly on to the film stock (the forming and re-forming dancing figures in *Jock MacDayen* for example). The word Oxygen, its chemical symbol O, is literally attaching itself to become Orkney and Ozone and even Oxyhaemoglobin, as well as being a lovely testament to the importance of Orkney to Tait. You might think of MacDiarmid's poetry of fact but MacDiarmid tends to pile up science as an aspirational simile for 'The Kind of Poetry' he wants: Tait is going in the other direction, trying to find comparisons to comprehend the material facts that science is disclosing. Francis Ponge's lyrical prose-poems come to mind, too, but Tait's line is much shorter, marking the breathing and then moving into the field of the page, playing that little step-down of 'Oxygen. Orkney. Ozone.' Tait's work really is a breath of fresh air.

A small selection of Margaret Tait's poems was made in the excellent A Margaret Tait Reader, edited by Peter Todd and Benjamin Cook (Lux, 2004), which rightly concentrates on the genius of Tait's films, and Carcanet has published Poems, Stories and Writings, *edited by Sarah Neeley (Manchester, 2012).*

Ear-jewels catch a glint: The Half-Year Letters

The Half-Year Letters[88] is an alphabet book designed and realised by the artist Ronald King using specially commissioned text by Roy Fisher. Each letter of the alphabet is made manifest as a pop-up which is not actually printed but ingeniously cut and folded from the paper of the page itself. Fisher's free verse appears under each letter. It is one of several collaborations King and Fisher have made over more than three decades of association, though these have usually been larger and more overtly complex works, such as *Bluebeard's Castle* (1972-3), *The Left-Handed Punch* (1986), and *Tabernacle* (1986).

Two short accounts of *The Half-Year Letters* by Cathy Courtney and Matthew Sperling give, respectively, musical and literary approaches to the book. Cathy Courtney describes the genesis of the book as a development of an earlier project with King, *Scenes from an Alphabet* (Circle Press, 1978). *Scenes* features pop-ups of A, B, and C only, with an acrostic poem by Fisher, the alphabet itself forming the first letter of each of the twenty-six lines. It was Fisher's encouragement that saw King extend the pop-ups in later years to the whole alphabet: 'Roy Fisher was integral to the idea, urging King to invent the full twenty-six letters.'[89]

---

[88] Fisher, Roy and Ronald King, *The Half-Year Letters: an alphabet book*, Guildford: Circle Press, 1983. British Library shelfmark: Cup.510.bha.7.
[89] Courtney, Cathy, *The Looking Book: a pocket history of Circle Press, 1967-96,* Circle Press, 1996, p. 140.

Courtney suggests that Fisher's experience as a jazz pianist is one way to approach an understanding of *The Half-Year Letters* and corroborates this with Fisher's reflection on his role:

> My accompaniment on 'The Half-Year Letters' was of a musical nature. Ron already had a very dogmatic master text, so I thought I would have a voice and a disposition muttering along with his letters.'[90]

Fisher's wry use of 'dogmatic' here affectionately imagines the alphabet and perhaps even King as strict taskmasters. It seems to me this way of seeing King's art is critical to how Fisher's texts, by contrast, behave. King uses capital letters, an aspect of their authority that Fisher is playing off and 'against'. Another authoritative aspect is the alphabet's 'given' nature — given in the sense that King has sent them to Fisher to work on but also because the sequence of the alphabet is canonical. Dogmatists tend to think their sequence of events is pre-ordained, in 'the nature of things', and are perhaps most dogmatic when their view's central assertions are in fact the most chancy. The alphabet has become so familiar that it seems unquestionable in that way, Fisher suggests, an irrefutable organic object instead of the artificial object it actually is. (Or perhaps the alphabet is neither one nor the other, and is, like a very old building, somewhere between nature and artifice?). In any case Fisher here signals a re-perspectivising of it (again, I stress that this is a humorous use of the word 'dogmatic').

In the nature of pop-ups, the letters jut out into the reading space of the page creating sculpture in a traditional place of contemplation — the book, not the temple or the gallery. However, far from the children's book genre in which pop-ups usually reside, King's are

---

[90] Ibid.

made only of cuts and folds in the paper and do not form an extravagant and brightly coloured structure (in children's books an elaborate boat, say, a tree, or an animal). In this sense King is himself playing off and against a 'given' but in the exact opposite direction from Fisher's. Fisher's texts, on the contrary, are busy — perhaps as busy as the pop-ups a reader might expect in such a book. As Matthew Sperling writes, 'Fisher's text imagines language as a material medium so alive with conflictual energies that it can rise off the page, and exist in three-dimensions, like a pop-up image.'[91] Fisher's poems describe a number of different (adult) activities which are nevertheless not dwelt on in detail; their texts are often rushing so quickly that they are syntactically incomplete. No verse is full-stopped at the end of the page, giving the jump from section to section sometimes a minimalist suspension (when the text has, despite my overview, a haiku-like staticity) but more often a kind of lurch.

These texts have been called prose poetry, or rather a 'species of 'poet's prose''[92], an observation which strengthens a link of affinity made earlier by Marjorie Perloff when she suggested that Fisher and the North American L=A=N=G=U=A=G=E poets shared a surprisingly close approach to avant-garde prose, Fisher anticipating the poets across the Atlantic in his *The Cut Pages* (Fulcrum, 1971), 'Roy Fisher's 'Language Book'' (Perloff, unnumbered). That may be, but I think the genre categorisation for *The Half-Year Letters* is incorrect: the lineation of the texts is almost always of poetry not prose, sometimes enjambed, sometimes endstopped, but always verse. Even the possible

---

[91] Sperling, Mattew, 'The Making of the Book': Roy Fisher, the Circle Press and the Poetics of Book Art, in *Literature Compass* 4/5 (2007), pp.1444-1459, p. 1451.

[92] Ibid.

exception, the text for 'N' (which I will discuss a little later), though it is among the most prose-like, has such suspenseful prepositions in key line-endings that it could still be defended as free verse. The others are much more clearly poetry. Here is 'H' for example, with the fertility of its searching line-end pauses:

> There's a belief to fix. It feels strong,
> it feels far off.
> There is no faith to defile by fragmentation,
> to fit into half faiths or less

This isn't necessarily a pedantic point: I think that Fisher's free verse, often linked to jazz aesthetics, leads to various effects on the meaning of the sequence, including its aural nature, to which I'll also return.

First, however, back to the visuality of *The Half-Year Letters*, and especially to the striking difference between King's and Fisher's approaches. The contrast between the two artists' contributions is so stark that King may have felt that each actually needed a little protection from each other: when Courtney interviewed King about the design of the book she asked him about the blue line that runs between pop-up and text: 'Well that was really to separate off the poem from the letter,' (King, p. 501). It's a blue line, not a black one, and I read it as gentler and more porous because of that, but a line it is (perhaps it could even be the 'thin blue line' of a police force separating, the Line might like to think, the alphabet's elite from Fisher's rabble, but that may be to carry things too far). Another effect is that the line evokes at the exposed outside edges of the book, in a modern, asymmetrical, way, binder's thread, a material actually absent from this elastic, bellows-like structure. When the illusion is discovered it serves to emphasise the non-conventional aspect of the accordion binding.

King doesn't mention another effect the line has, which is to complement, rather than contrast with, the bustling ever-onwards nature of Fisher's text: internally the line visually moves the book across each page and then onwards from page to page. Fisher's choice of making the work a calendar or diary — each opening corresponds to a week (there being fifty-two weeks in a full year, hence the 'half-year letters' of the twenty-six letter alphabet) — means that King's blue line is a *time*-line, contributing to the book's propulsive call to turn from the one page into the next, and so into next week. It is likely that King added the line later and so was in turn responding to Fisher's text, the genuine to-ing and fro-ing of collaborators in art.

King is celebrated for, among other aspects of his work, his use of exuberant collaging and warm colour (which has been variously associated with his Brazilian upbringing, his interest in African masks, and, later, his London studio's location on the route of the Notting Hill carnival). However, these pop-ups display a quite different but enduring element that has perhaps been under-acknowledged: austerity, abstraction; depth in the minimal. This is something that Fisher, in interview, does identify in King's solo works but, perhaps because of the highly complex larger scale works he was also involved in with King, doesn't associate with their collaborations:

> I don't see myself as restraining Ron, explicitly or tacitly. I think rather, that by inviting me to be his collaborator he implicitly asks me to hold his coat, that is to say to embody for a while the classical or austere part of himself while he indulges in freedoms he might otherwise feel inclined to rein in. In his non-collaborative works the purity is often clearly central. You could reverse the proposition and say that in our collaborations I can indulge my passion for parsimonious writing to the full, safe in the

knowledge that sustained invention and feats of technical virtuosity can be counted on to be provided by the artist.[93]

Fisher is of course right, though, about King's extraordinary technical accomplishment as anyone who contemplates the elegance and concealed complexity of the folded cut-out pop-ups will realise. The result is a breathtaking purity but one that is soft-edged, delicate: that there is no actual printer's ink used for the cut-outs means that the letters rely on subtle contrast and shadow for their definition. Fisher's verses allude to the joint project as a sculptural one, the initiating letter A suggesting that the book at this stage is the block of stone that begins a sculpture or other work of construction — 'Half-year starts out of the quarry' — but the sculpture is as light as a feather. Further along in the sequence the fragmentary sentence in the letter M, 'In a book of marked megaliths', captures the sculptural (and mysterious) nature of King's lettering. Perhaps even this, however, does not quite touch the paradox of the letters' forceful yet delicate imposition. Instead Fisher arguably finds an analogue across the whole of his text in the many references to part-states, half-ness, compromises in clarity (smoke, veils, and glints that actually emphasise the murk of their surroundings); like the letters these descriptions seem to rely on the emergence but weightlessness of light for their discernment.

There is also the aural to think about. Fisher's reference to himself 'muttering along' to the letters confers a kind of sound quality not just to his own poetry but to King's shapes: it's as if the pop-ups

---

[93] Lambirth, Andrew, with descriptions and commentary by Ron King, *Cooking the Books: Ron King and the Circle Press,* New Haven: Yale Center for British Art, 2002, pp.141-4.

aren't just visual but are powerful one-letter utterances, thought-clarifying not just as physical works of art but as the one-syllable words of meditative practice. Fisher's 'muttering' also implies the eyes-to-heaven attitudes of the bright resentful servant (think of Muttley and Dick Dastardly if you like), though of course Fisher's is a mock-resentment here, and it foregrounds distorted speech as a response to the breathtaking clarity of King's letters. Such creative accompaniment only confirms, as Courtney rightly suggests, that Fisher is here as much the jazz player elaborating around a rock-steady bass as he is the poet.[94]

Yet the story is more complex on both sides of the partnership. In a note by Fisher on the last page of the book a further structuring device is revealed. The reader now finds out that it was not just that the text had to relate to the alphabet, but that there was a controlled vocabulary to be peppered throughout the work. Moreover, as the reader might now expect, even the relationship to the alphabet was never intended to be straightforward. Fisher now confirms what will have gradually dawned on the reader: that acrostics were always going to be out because he had set the rules in such a way that the letter in question could be within the body of a word rather than, as in more traditional alphabet books, always at the beginning.

The text treats the rigorous forward movement of an alphabet as a movement through time, as if it marked the twenty-six weeks of a half-year, April through September. The vocabulary for each letter, a week, is governed in part by the pervading presence of the letter, in a variety of uses; in part by a chance operation based on a set of key words – half, year, quarry, bread, candle, swan, blunder, job, booze, burnt, trick, door, rider, wild, glisten, veil, lope, vigil,

---

[94] Op. cit., p. 140.

smoke, vex, prize, open, swift, fit, fix – each of which is particularly likely to occur in the company of one of the letters which spell it.

The restricted set of terms contains several words of the kind I've already mentioned: they are to do with reduced light, or points of illumination within an environment of otherwise subdued light — candle, glisten, veil, smoke. In the book at large, Fisher adds to the atmospherics of these using cognate words that are not on his self-imposed list (such a list is also a kind of 'dogma' by the way — clearly Fisher relishes such parameters to work with): pall, twilight, dull, dusk, and glint. Others words from the locked-down kist of special words suggest movement implictly or explicitly — blunder, rider, wild, lope, open, and swift.

There are several mysteries associated with this list. Is there something drily amusing in having such a large 'restricted' list for such a minimal text? Surely there is something odd about having 25 words, just one short of the number of letters in the actual alphabet, rather than the full 26. A further curiosity is the underplayed use Fisher makes of this vocabulary. Several of his words could double as two different forms of grammar (especially, both verb and noun), a quality that poets would normally exploit for switches of meaning in the sort of permutational form that *Half-Year Letters* is. Perhaps this is Fisher again avoiding another kind of expectation, or demonstrative simply of the fact that the verb-noun 'flick' is not part of Fisher's poetry scape, not part of his sensibility: in this way in *The Half-Year Letters* 'swift' is fast but never the flitting creature; 'smoke' is never an active verb but rather drifts in and out of the sequence solely in nouny clouds. Perhaps the conclusion to be made here is that although there is clearly play and humour in the text, some of which is based on the re-use of vocabulary in surprising contexts, such play seems relatively low down in the mix, an obliquity without the demonstrative tease of such grammatical pivots.

So far this vocabulary gives a greyish, glimmering palette to Fisher's poetry, but what, some pre-readers may ask, is the sequence actually about?

For some this will be a crass question: because the text could be said to be so abstracted as to be, as it were, musical, so making the reception of tone all (in which case that glimmer-in-the-grey and its metaphoric diffusions *is* what the text is about); because to talk of pressing quickly on to 'a' 'subject' is to give in to a satisfaction-on-demand culture characterised by the bold philistine certainties of both retail and the media (certainties which nevertheless seem invested with caprice); and because the pedagogy of poetry should emphasise formal qualities above informational substance ('Mere subject matter? Go to the novel and the film for that...').

My own view is that a praising of the paratactic should not obliterate the fraught and minute interaction of detail that these texts carry, especially as to do so may encourage an ideological interpretation on a category-praised but essentially unscrutinised text (old fashioned parataxis as the continuous revolution in literature).

What is *The Half-Year Letters* about? In a sense, the title is the label. Nouns first: 'Letters'. We've already seen indications of how self-conscious the text is about the book itself — as well as the sculptural examples above, think of the letter M's sentence 'By empty morning roads to a hump-backed / bridge.' As if it contained a shadow of an Anglo-Saxon riddle, this seems to me to be a quiet reference to M as the last letter before the doubled book needs to be turned over for the remaining half of the alphabet: 'M', sharing an intervening silence with 'N' — that silence is the true halfway of the even-numbered alphabet — is the beginning of the book's bridge. Is there even an allusion to the letter M, King's cut-out, as looking like a bridge? It certainly does. The reader might also note Fisher's enjambment of 'hump-backed / bridge' — that's an apt jolt for such a crossing and again reminds the reader that free verse rather than prose poetry is the active genre here. In the letter H, Fisher again seems to be talking about the book when he says 'Half reconciled, half healed: but two / different sets of halves that won't match''. (Of course he is talking much more generally as well, with a melancholy sense of unease.). Again look at the function of the enjambment as it pressures the word 'different' at the beginning of that last line. All this suggests that one of the topics of this book is the nature of the book...

Adjectives second: 'Half-Year'. Time's registration is a theme in the book, as the calendar element demonstrates. There are diary-like entries — 'A queasy request in the mail' ('Q'), 'Then in hard-blown sun to the uplands / above the used-up quarries and burnt houses' ('U'). This betrays one of the origins of the text — Fisher 'took a random starting date from his own diaries and extracted events and observations from a twenty-six week span. From these he selected a group of words associated with the notes [...]' (Courtney, p. 140). That said, many of the poems in the sequence are less direct than this, or suggest not a single event but, montage-like, a continuousness of activity across a more extended period of time: 'Open season for old wounds, odd jobs; / loping from door to door, hovering, / hamming it up, on the booze' ('O'); 'A burnt year. Trick riders blunder about / the concrete, without quarry or prize.' (from 'R'); 'Burnt sugar; / and blunder to London, lie frog-flat under / a black pall, wake in the after-smoke, / a huge bee at the window' (for 'B'... playfully). In one poem, 'G', Fisher's text seems to be reaching towards a sensual understanding of time, a palpability and freshness that tries to elude the strict measurement that time of course is: 'Vigil glistens through into the night, / under a veil of vagueness. Still left in it / there's a virginity that won't tell the time.'

'Vigil', one of the recurring words from the given set of vocabulary, is a temporal word that offers, as it were, slow time, the state of concerned waiting: initial impressions of hyperactivity in Fisher's sequence really do need to be modified to convey a greater sense of the different time signatures occurring across the work, rather than relentless full speed ahead. In the same way there is nothing hyperactive in the letter N:

> The spirals of the snail shells I found in the
> dawn, scattered in the carbonized stubble
> of the charred canal bank at Swanbank:
> some shells burnt white, others still
> patterned, a glisten of mucus left at
> their openings

There is after all something awkward, interim, and certainly unliterary about a half-year diary, normally a form of business stationery. I think the sequence's internal moving from images of bluster and the frantic to solitary reflection and back again reflect at micro level the abbreviated diary's insecurity of balance, a restlessness which encompasses a spectrum between the frenetic and the static, the exhausted, even.

There is much more in the text, however, than is signalled by the title. The visually reduced palette of whites, blacks, greys and glimmer certainly resonates with the post-industrial landscape that this and other poems by Fisher describe even as the focus veers between the close-up-and-personal (the glint of earrings, a ringed hand on a page) to broader scapes (a quarry-side vista). To me the text, as with the artist's book as a whole, becomes in itself a metaphor for the reduced knowledge that one can only ever have of anyone else, with the compressed entries for each letter offering not only a tone of intrigue, evidencing such unknowability, but, as with a particular perhaps Beckettian strand of minimalism, suggesting with more than a pang vast emotional depths. As such the text proceeds as much in a series of dreams as in a series of recorded facts. The scorched snails by the canal-side in 'N' are intensely if imagistically 'real' but there is the mystery of what precisely the voice was doing there as a witness. On second look there is also that lyrical aestheticisation of the shells in the observation of their heat-wiped pallour and the remains of 'pattern' (I think of the blank pop-outs again and the pattern of words beneath them, and the suggestion that time can be experienced not only as a measure but as heightened feeling, perhaps called art). A third look and there is the curious placing of that text between two other quite different verses, 'M' and 'O', all of whose connection only seems to make sense as a function of the voice's (and book's) wayward momentum, the nearly discontinuous in the human now marshalled and propelled by the book.

There is of course much more to say about *The Half-Year Letters*, and much more than can be said here. The odd temperature variations in tone, it seems to me, need more scrutiny. Take for instance the spiky contempt the text reserves for academic careerists ('A thesis to turn a trick comes swiftly to / trial. The fate that fits it is to be burnt' (from 'T'). Elsewhere there are troubled ('vexed') responses to faith and belief; there is the recurrence of a Rider figure, 'The Rider Interrupted by Anniversaries' as the voice in the letter 'I' puts it; and there are instances of hearing impairment — sometimes deafness figured as hapless gaucherie ('Blundering in deaf through the door'). All these and more contribute to a text which manages to be leaf-light and 'rich' at the same time, a feat entirely in keeping with Ron King's realised design, making it a book to return to again and again.

Acknowledgements and further references
The collaborations made by Ron King and Roy Fisher over the decades can be seen in the collections of the British Library. I am grateful to the Library for allowing me time to work on this article, and to the poet Peter McCarey for his comments on an earlier draft.

King, Ronald, with Cathy Courtney, *Ron King interviewed by Cathy Courtney*, London: British Library, 1996. Transcript of recording C466/47/01 F5422A.

Perloff, Marjorie, 'Roy Fisher's 'Language Book'', Electronic Poetry Center,

http://wings.buffalo.edu/epc/authors/perloff/articles/fisher.html, Unnumbered, undated; accessed 21/8/09.

Beyond La Grille: France and Four Contemporary Poets

There is an episode of the TV cartoon show *The Simpsons* that, with a little reflection, encapsulates Scotland's recent relationship with France. Homer Simpson, the overweight, feckless father-figure, decides to build a brick barbecue in his back garden. His hardworking and intellectual daughter Lisa has already laid the concrete base for the new structure. All Homer has to do is build the self-assembly barbecue into the concrete. As loyal viewers and flat-pack victims will have expected, the plan quickly goes awry. Homer's structure slips and then topples into the grey porridge of Lisa's carefully designed foundations.

Homer is not deterred. The series is testament, after all, to his overcoming greater problems than a subsiding barbecue, even if the problems are often self-imposed (see the recurring nuclear meltdown theme). A 'triumph' means that he is usually returned to right back where he started. This time, he manages to rescue the instructions. Although the English text has been obliterated by wet concrete the French version is still intact. Finally, it is time to despair: ' "La grille"?!' he shouts, angrily, only to add, with a whimper, 'Oh, why are foreign languages so hard to understand!'

That's not quite the end of the story, though. The next time we see him, his barbecue has been completed. It's utterly unusable — bricks and tools and 'la grille' stick out from a concrete composite. With the luck inherent in the glorious fiction that *The Simpsons* is, an art collector happens to see it. She loves it for its 'raw energy' and persuades Homer to have it installed in the most fashionable art gallery in town. It is a great success, particularly with the art critics. In one of the many instances in *The Simpsons* where American anti-intellectualism is pitted against European pretentiousness the adoring reviewers speak with snobbish mittel-European accents. Homer Simpson's art, an object built through his faulty but energetic misunderstanding of French, has, briefly, found validation.

In *La Nouvelle Alliance* (Ellug, 2001), David Kinloch and I assembled a number of studies of French influence on modern Scottish literature. There has been limited but real engagement with French literature in Scotland in the last hundred years or so, and the essays each showed very specific connections. Perhaps of all the poets covered in the book, though — including Hugh MacDiarmid, Sidney Goodsir Smith, Frank Kuppner, and even Kenneth White — only Ian Hamilton Finlay could be said to have made a connection to French culture as a directing force in a large swathe of his work. This essentially confirms the subtext of Kenneth White's essay 'The Franco-Scottish Connection': after centuries of cross-cultural influence, there are very few significant links in the twentieth century.[95]

Perhaps a few other names could be added. Veronica Forrest-Thompson, for one, clearly engaged with the work of theorists Barthes, Derrida, and Kristeva; and with the poetry of Marcelin Pleynet, Denis Roche, and with the literary magazine *Tel Quel*. However, how much Forrest-Thompson's acknowledged debt to William Empson modified or complemented her relationship with French literature and theory would also be worth considering. Indeed the English avant-garde context in which Forrest-Thompson can also be placed, 'The Cambridge School', was probably as much a conduit for French translation as any in

---

[95] *On Scottish Ground*, Edinburgh: Polygon, 1998; pp.115-128.

Scotland at the time (see, for example, Peter Riley's magazine *Collection*, published in the late sixties, with its translations of Cendrars, Apollinaire, Soupault and Francis Ponge; Forrest-Thompson was herself a translator of Pleynet and Roche).

Edwin Morgan's extremely early contact with French — a poem of Verlaine's being the first poem he translated, in 1937 — and the appropriately different modes of translation he employed in *Cyrano de Bergerac* and *Phaedra* — suggest that, here is another of the few modern Scottish writers whose relationship with France has been profound. Yet this is true at the level of Morgan's *respect* for French literature: unlike his enthusiasm for Anglo-Saxon, Elizabethan drama, and modern American literature, it is difficult, I think, to see either a stylistic or thematic influence from French literature affecting Morgan's work.

Other Francophile writers warrant further study, of course — Seán Rafferty, Gael Turnbull, and Stephen Mulrine come immediately to mind, and among younger writers there are Guillevic's and Houellebecq's influence on Gavin Bowd, and James Robertson's use of Scots in his translations of Baudelaire. Most recently, Peter Manson's acclaimed translation of Stéphane Mallarmé, *The Poems in Verse*, translated (Oxford, OH: Miami University Press, 2012) has led to his *English in Mallarmé* (BLART Books, 2014), a procedural work which only 'sees' English words in the French originals, in the words of Rebecca Varley–Winter, compelling the reader 'to exist out-of-place, between languages'.[96]

---

[96] Rebecca Varley-Winter, 'The bark of the language forest: Peter Manson's "English in Mallarmé"', *Glasgow Review of Books,* 13th Aug 2015. https://glasgowreviewofbooks.com/2015/08/13/the-bark-of-the-language-forest-peter-mansons-english-in-mallarme/

Nevertheless, considered as a phenomenon that would affect writer after writer, not just as writing which they enjoyed or even translated (translation in any case can often be more about affinity than influence), there is little of substance to be said here. Or rather, there is nothing of the order of influence that one finds in, say, the Francophile Castilian poetry of James V, where almost the entire frame of expression is derived from French models.[97] These exceptions are just that, and — given the changed cultural and political times — it would be a great surprise if Scotland did come within France's gravitational pull.

Yet there are several more recent poets who buck the trend of negligible French influence on Scottish literature. Their number includes Donny O'Rourke, David Kinloch, Iain Bamforth and Peter McCarey.

Donny O'Rourke's song 'Like Simone Signoret', collected in *The Waistband* (Polygon, 1997) is a particularly good example of the way in which French influence is transformed in Scottish literature. This beguilingly simple song is in fact a subtle expression of hopes for a sophisticated intellectual and artistic culture within Scotland, even if those hopes are to be dashed by the time the song is over. The first stanza in 'Like Simone Signoret' sees the poet's persona watching a woman buying a collection of poems by Prévert, and likening her to the French actress of the title:

> Perhaps it was the weather
> Wet and hot
> Or the poems of Prévert

---

[97] See, for example, R.D.S. Jack 'The French Connection: Scottish and French Literature in the Renaissance' in *Scotia: American-Canadian Journal of Scottish Studies* 13 (1989), pp. 1-16.

> She'd just bought
> Watching her browse
> I decided now's
> the time to make a play
> But I just let it pelt
> while she knotted her belt
> just like Simone Signoret

The hesitation here changes in the second stanza and the voice becomes more confident in attributing a specifically French kind of experience to the encounter.

> When she asked the quickest way
> To Buchanan Street
> I suggested coffee
> If she'd no-one to meet
> Sharing her umbrella
> I was that Montand fella
> Très distingué
> A boulevard romance
> A Glasgow Saturday in France
> with Simone Signoret

'If she'd no-one to meet' is a gentle noseyness: the speaker or singer is asking shyly if the woman is single. There is a charm and delicacy to the whole song, in fact, and this is complemented in both versions of the music where the hesitancies are beautifully captured, whether it's Dave Whyte's composition on the album *Still Waiting to Be Wise* (Last Track Records, 1999) or the poet's own version in his remarkable solo performances. (It is no exaggeration to say that the Provençal troubadour tradition is alive and well and living in Glasgow, as far as O'Rourke's art and practice is concerned). This and the next stanza form a sweet fantasia about Glasgow-as-Paris, where it's even possible to imagine 'Sartre's making speeches / in George's Square.' But the final stanza returns the singer to the cold light of day:

> She'd bought the poems for a friend
> Didn't read that much
> Though in the café our heads were close,
> They didn't touch.
> Waving her goodbye
> I wonder why
> I'm still a fool this way
> A look over her shoulder
> That self-sufficient smoulder
> Simone Signoret

The turnaround and economy of those first two lines is especially devastating: 'Didn't read that much' is as crushing as it is beautifully observed. The singer's new acquaintance clearly regards reading as simply another leisure pursuit that you might or might not like to do — indeed, for many, this is exactly what it is. For the poetry-reading Francophile persona, such an admission announces the closing down of romantic possibility. It also brings the realisation that a whole other world exists, largely without books and largely without engagement with other cultures, a world that indeed appears 'self-sufficient'; that is, in fact, a world so foreign to him that it's outside his means of understanding, grasping as he does for the Simone Signoret analogy — one that all evidence suggests would be lost on the woman it is meant to describe (Larkin uses a similar abbreviated phrase, 'Don't read much now' in the poem 'A Study of Reading Habits' to slightly different effect: the speaker has turned away from reading, after finding that books do not offer the self-protection and satisfying fantasy that they once seemed to promise; *Collected Poems*, London: Faber, 1988, p.131). In O'Rourke's text, 'Didn't read that much' is a fragment of a sentence both because the singer is choked — gulp, [he] can hardly bring himself to tell us — but perhaps also because the woman is a mumbler, perhaps even an apologetic one, a semi-articulacy which again is against the extraordinary fluency and confidence of O'Rourke's poems.

The ambiguity of why the singer is a 'fool' is balanced between his romantic love of French culture, and just a hint of disgust about the Glasgow (and Scottish, and British?) way of life. He is a 'fool', largely, for being excitably sentimental about France, but also for thinking anyone he's likely to meet at home would actually be interested in foreign cinema, philosophy or poetry. Perhaps there are gentle shades of Apollinaire's 'La Jolie Rousse' here: 'Mais riez riez de moi / Hommes de partout surtout gens d'ici' ('But laugh at me laugh / Men from everywhere especially folk from here').

The Waistband uses references to France in similar ways in several other pieces, too. It is fair to say that there is a French atmosphere across the whole book. O'Rourke's translations of Soupault, Larbaud, Desnos and Cendrars into Scots from the collection *Eftirs /Afters* (Au Quai, 1995) are included, there's an epigraph from Camus, and even the other strong flavour of the collection — tributes to and reflections on the New York School poets James Schuyler and Frank O'Hara — are refractions from poets whose work owes so much to French predecessors.

A sense of a living boulevard where there are independent cafés, restaurants, old-fashioned shops like butchers and fishmongers, galleries and bookshops is important to O'Rourke. Many of his poems are about walking in the city — alone, with friends, with lovers — and the improvisatory quality of the prosody, with its underlying assurance, matches the theme beautifully. The rich intermingling of themes in and across poems — friendship, love, family, what constitutes 'culture' — is again entirely appropriate to the flâneur persona. The most extensive of these Scottish boulevard poems is 'Great Western Road', which opens:

> Glasgow, you look beatific in blue
> and I've a Saturday before me
> for galleries and poems,
> a house full of Haydn,
> and beneath my kitchen window,
> tennis stars in saris
> lobbing backhands at the bins.
> French coffee, and who knows maybe
> Allen Ginsberg in my bath!

The poem then imagines the whole day enjoying Great Western Road and its environs, 'where, today, everything is redeemable / because tonight there'll be guitar poets / from Russia playing at the Third Eye Centre.' Like so many O'Rourke poems, this is poetry about how one might live one's life: the flâneur persona is used to express a sensibility that is discriminating but open to all manner of the arts; it is a very human poetry — the poet is often accompanied by others, or bumps into them in his travels — but it is sensitive to the varying degrees of seriousness within the art and other cultural matter it encounters, joking and delicately elegising within lines of each other. It *almost* goes without saying that O'Rourke's Francophilia is matched by a very keen concern to shift sensibility in Scotland, so that there are poems and songs that bring France to Scotland, but there is also work which pointedly, even programmatically, addresses itself to Scottish material, such as the anthemic bid to resurrect a Scottish festival in February in 'St Brigid's Day', or the song to celebrate the Edinburgh Book Festival, 'Charlotte Square'.

That O'Rourke is able to dissolve 'high-', 'middle-', and 'low-brow' concepts in the space of a single poem is perhaps reflected in the popularity of 'Great Western Road' which, as well as being an anthology favourite, has actually been pirated. This culminated in the spectacle of O'Rourke sitting in a café on the eponymous street, only to be offered a free photocopy of his own poem by a liberator of the text who wanted as many people as possible to enjoy it. Charges were not pressed.

With a title like *Un Tour d'Ecosse* (Carcanet, 2001), David Kinloch's second full-length volume of poetry announces a Franco-Scottish link with style. The book before that did, too: *Paris–Forfar* (Polygon, 1994). The engagement isn't title-deep: apart from the fact of Kinloch teaching French at the University of Strathclyde, his interest in Mallarmé, and work on Joseph Joubert, the author of the textually-idiosyncratic *Carnets*, his poetry is obviously informed by an in-depth reading of French literature. Among other work, his remarkable prose-poems openly owe a debt to Rimbaud, for the form as such, but also for their often exclamatory, ecstatic nature. Kinloch also attributes his interest in the prose poem's ability to work as a theoretical text to the personal encouragement of the poet Michel Deguy, whom Kinloch knew in the 1980s. Indeed, at this time Kinloch was a *lecteur d'anglais* at the Ecole Normale Supériere when Derrida was also on the staff. His poems emerge from a spirit of creative philosophy more common in France than in the British Isles, to say the least. Yet, for all that, a good deal of the poems' power derives from Kinloch's inspired use of barely recoverable Scots:

When I opened the window and reached for the yoghurt cooling on the outside ledge, it had gone. All that remained was a single Scottish word bewildered by the Paris winter frost and the lights of the riverbank motorway. What can *dustie-fute* say to a night like this? ('Dustie-fute', *Paris-Forfar* p.30)

There is the gentleness of genuine enquiry in these poems, as well as a mixing of many different kinds of text, a reaching-out to theory-by-poetry, exemplified by the comic-melancholic figure of the student reaching for that transformed yoghurt ('dustie-fute' is a traveller-figure, a stranger, a juggler, an acrobat). The rewarding density of a sequence such as 'Dustie-fute', where a *dérive* meets MacDiarmidian lexicon-love on board W. S. Graham's language trawler is impossible to detail here, except to say that my description should be taken merely as a temporary range-finding device.

The relationship between France and Scotland is itself one of the risk-taking metaphors in *Paris–Forfar* where 'the auld alliance' is between 'words and things' (30). In an interview I conducted with him for *PN Review* (Vol. 27 no. 3 (Jan./Feb. 2001), pp.23-5), I asked Kinloch about the French aspects in his work. It was clearly important to him to emphasise the particular human moments of his coming to terms with France (in the same way that the poems that engage with French life and culture are also, tenderly, about and 'through' actual people, the poet-as-student, the speaker's aunt and so on).

> Well, France for me has always been about people and places first and foremost. I first spent a year in Paris in 1979 and the first man I fell in love with, who was about five years my senior and heavily into most kinds of literature, more or less gave me a crash course in 'the books you ought to read' or rather the ones he thought I ought to read. I can remember achingly romantic walks to visit Chateaubriand's tomb at St Malo and lazy picnics reading passages of Flaubert and Proust to each other. Sadly the romance was all on my side but he put me onto Joubert so I suppose he had quite a long term effect! In this sense books have usually come to confirm things I've already felt or experienced and that has been a pattern in my life.
>
> (*PN Review*, p.23)

This is an important element of Kinloch's self-classification, and one that is palpable in his poetry: the mediation of literature through human contact, usually through love; occasionally through the lack of it. In the poem, the word 'dustie-fute', like an old forgotten luggage label that has temporarily been given animation in an art-house cartoon, is created as part of the poet's sense of isolation in Paris: it is both a delightful literary conceit and a tentative answer to a real human need (the need to *place* oneself, knowing that this may be an act of will as much as a realisation of what already 'is'). The word, as a Scots word, connects Kinloch to the Scotland he misses, to a Scotland that probably can't exist except in the imagination (it is a word from an obsolete kind of Scots), and, paradoxically, it connects him to his sense of alienation in Paris, since the word means a foreigner. Aspirationally, however, the word eventually answers itself, as the poem explains, 'triumphantly': it is 'the dustie-fute of 'revelry', the acrobat, the juggler who accompanies the toe-belled jongleur with his merchant's comic fairground face' (here I think of Edwin Morgan's 'Cinquevalli').

Nevertheless, Kinloch's relationship to Francophone literature, notwithstanding his interest in those traditionally seen in particular and different ways as 'outsiders', Joubert and Rimbaud, is far from straightforward:

> Latterly, I have experienced a certain fatigue with metropolitan French culture and literature and I've struck out in the directions you've mentioned [other Francophone territories] although my interest in Quebec and the Caribbean has as much to do with Scotland and Scottish literature as with France. [...] Where I differ from other writers perhaps, is that for me France is also French, and the foreignness is also a linguistic foreignness and although I have come to speak and write that language quite well

> it remains tantalisingly foreign for me.
> (*PN Review*, p.24)

The concern with apparently anomalous states of being, as fundamental as the 'wrong' kind of sexuality, is central to *Paris–Forfar* and is surely linked to a kind of synaesthetic existentialism, in which 'to be' can only be understood through analogy, and analogy itself can only be understood through the exercising of unfamiliar and conventionally inappropriate senses. Of course, *Paris –Forfar* represents a startling and, to some, provocative use of the traditionally macho, hide-bound Scots language, now rewritten within a gay discourse, but that is surely concomitant with the rich text that it is: as with the affectionate relocation of Whitman and Hervé Guibert and their techniques in *Un Tour d'Ecosse* (and, in a single poem, a homage to O'Hara and Apollinaire — that American-French matrix again), it is a poetry available to but not circumscribed by meta-poetry.

An important part of *Paris–Forfar* is Kinloch's elegiac poetry for victims of AIDS and for victims of anti-gay prejudice. This includes moving poems centred on the experience of an AIDS sufferer in hospital, as well as 'Warmer Bruder'. The latter reminds the world of the Nazi treatment of gays who were killed in concentration camps *en masse* during the Second World War. At the same time it very clearly connects that genocide to the AIDS crisis, through the at-first mysterious recurrence of the word 'Grangemouth': only later does the reader realise Kinloch is talking about a modern-day hospice, a link made through the visual hinge of 'snow', snow being moved by forced gay labour in the concentration camps, snow being moved by hospice employees (or perhaps council workers) in Grangemouth to keep the hospice open to visitors.

There is no rivalry among the dead, but 'Warmer Bruder' is surely an intervention in the politics of interpreting the Second World War and contemporary life through each other. Again, the poet relates such involvement in gay politics to a specific French experience. In correspondence, he speaks of becoming politicised through the unexpected route of co-editing Joubert's *Carnets* with Philippe Mangeot:

> Philippe was one of the founder members of the Paris Act-Up coalition of AIDS activists. I was collaborating with him on our edition of Joubert's *Carnets* while he was busy organising and taking part in some of the AIDS direct action campaigns. [...] There was a recognition that AIDS posed society some very real ethical dilemmas in France and gay men and women were vociferous in trying to force these issues into the public arena and stimulate debate. I was very aware when I was living in France that I was taking part in an unfolding drama, whereas here so much was just not mentioned, swept under the carpet or treated as of marginal interest.

This also forms the background to *Un Tour d'Ecosse*, a book nevertheless characterised by a greater formal range and, frankly, levity. The greater number of comic poems — satirical, affectionate, and marked sometimes by a quite broad sense of humour — might be perplexing at first, given the seriousness of Kinloch's recurring theme, but the effect is to assert 'the love that dare not speak its name' within all areas of discourse, not just the elegiac mode. In this way, *Un Tour d'Ecosse*, as the title suggests, is a deliberate and self-conscious import into Scotland, in which France's versatile treatment of homosexuality in literature, especially as represented by Hervé Guibert's books, which blur the distinction between fiction and documentary, can now be adapted for Kinloch's own concerns.

Like David Kinloch, Iain Bamforth also has a France-orientated poem that is key to his work overall, and which involves a stylised autobiographical episode in Paris: 'Alibis', collected in *Sons and Pioneers* (Carcanet, 1992). As in 'Dustie-fute', the idea of the individual before a window is important. At the beginning of the poem it introduces the hopes of Enlightenment France, represented by the Pont Neuf, to one of side it. Bamforth tells the reader the bridge was unpopular for centuries: 'those bourgeois sins, complacency and self-regard, / strode out of their century, asking why we needed this.' (p.59). To the other side is 'a tour through the skin trade: fast food, fast sex / and a gallic Punch giving Judy the once-over; / little secrets Maigret might have kept from his wife / and the big-time vendors of the naked truth.'

The window therefore dissects rational idealism from the physical 'limitations' from which the Enlightenment spirit can't quite escape, and the poem seems to understand each as socially-mediated phenomena. Such an analytical process, its reversibility, and its interstices, are critical to Bamforth's poetry in general. This is no doubt in part to do with his profession, a doctor and scientific translator, but Bamforth has also long been engaged in the reading and re-interpretation of the history of philosophy, a subject which surely feeds his convincing abstractions (and his satire) — 'Those bourgeois sins, complacency and self-regard' — and which, in other poems, are foregrounded a great deal further.

In fact, a willingness to use abstract nouns, to generalise without need of a Movement-style observing persona, and to change metaphor and simile again and again in the same poem, allies Bamforth closer to a French (and much wider European) tradition than to any other British poet I know — even if aspects of such an aesthetic were of course familiar to English Renaissance drama and may not yet be lost to poetry in Britain in general. This can make some of Bamforth's poems seem difficult because they appear so obtuse (especially when there is a suggestion that something very specific is actually meant), but it can also lead to stunning effects: a sense of lyric authority and so propulsion, exhilaration; a match of a series of different analogies to the theme of mutability itself — as in the appropriately shape-changing qualities of the nation-state of 'Men of Fire' (*Sons and Pioneers*, p.11); and a suddenly burning, mordant, use of colloquialism, renewed because contrasted within the abstract frame.

If there is a stylistic affinity with French poetry, however, Bamforth's relationship with French culture is far from simple. He certainly expresses an interest in French poetry, and, like all the other poets I discuss here, is especially interested in Baudelaire (this may simply be a kind of minimum requirement for writing modern poetry, though, and can hardly be ascribed, I would have thought, to a 'Scottish' affinity, whatever that may be), but it is clear that France's past glories are the problem for Bamforth, especially France's memorialisation of itself.

In 'Alibis', Paris is seen as a meeting point of very different ways of viewing the world; very different, but unified by the fact that each is simply out-dated; each trades on ways of perception that may once have meant a great deal, but which can no longer have such purchase; they are merely the alibis of the title. The city is 'a place my grandpa called Babylon, the Antichrist *chez lui*' but, to the poet, it doesn't even have the vitality of the Devil. It's on its uppers, resorting to various kinds of myth-peddling, a 'storyline [...] scraping by on Piaf-naïf dreams of glory'.

Whereas in 'Dustie-fute', the magical, iconic, yoghurt cools refreshingly on the windowsill, and Kinloch's persona experiences Paris as a liberator of self and of text, Bamforth's vision of Paris is one of disenchantment, of disgust. Paris's history is seen as typical of Europe's, 'the snore of the old world outliving itself', and the sentence 'Curdled leftovers occluded the windowsill' both observes, with some humour, a detail of student life while symbolising a history whose own decay prevents perspective. This is capped, in the final stanza, by the behaviour of one of the poet's neighbours. Winning through to a clarity of a kind, 'the ultimate collector' surely embodies Bamforth's anger and disappointment at 'progress' since the Revolution. As the satire draws down to its final lines, the neighbour is revealed to have devoted years to amassing a museum... of excrement:

> Beside me, in the next block, lived the ultimate collector.
> I never saw him, only heard the poisoned whisperings:
> one day they called the *pompiers* in to clean him out,
> houseproud among a decade's scatological relics,
> each one labelled, wrapped and catalogued.

The presence of the first person singular here is untypical of Bamforth's work — 'Alibis' is a revealing exception. This — despite the regretful tone of the poem — must surely come from an almost wholesale rejection of introspection, both as a worthwhile philosophical practice and as a mode of writing poetry. As Bamforth says in his note to the poems collected in *Dream State: the New Scottish Poets*[98] 'I [...] find myself impatient to pin my poetry to the conventionally "non-poetic", to indeterminacy and process, since poetry seems to me, not least in its attitude to the self, still assiduously Romantic.' Perhaps the 'impersonality' of a French-like poetic diction is attractive to Bamforth for this reason.

The experimentation of the Oulipo author George Perec certainly made an impact on his sequence of 101 short prose poems, 'Impediments' (*Open Workings*, Carcanet, 1996; p.80). He told me:

> I wrote 'Impediments' under the influence of Perec, and what I tried to do was produce a cognitive self-portrait sitting one fine

---
[98] ed. Donny O'Rourke, Polygon, 1994, p. 94.

August day in the office of the translating agency in Paris that used to send me work. In other words I would have been working instead of playing when I wrote the sequence. I co-opted the word Impediment in at least two ways. You have it as a homophonic building block in 101 — 'un pays de menthe', démente', 'de monts', etc., and as a kind of exchange system, in the sense that what attracts is what resists, a kind of mimetic stumbling block. 101 aphorisms seemed arbitrary, but just after I'd published the book I found a sentence in the Upanishads which suggests it perhaps wasn't. It's even more suggestive than the Calvino quote ['Nobody excluded the possibility that things could proceed in other, entirely different ways. You would have said that each individual was ashamed of being the way he was expected to be' - from *Time & The Hunter*, quoted at the beginning of the poem]: 'There are 101 arteries of the heart, one of which penetrates the crown of the head. Moving upwards by it, a man at his death reaches the immortal: the other arteries serve for departing in different directions.'

'Impediments' begins as a kind of 3-D mapping exercise, with chance as one of the vectors. Bamforth's phrase 'cognitive self-portrait' captures objectivity's meeting with the subject, and again in 'Impediments' there is his ambivalence towards the Romantic, as the opening section suggests:

Capture, recapture and maximum likelihood: those are my guiding principles on each excursion across the salty pavements of Paris to a room where I plot my three *points de repère:* M1, M2 and M3.

However, it soon becomes a project of very different kinds of text; a miscellany, certainly, but one in which the preoccupations about the body, about substance itself, and about knowledge-organising structures recur. In this way, there are, for example, tightly-focussed images where the individual meets generalising science ('...a wax model of a woman with her spine arched like an exocet.

Her hand is draped across her body to the supernumerary rib indicated with a pointer.'); reflections on even the reflective sense as an off-the-shelf genre ('Dissatisfaction follows me home, a fictive lack deliberating what it might have done before remorse charged the air of a bare room...'); and a sustained flickering of ambiguities, in which Paris itself is an exemplar ('To take a leaf from Rabelais' book. Paris's marriage of architecture and amnesia takes two names: *Lutetia*, meaning city of mud (*lutum*) and *Parisis*, city of Iris, mysterious sidelong goddess of truth.')

Yet Oulipo need not be so hard-edged a tool. Bamforth remarked to me that he considered 'Between the Rhinns and the Machair' (*Open Workings*, pp.20-23) as every bit as much in the spirit of Oulipo as 'Impediments', and its homage to Galloway life, where Bamforth was briefly a G.P.; its incantations and brief meditations, create an elegiac quality far removed in spirit from Bamforth's Parisian poem.

Oulipo, with its characteristic play between rule, accident, and individual determination, is one of many links Bamforth shares with Peter McCarey. These include post-religious sensibilities after a devout religious upbringing — Bamforth by Plymouth Brethren parents, McCarey by Catholics; day-to-day work as professional translators; day-to-day work within the medical world, Bamforth as a G.P., McCarey running the language service of the World Health Organization; location within anomalous French-speaking regions, to Bamforth's Alsace, McCarey may reply with his many years in Geneva; and first-hand experience of international organisations – Bamforth, in Strasbourg — McCarey, the many international bodies on his doorstep, one of which employs him. If Bamforth is interested in philosophy of the Romantics and of the Enlightenment, McCarey is especially interested in the Nietzsche-influenced Lev Shestov, Berkeley and Hume, and George Davie and the Thomist Alasdair MacIntyre. Their poetry also shares a prosodic quality — broad, world-analysing gestures which swoop down to short, pithy sayings, before flying back up to the heights of a cooler rationality.

McCarey's early poem, 'Sous les pavés — la plage', what we may now take as one in the genre, 'the young male Scottish émigré at Paris window poem', is one such example:

> Urban sunlight comes in the window
> staggering up to its knees in sand
> banknotes blowing out of its seams
> like scarious leaves and carious buildings
> [...]
> Frontiers, harbours, roads, currencies
> crowd control and corpse disposal.
>
> Money is busy buying itself up
> using what there is for collateral.
>
> Light is said to be sculpting itself
> with its only sense
> of touch.
>
> (*Town Shanties*, Broch Books, n.d., p.36)

In passing, it's worth noting the Rimbaud-like synaesthesia of light's 'sense of touch'. More importantly, look here at the very characteristic presentation of McCarey's individuals as caught within a net of capital and its enforcement systems. The apocryphal chant of the students of '68, 'Under the pavings, the beach!', is examined more coolly — the image becomes closer to quicksand, to the desert, than to a summer holiday. The enigmatic, slowed-down, last stanza is offered, it seems to me, as a mystical and carefully paced answer to the faster but equally abstracted concept of 'money buying itself up'.

If Bamforth's at times similar prosodic dynamic is founded on body/rationality and pre-modern/post-enlightenment divisions, McCarey's emerges from somewhere else: a sensitivity to overbearing power structures and their warping of individual will. Both Bamforth and McCarey, of course, are attentive to materiality — both, for example include medical and chemical data in their work — but whereas Bamforth may be said to have been affected by Oulipo in texts such as 'Impediments', which is in part about the anthropology of science, McCarey's Oulipoean use of, say, the English spell-checker that 'corrects' the great Scots poem 'The Flyting of Dunbar and Kennedy' ('Dhow', in *Town Shanties*, Broch Books, n.d., p.68) is less about technology than about the power relationships between speech-delineated groups (and, implicitly, between unequally matched nation states).

Like Bamforth, McCarey is candid about his connection with Oulipo. Responding to a question I put to him about French influences, he traces his connection to this world to a chance acquaintance with the creative partnership of poet-printer John Crombie and artist Sheila Bourne (together, Kickshaws Press):

> So: place Fontenoy, then, in 1983. I shared an office with John Crombie on my first contract in UNESCO. A big guy with a walrus moustache and a mid-Atlantic accent influenced, I guess, by his partner Sheila Bourne. John would get in at nine and whack out a tirade of translation on his mechanical typewriter. He loathed and despised the stuff he had to translate, but the occasional contract gave him just enough money with which to keep writing, printing and publishing books in Kickshaws Press, which he and Sheila ran from a small flat in Montparnasse. A very small flat, in rue de la Grande Chaumière. He showed me the press: a thing of beam-bending weight, half steam engine, half bicycle, that squatted one of the rooms. And the books: evolving from Edward Gorey meets Alphonse Allais towards a convergence of typography, Beckett, Queneau and Oulipo.

There's much more to Kickshaws than what I've learned from it, which is this: random rules, and don't let that stop you.

McCarey sees the work of Kickshaws Press of which there is a fine collection, incidentally, in the British Library — as one of the key inspirations for his long-standing *Syllabary* project, in which it is intended there will be a poem built around every syllable within the contemporary Scottish English lexicon:

> As I look through the books, I find the level of presentation and invention I'd love to see in my Syllabary, and I find the push away from linear narrative that's been running my own work for quite some time.

As far as Oulipo is concerned, Roubaud is more important to McCarey than either Queneau or Perec:

> The central writer of the group, for my purposes, is Jacques Roubaud. I first came across him in *Verse*, where David Kinloch (I think) translated extracts from *Quelque Chose Noir* [in fact, translated and introduced by Rosmarie Waldrop, *Verse* vol. 6 no. 2] — that powerful book of elegies to his wife, Alix Cléo Roubaud. I then read — on Peter France's advice — his *La vieillesse d'Alexandre*, which is *the* book on French prosody; it unlocked French verse to me twenty years after I'd read the stuff. Then I read *La Fleur Inverse*, an inspirational work on Provençal poetry, and anything else of his I could find on verse and the writing of it, since the man thinks hard and well on the matter. He's written on Petrarch, he's worked with Douglas Oliver; with Sorley Maclean...

It is significant that the *sound* of French poetry — its prosody and, for speakers of Scots and Scottish English, the seeming lack of phonic vigour in French's vocabulary — should be one of the barriers to its appreciation within Scotland. This is surely why

Bamforth stresses the fascinating exception of Rabelais, and why McCarey, despite having a degree in French, sees Roubaud and his work on the alexandrine as a turning point in his previous underestimation of French poetry. Without wishing to yoke very different poets like O'Rourke, Kinloch, Bamforth and McCarey together, I think they would all agree with a significant amount of what McCarey says when he talks about his natural disinclination towards French poetry. Perhaps this would also be the case for many others, too:

> I was never much taken by French poetry. It's rhotic languages that resonate most in me: Russian, Italian, Scottish English, some Provençal. French Gothic *architecture*, yes, and Romanesque; cosmopolitan Paris in its existential void — all of those have moved me. But not much of the poetry, magnetised as it was between a sinister religion and secular imperialism, poetry that was cerebral and measured, manipulative and nostalgic.

Of course, the important thing for all these poets is that they did overcome such distrust, reading French literature with an approach that is far from a tourist version of Francophilia, but, thankfully, is also light years from Homer Simpson's construction of la grille.

Robin Fulton Macpherson: Light Years

Light Years

The loneliness of a blue sky is extreme.
There's no depth on earth like it we could fall down.

What relief, then, when night comes, to see the stars
once more, Aldebaran, Regulus, Deneb

close to hand like marks on my childhood ceiling
measuring how the day's last paleness took so

long to darken over the line of pine-tops
west of the manse, over the rise of the moor

its skein of thready tracks, beyond the moor then
over Kilbrannon Sound, and remote Kintyre.[99]

This poem by Robin Fulton, or rather Robin Fulton Macpherson as he is now known, reflects on stellar distances but the poem is also about the concept of time folded into the constant. It reflects, too, an understanding of the poetic qualities of the apparently objective, the way that symbolic language is very difficult to elude, even within terms specifically designed for mathematical precision.

---

[99] *From* Grenzflug, Editions Rugerup, 2008, p. 106, republished in full with the permission of the author.

Many of RFM's poems, perhaps most, unfold from a declared observing 'I'. Sometimes, as with 'Light Years', the personal is generalised, momentarily transferred to an objective exterior with the assertiveness of a natural law, hence the arresting opening line: 'The loneliness of a blue sky is extreme.' This is a transferred attribute: it is of course the poet's 'loneliness' here, not the sky's, and because RFM has depersonalised the sentence there is also a sense that this might actually be everyone's sense of loneliness before and beneath and within the awe of blue. With a headlong, appropriately awkward second line, delaying, teetering-style, the verb and preposition to the end, 'There is no depth on earth like it we could fall down,' the poet expands on the angst of a clear sky, reversing up with down and challenging the conventional view: after all, for many, the same clear sky, might simply, unproblematically, be beautiful.

RFM's poems are almost always concerned with solitariness, a quality that surely needs to have known others to be able to talk about itself since it would mean nothing without the knowledge of absence. The others in RFM's poetry are other apparent solitaries, his minister father, composers such as Shostakovitch and Beethoven (so perhaps artists in general), and, most of all, his past self it — or himself, the two near-distinct beings of the poet in the past and the poet of the now. (In a parallel doubleness, for decades the poet was 'Robin Fulton' but now, in retirement from his teaching career, he has become 'Robin Fulton Macpherson', as if another, equally essential person, always latent, has finally revealed himself, and the two Robins can now co-exist publically.)

To be solitary, alone, is not necessarily to be lonely. In RFM's work there is a very special ability to adopt a philosophical lyrical stance, a certain outward stoic serenity even, while bearing witness to what can at times be the inward slow motion of a deep-seated panic attack. Vast expanses — the sky, the sea, or the moor — can simultaneously fascinate and terrify. As the poet says in the poem 'Rain', which recounts his youthful ambition to climb Morven, in Caithness, in a day: 'What stopped me was not the gradient / but the unbearable loneliness / that would crawl in on me from the moors / and would stare at me and not say one word.' (*Grenzflug*, p. 136). The personification of the absence of persons is a witty response, even so, to such existential terror.

In 'Light Years', RFM again reverses expectations when daylight recedes and the stars begin to appear. They, of course, are far bigger and much further away than the blue light of infant Earth's atmosphere but the poet instead makes the stars small-scale and homely, paradoxically far nearer than the sky and therefore far more reassuring — 'close to hand like marks on my childhood ceiling.' Even here, though, the poetic device is complex, expressing several otherwise irreconcilable ideas at the same time. The reader knows that the poet's childhood is in fact well beyond reach, as all past events are, and so that 'close to hand' is at best meaning in memory only until another sense clarifies — it is that the particular marks on the ceiling were 'close at hand' to the young poet not only to the older poet in the act of remembering. There is also the suggestion that these marks, by a trick of light, may themselves have been a way of tracking the coming darkness as light seeped away from the childhood bedroom at dusk, an invention of measurement, the poem seems to hint, by someone used to having time on their own from an early age.

Despite the initial sense that this childhood was as reassuring as RFM's old friends the stars Aldebaran, Regulus and Deneb, the childhood vignette is presented rather coolly. The child waits, waits, waits for the comfort of nightfall, a series of images which hardly suggests unalloyed happiness in the day. The poem then tracks the disappearing light, naming the places it deserts one by one, a film sequence of silent observation, with the final irony that 'remote Kintyre' — in reality, a local place just across a narrow stretch of water — is emotionally further than Aldebaran, which really is light years away. And so 'Light Years' concludes another poem by a master witness of the unsettling dizziness of being, responding with simplicity of language and complexity of thought.

Afterword

Poetry is the gift-tag, people are the gift.

Readings are about 'aliveness'. For the author, there they are, actual people in front of you, listening to this poem or song or story you appear to have made.

Later, at a question-and-answer session or at the book table or at the café or sometimes just in the street, you're together, talking about anything and everything, and you can hear other conversations rippling out, going well beyond the starting point of your own words. The quiet work that you spent so much time on turns out to have been much more sociable and in a funny sort of way much more transient than you thought: it was only a way of helping in its limited way to keep the bigger permanence — people — thinking aloud, disagreeing, laughing, finding the company of other people via the company of ideas and enjoyment.

I said 'works you appear to have made' just there because I find, as I've been writing I've often been concentrating so hard on making a poem or a song or novel that I can't actually vouch for the precise process that allowed the work to be created — I was too 'inside' it to realise what it was becoming, even how I was making it. Sometimes you can recall starting-points and later finessings, but the intimate act of creating a work designed to be shared can actually be private even to the person making it.

Now, though, at a festival, say, it's being presented through this living breath, this voice, and surprise — it's *your* voice! You like the sound of your voice, sometimes — at least it's a very you part of your you —and you also find it a curse, a limitation. Once actors get the training they need for contemporary poetry, maybe they could deliver great alternative versions. And, wait, maybe there's a polyphonic approach to the lyric poem we haven't quite addressed yet (it doesn't have to be a single voice every time), maybe, maybe, maybe – with the right electronica and a choir the size of the Royal Festival Hall...

And so the artistic megalomania begins. No, it's you, just you, reading your work, you're walking the plank when you're walking out onto that stage, and now if you can't always make eye contact with the audience, on a good day or night you know you are making *word contact*. They can hear the word-play, the pathos, the spoken word melody, the structuring rhythm — sometimes they are actually interrupting (it happens!); even then at least you've provoked an action across air — but hopefully, mostly, at the end they are actually clapping (it happens!).

So that's a validation: sometimes it feels you do need in-person validation; sometimes you feel more aloof.

You'd been self-editing the choice of texts, the sequencing, you'd been trying to get the articulation right for what seems like days and it's not as if you haven't got writing to share, but even so — the greatest element of festivals isn't the texts. It really is the actual people.

They have convened — it might have seemed like simply a transaction, an act of individualism, buying that ticket but it was also a conscious act in the direction of the collective. The audience have *gathered* and they have done so to know more and to take pleasure in what they see and hear but very importantly they have done this simply to be together. In a way it is a literary version of a bacchanalia, a word rave, a non-religious religious meeting (and sometimes a religious, religious meeting — almost anything goes and should go).

The recent history of festivals in the 'United Kingdom' probably derives from one key post-war event, the first Edinburgh Festival in 1947. That was when one city decided it would help rebuild itself and its country in a way that ambitious schemes of house-building were in the physical world: the festival would do it through assembling people around, and in and through, culture. Since then many cities, and many other smaller locations, have taken that example to heart and with good reason: yes, there is certainly an immediate economic benefit to live literature, but the other benefits keep radiating out, educating in old and new kinds of articulacy — which is a political benefit in the deepest sense of politics, and, almost as importantly, sharing old and new kinds of pleasure.

Occasionally I am asked to describe the traditional publishing model for poetry — how a poet becomes a published poet, for example. I explain as best I can the conventional routes to publication but then go on to describe all the different activities that go on in the poetry world beyond the idea of a standard trajectory or 'career'. Created by these relatively small texts is an extraordinarily rich world of interchange, surprise, and enjoyment in which actual publication takes a minor role — translations, broadcasts, magazines, single author collections, anthologies, newspaper articles, sculpture and murals, and music — all of these, like poems themselves, are physical, inert materials which nevertheless give life. I do believe that poems are gift-tags, simple, beautiful, complex, thought-provoking, all that, while the real gifts are what all the people involved make together as they convene. Much later, the poems still have the power to catalyse individuals to think and enjoy and, finally, to make gift-tags, poems, of their 'own'.

Index

Adam, Helen, 197
Akhmatova, Anna, 98
Allais, Alphonse, 232
Andrews, Bruce, 153
Apollinaire, Guillaume, 16,
　17-23, 29, 31, 147, 215,
　219, 224
Arts and Crafts, 98, 102
Ashbery, John, 153
Atkins, Tim, 14
Auden, W.H., 71, 79, 80, 138
Baird, John Logie, 115-18,
　130, 134, 136, 140
Balashova, Elena, 171
Bamforth, Iain, 3, 216, 226-30,
　232, 234
Barthes, Roland, 65, 121, 214
Baudelaire, Charles, 215, 227
Bean, Victoria, 3, 156, 157,
　159
Beatles, 63, 178
Beckett, Samuel, 48, 211, 232
Belli, Giuseppe, 184
Bergvall, Caroline, 15
Berkeley, George, 20, 230
Betjeman, John, 71
Black Mountain College, 106
Blackburn, Paul, 106, 107
Blake, William, 30
Bleitz, Karen, 3, 156, 158-59
Blok, Alexander, 98
Bloy, Leon, 110

Bomberg, David, 16, 33-38
Bourne, Sheila, 232
Bowd, Gavin, 215
Boyle, Mark & family, 129
Brasca, Clara, 145
Breakwell, Ian, 124, 126
Browning, Robert, 48
Brownjohn, Alan, 110
Bunting, Basil, vi, 40-59, 108,
　114, 119
Burroughs, William, 133
Buzzcocks, 174
Cambridge School, 113, 214
Camus, Albert, 219
Carlos Williams, William, vi,
　11, 43, 78, 108, 110, 117,
　172
Carswell, Catherine, 81
Cendrars, Blaise, 44, 147, 215,
　219
Chekhov, Anton, 43
Claire, Paula, 15
Clark, Leonard, 144
Clark, Thomas A., 123, 132
Clark, Tom, 70
Cobbing, Bob, 68, 79, 84, 88,
　89, 124, 126, 132, 139
Conrad, Joseph, 43, 48, 93
Corcoran, Kelvin, 174
Corman, Cid, 78, 106, 107,
　110, 132
Corso, Gregory, 108, 197

Cox, Ken, 124
Crawford, Robert, 141, 149–53
Creeley, Robert, 71, 78, 106–10, 113
Creighton-Hill, Hugh, 110, 111
Crombie, John, 232
Crosbie, William, 148
Crozier, Andrew, 86
cummings, e.e., 105
Cutler, Ivor, 127, 131
Cutts, Simon, 124, 126
Dallat, C.L., 5, 142, 145
Daniels, Peter, 143
de Chateaubriand, François-René, 222
de Melo Castro, E.M., 125
de Saint-Denys-Garneau, Hector, 106
Deguy, Michel, 221
Delattre, Pierre, 110
Demarco, Richard, 127
Derrida, Jacques, 121, 214, 221
Desnos, Robert, 147, 219
Diaghilev, Sergei, 34
Donne, John, 14
Donovan, 131, 135
Dorn, Edward, 89, 110, 111
Dragomoschenko, Arkadii, 171
Drinan, Adam, 119, 120
Drunk Man Looks at The Thistle, A, 43
Dudek, Louis, 111
Duffy, Carol Ann, 139
Dufy, Raoul, 28
Dunbar, William, 232

Duncan, Andrew, 119, 135, 151–55
Duncan, Robert, 106, 108, 110, 111, 120, 129, 197
Dürer, Albrecht, 179
Dylan, Bob, 31, 56, 79, 138
Ecclesiastes, 191
Eigner, Larry, 110
Eliot, T.S., vi, 42, 44, 56, 87, 117
EMI, 63
Empson, William, 214
Epstein, Hugh, 142
Euripides, 97
Fauve, 98
Feinstein, Elaine, 86
Ferlinghetti, Lawrence, 108
Filonov, Pavel, 145
Finlay, Alec, 134
Finlay, Ian Hamilton, vi, 36, 67, 72, 79, 85, 96, 107, 111–13, 124, 125, 127, 132–34, 131, 158, 197, 214
Finnegans Wake, 43
Fisher, Roy, vi, 79, 85, 89, 107, 108, 110, 127, 139, 200–212
Ford, Ford Madox, 59, 81
Forrest-Thompson, Veronica, 214
Fraser, Antonia, 189
Friel, Raymond, 149
Frost, Robert, vi
Fulton Macpherson, Robin, 14, 124, 133, 235–38, 236
Furnival, John, 124

Gardiner, Michael, 121, 150
Garioch, Robert, 132, 184
Gibbs, Michael, 126
Ginsberg, Alan, 108, 197, 220
Glen, Duncan, 118, 123, 129, 130, 131
Goodwin, Fay, 144
Gordon, Giles, 123
Gorey, Edward, 232
Gorky, Maxim, 98, 101
Graham, W.S., 222
Grassic Gibbon, Lewis, 81, 134
Graves, Robert, 70
Gray, Alasdair, 141
Guibert, Hervé, 224, 225
Guiguère, Roland, 106
Guillevic, Eugène, 215
Gumilev, Nikolai, 98
Gunn, George, 151–55
Gunn, Neil, 3, 81, 132, 198
Guthrie, James, 38
H.D., 80
Hall, John, 126
Hancock, Herbie, 15
Hardy, Thomas, vi, 11, 43, 50
Heaney, Seamus, 3, 139
Hedley-Dent, Chris, 142, 143, 145
Hejinian, Lyn, 14, 171
Hemingway, Ernest, 42, 43
Herbert, W.N., 145, 147, 149, 150, 151–53
Hills, Joan, 129
Hollo, Anselm, 111, 113
Houédard, Sylvester, 124, 159
Houellebecq, Michel, 215
Hughes, Ted, 71, 96, 133, 139, 144
Hulse, Michael, 146
Hume, David, 230
Informationists, vi, 149–54
James V, 216
James, Elizabeth, 142, 143
Jamie, Kathleen, 79, 80
Johnson, Linton Kwesi, 139
Jones, David, vi
Joubert, Joseph, 221, 222, 223, 225
Joyce, James, 68, 105
Kelman, James, 49, 134, 141
Kennedy, Walter, 232
Kenner, Hugh, 110
Khalvati, Mimi, 15
King, Ron, 200
Kinloch, David, 3, 14, 145, 149–54, 153, 214, 216, 221–25, 227, 233, 234
Kristeva, Julia, 214
Kuppner, Frank, 15, 214
L=A=N=G=U=A=G=E, 149, 202
Labé, Louise, 183, 184, 185
Laing, R.D., 131
Larbaud, Valéry, 147, 219
Larkin, Philip, 9, 12, 29, 79, 80, 110, 138, 139
Lawrence, D.H., 43, 189, 194–97
Leonard, Tom, 15, 131, 132, 134, 139, 141, 183
Leray, Jean-Pierre, 145
Lettrist International, 132

Levertov, Denise, 106, 110
Lewis, Wyndham, 67, 71, 93
Lijn, Lilian, 124
Lissitsky, El, 123
Lochhead, Liz, 141
Lowell, Robert, 71
Loy, Mina, 80
MacCaig, Norman, 14, 122, 132, 172
MacDiarmid, Hugh, vi, 81, 119, 121, 189, 197, 199, 214
Macgregor, Miriam, 144
MacIntyre, Alasdair, 230
Macleod. *See* Adam Drinan
Macpherson, Jay, 110
MacSpaunday, 81
MacSweeney, Barry, 80, 86
Maigret, 226
Mailer, Norman, 133
Mallarmé, Stéphane, 215, 221
Mamet, David, 48
Mangeot, Philippe, 225
Manson, Peter, 154, 215
Martial, 165, 169, 170, 171
Martian School, 14
Mass Observation, 110
Mayakovsky, Vladimir, 110, 134
McCarey, Peter, 3, 106, 145, 147-51, 154, 171, 212, 216, 230-34
McGibbon, Duncan, 142, 143
McGrath, Tom, 127-30, 132
Medlin, Leona, 142, 144
Melville, Herman, 47
Mew, Charlotte, 43

Michaux, Henri, 111
Middleton, Christopher, 71
Migrant, vii
Miller, Henry, 133
Mills, Stuart, 126
Milne, Drew, 154
Monet, Gustave, 102
Montale, Eugenio, vii, 171
Morgan, Edwin, vi, 110, 111, 113, 120, 122, 124, 125, 130-34, 139, 141, 177-87, 215
Morits, Yunna, 148
Morrissey, Kim, 142, 143
Motion, Sir Andrew, 76
Motler, L.A., 98
Muir, Edwin, 81, 96
Muldoon, Paul, 139
Mulrine, Stephen, 215
Niedecker, Lorine, 113
Nipkow, Paul, 118
Nuttall, Jeff, 127
O'Hara, Frank, 219, 224
O'Rourke, Donny, 15, 140-47, 216-21, 234
Objectivism, 46
Olson, Charles, 89, 106, 107, 108, 111
Oulipo, 157, 228, 230, 232, 233
Owen, Wilfred, 16, 17, 23-28, 31, 37
Pankhurst, Sylvia, 91-103
Pasternak, Boris, 111
Perec, Georges, 228, 233
Perloff, Marjorie, 202, 212

Phillips, Tom, 124
Pickard, Tom, 59
Picking, John, 131
Pink Floyd, 129
Pinter, Harold, 48, 49, 51
Pisarro, Camille, 102
Pisarro, Ludovic-Rodo, 98
Pleynet, Marcelin, 214, 215
Pound, Ezra, vi, 12, 37, 41, 42, 44, 50, 56, 57, 81, 117, 132, 167
Pre-Raphaelite, 98
Prévert, Jacques, 216
Prynne, J.H., 15, 59, 79, 80, 86, 89, 139
Puffin Club, 125
Queneau, Raymond, 232, 233
Rabelais, François, 230, 234
Redgrove, Peter, 86
Riach, Alan, 150, 153
Riding, Laura, 139
Riley, Denise, 12, 79, 80, 139, 174
Riley, John, 86
Rimbaud, Arthur, 221, 223, 231
Robertson, James, 215
Robinson, Peter, 145
Roche, Denis, 214, 215
Rodker, John, 34
Ronnie, Stevie, 14, 15
Roubaud, Jacques, 233, 234
Russian Futurists, 126
Sampson, Fiona, 76
Sappho, 3-13
Sartre, Jean-Paul, 218

Sassoon, Siegfried, 27, 28, 29, 38, 95
Schmidt, Michael, 76
Schuyler, James, 219
Seán Rafferty, 215
Selerie, Gavin, 128
Shakespeare, William, 186
Sharkey, John, 124
Shaw, George Bernard, 98
Shayer, Michael, 80, 85, 104-14, 104, 125
Shepherd, Nan, 134
Shestov, Lev, 230
Shostakovitch, Dmitri, 236
Shuttle, Penelope, 139
Signoret, Simone, 216, 217, 218
Simpson, Homer, 213, 214, 234
Situationist International, 132
Smith, Ali, 120, 189
Smith, Sydney Goodsir, 214
Snowden, Peter, 143
Snyder, Gary, 144, 197
Sophocles, 97
Soupault, Philippe, 147, 215, 219
Souster, Ray, 106, 108, 110
Spence, Alan, 141
Spender, Steven, 80, 138, 139
Spenser, Edmund, 20
Spicer, Jack, 120, 197
Steadman, Philip, 126
Suffragettes, 93
Tagore, Rabindranath, 98
Tait, Margaret, 120, 188-99
Tel Quel, 214

Templeton, Fiona, 14
The Waste Land, 44
Thomas, Edward, vi, 9–12, 16,
  28–33, 38, 43, 79, 80, 138,
  172
Toller, Ernst, 98
Tomlinson, Charles, 110
Trocchi, Alexander, 121, 130,
  132, 134, 135
Turnbull, Gael, vi, 59, 80, 85,
  104–14, 125, 148, 170, 215
Ulysses, 68
van den Beukel, Karlien, 174
Verey, Charles, 124
Verlaine, Paul, 215
Villon, François, 57
Vorticists, 48, 65, 93

Webb, Phyllis, 106
Weissbort, Daniel, 96, 133, 148
Welles, Orson, 171
Welsh, Irvine, 134
White, Kenneth, 130, 132, 214
Whitman, Walt, 100, 191, 224
Whyte, Hamish, 143
Williams, Jonathan, 108
Winston, Sam, 3, 156, 159,
  160, 161
Woolf, Virginia, 15
Yeats, W.B., 41, 50, 138
Zola, Emile, 98, 101
Zukofsky, Louis, 106, 108,
  113, 133
Zurbrugg, Nicholas, 126

Lightning Source UK Ltd.
Milton Keynes UK
UKOW02f0821200916

283395UK00004B/103/P